# South Asian Racialization
# and Belonging after 9/11

# South Asian Racialization and Belonging after 9/11

*Masks of Threat*

Edited by Aparajita De

LEXINGTON BOOKS
Lanham • Boulder • New York • London

Published by Lexington Books
An imprint of The Rowman & Littlefield Publishing Group, Inc.
4501 Forbes Boulevard, Suite 200, Lanham, Maryland 20706
www.rowman.com

Unit A, Whitacre Mews, 26-34 Stannary Street, London SE11 4AB

British Library Cataloguing in Publication Information Available

Library of Congress Cataloging-in-Publication Data Available

The hardback edition of this book was previously catalogued by the Library of Congress as follows:

Names: De, Aparajita, editor of compilation.
Title: South Asian Racialization and Belonging after 9/11: Masks of Threat / edited by Aparajita De.
Description: Lanham : Lexington Books, [2016] | Includes bibliographical references and index.
ISBN 978-1-4985-1252-7 (cloth: alk. paper) | ISBN 978-1-4985-3814-5 (pbk.: alk. paper) | ISBN 978-1-4985-1253-4 (electronic)
Identifiers: LCCN 2016010023 (print) | LCCN 2016024258 (ebook)
Subjects: LCSH: South Asian Americans--Social conditions--21st century. | September 11 Terrorist Attacks, 2001--Influence. | War on Terrorism, 2001-2009--Social aspects--United States. | South Asians in literature. | Race in literature. | Literature and society--History--21st century. | Racism--United States--History--21st century. | Identity politics--United States--History--21st century. | Imperialism--Social aspects--United States--History--21st century. | United States--Race relations--History--21st century.
Classification: LCC E184.S69 S68 2016 (print) | LCC E184.S69 (ebook) | DDC 305.800973--dc23
LC record available at https://lccn.loc.gov/2016010023.

Printed in the United States of America

Dedicated to Sanghamitra and Nabendu, my partners in learning

# Contents

# Acknowledgments

This book came out of a panel proposal I put together during a NEMLA (Northeast Modern Language Association) meet in 2012. While the process of getting it to print has been long and tedious, I want to thank all those who participated and were patient with me. I want to thank all of my contributors, Reshmi, Chandrima, Lopa, Stanley, John, Sarah, Zayed, and Nitasha who kept up with my strict deadlines and calls for repeated revisions. This is the fruit of our labor. I would also like to thank Surbhi Malik who helped me during the initiation of the project. I owe my thanks to our wonderful publishing team at Lexington Books, Lindsey Porambo and Marilyn Ehm, for working tirelessly with us. My colleagues at CUNY Kingsborough: Amy Karp, Eileen Ferretti, Brian Katz, Maureen Ruprecht Fadem, and Anthony Alessandrini, who continue to inspire and support me. I thank my current colleagues at UDC: Cherie Ann, La Tanya, Wynn, and Alex, who invested in my project and in my scholarly activities. To my Dean, Dr. April Massey, who unequivocally supports my projects and continues to assure me that I can make it work. Thank you all. My sincere thanks to all my friends, teachers, and peers for their valuable inputs during the conversations we had during the making of the project.

Last but not the least, I owe my deepest gratitude to my family, Nabendu, Maa, Baba, Sanghamitra, Rajiv, Moumita, and Rajarshi, whose love, understanding, unflinching support, and faith in me, humble me. Every time. All the time.

Overall, our endeavors contribute to the burgeoning scholarship in the field of South Asian studies, critical race and cultural studies. We hope that this volume continues the discussion and encourages more scholars and students within the humanities and social sciences to ask and review important questions on identity, belonging, and citizenship within our changing landscapes, especially in the light of events following September 11, 2001.

# Introduction

*South Asian Racialization and Belonging after 9/11:*
*Masks of Threat*

## Aparajita De

"Mama, see the Negro! I'm frightened!" (Fanon 1986, 112). It was Franz Fanon describing the objectification of threat in the black racial body. Fanon noted that the association of peril, among other things, was always already overdetermined from the outside through a paradigmatic, white colonialist perspective. In the current era, race continues to be a determining factor in signifying terror or benevolence, however, religious and cultural identities are increasingly becoming major scripts inflecting "goodness" or "evilness" within racial identities. I have the Arab, Muslim, non-Muslim Sikh, and Brown identities in mind, that are increasingly the focal point of assumptions of violence and threat. After the epochal attack against Western imperialism on September 11, 2001, Arab Americans, South Asian Muslim Americans, Sikh Americans, and South Asians in general find themselves under scrutiny—often leading to the juvenile conclusion, reminiscent of the Fanonesque moment. Thus, veiled women, Sikh doctors, or, "Arab-looking" Americans become targets of racial attacks and assaults.[1] While it is beyond the scope of this collection to include the heterogeneous voices of Arab American and/or Muslim American perspectives on the reconstruction of their identities along racial, ethnic, political, and economic lines following 9/11, or to comprehensively examine when Arab, Muslim, and terror became interlinked, this volume will put into focus the narrative of belonging and racialization among South Asian Muslim Americans and South Asian Americans by focusing on their empirical experiences through film and cultural texts, public events, and in popular writing and fiction. This focus distinguishes the volume's content and perspective from Muslim and Arab American Studies and scholarship, while entailing the revivification of a conversation specifically along these lines. Such a simultaneous discussion separated from and provoking engagement, along side Arab American and Muslim American scholarship, underscores regional, economic, historical, cultural, political perspectives, and tactics of surveillance and policing. By implication, these are discursive domains that are also patriarchal, sexist, conservative, and classist. Ultimately, this discussion informs, enriches, and expands current race and cultural studies as it addresses debates around issues of belonging and citizenship.

It has already been widely acknowledged that the comprehension of racial development and identity studies in the current global context cannot be insulated from cultural, geopolitical, historical, and phenomenological markers (Omi & Winant 1994; Ong 1999; Goldberg 2002; Maira 2009). Thus, while the scope of this volume of essays is focused on the reconfigurations of South Asian American (and South Asian Muslim American) identities after 9/11 it is also primarily engaged with intersections of gender, sexuality, socioeconomic class, and religion in the formation of these identities. Understandably, the new racialization of South Asian Muslims implies a reconfiguration of the indices of belonging to the American polity. Such a premise echoes cultural studies scholars' insistence on understanding the terrains of cultural citizenship alongside sociopolitical affiliations to forge belonging (Appiah 1994; Maira et al. 2004; Goldberg 2009). The title of the volume underpins the strategies and factors redefining belonging and racialization of South Asian Americans following 9/11, simultaneously putting the events and policies of the events in context with contemporary and past incidents throughout the globe. This enables studying brown racialization post 9/11, not as an isolated incident limited within a geopolitical terrain, but as an event which resonated as *part* of a wider politics restricting the boundaries of belonging, in doing so, the volume reexamines the issues of race and identity politics in current times.

The term "racialization" used in the title is, however, both nuanced and different from the term "racial formation" that Michael Omi and Howard Winant (1994) use in their seminal work to connote a process through which "social, economic, and political forces determine the content and importance of racial categories, and by which they are, in turn, shaped by racial meanings" (Omi and Winant, 61). Neither of them describe how "racial meanings" may change over time and in the context of epochal changes reconfiguring indices, based on national, ethnic, spatial, gender, and religious signifiers. For these early scholars, race was a sociohistorical construct to maintain and justify sociopolitical hegemonic ordering, a way to ascertain power relations; where race was only sparingly connected to religion, gender, or sexuality. This early work is restricted in foreseeing the importance of bodily experiences *while* being raced or experiences of race in historical time; so, in their understanding, racial embodiment or experiences of a body due to her racial and cultural markers, shaping perception and consciousness, were not as important as the organization of the structures of powers. Neither were they more interested in reexamining sociohistorical and cultural periods when inter- and intraracial relations become more distinguished or forge (temporary) alliances against minority citizens. Thus, in the compass of this current volume of essays, the term *racialization* has come to refer to the processes and experiences through which race becomes integrated as a default marker through attire, behavior, cultural and religious practices, an ascription through ethnographic, geopolitical, economic, religious, and immigration category ultimately segregating or integrating, classifying, or (dis-) identifying a group or community over others. Racialization is distinct from the way biological racial distinctions work. It may be argued to be a symptom of the sociocultural production of race, making race and religion one and homogeneous, although due to its cultural associations, racialization is also spatiotemporally determined and in flux.

Racialization is as much about the racial interpellation of others (black, brown, or minority bodies), as it is about the ways in which domains of sociopolitical power structures construct the experiences of these bodies. The consequences of racialization due to empirical experiences within these structures of power reveal the banality of racism while cautioning us about nuanced exclusivities within global democratic spaces. Current racialization politics in the United States intensified after the terrorist attacks of 9/11. In fact, the thin veneer of multiracial solidarity collapsed after the 9/11 attacks and revealed the fissures within and among working class, minority, and diaspora communities. Thus, the new and evolving racialization of minority identities both within their communities and within the greater U.S. polity, reinforces migrant indeterminacy—a framework underpinning the binaries of minority belonging to be either inclusive and aspiratory (model minority) or extraneous and transgressive (the "other" minorities). In the context of 9/11, the easy grouping of belonging was sounded in current political ideology, "Either you are with us, or you are with the terrorists."[2] Eventually, the war on terror got quickly reconfigured in popular narrative as a war against minority articulations of identity, especially if they were Muslim, brown, bearded, veiled, head-scarved, practiced a different religion or culture, spoke languages other than English, or had other sociocultural markers denoting their "otherness." In the sociohistorical context of the United States, and in the overall rhetoric supporting the maintenance of empire, the racialized body of the Muslim has been a socioculturally constructed entity, which has straddled over time, biology, and culture (since the association of Arabs and Muslims with threat, however essentialist, also refer to the spread of a historical racism stemming from medieval Europe, see Deepa Kumar, 2012). This metonymic projection eventually led to "Islamophobia" which was reinvigorated by 9/11, and thus, the religion of Islam and the body of a racialized Muslim became centers and objects of terror and threat emanating from an intersection of discourses that were neoliberal, capitalist, historically situated, and imperial, such as in the United States and Europe (Majid 2009; Mufti 2007; Kumar 2012). Thus, as a term loaded with subjective and empowering possibilities, racialization may also, paradoxically, seem to reject plural belongings, in the same way in which all Sikhs in the current Euro-American context become identified as Arabs, all South Asians *are* Indians and Hindus, or all Pakistanis Muslim, Middle Eastern terrorists. Thus, racialization is emblematic of the polarization of public rhetoric, espousing judgment— arbitrary or not—with serious and concrete consequences—justifying segregation, disenfranchisement, oppression and, in light of recent cases, even extermination.

In the context of this volume, racialization has thus recast itself as a more dynamic category of belonging and identity based on sociocultural and political-economic experiences than the earlier perceptions of pheno-typical codes. It is a category that silence and make invisibile, minority exclusion and oppression in order to highlight either perceptions of their threats to the greater body politic or their contributions to it as "good" citizens. Racialization has evolved as a category of difference that is thrust upon minority bodies in the U.S. context, due to strategic sociocul-tural codes (i.e., determined through sight), and political-economic per-ceptions (i.e., those determined by site or positionality). In the context of 9/11, scrutinous generalizations of the immigrant's body, cultural attire and practices, religious markers, gender, sexuality, and economic spaces become ways of revising and reexamining spaces of their belonging and racialization. In this politics of new thematization of those *that examine* and those *who are examined*, racializations too expand and get reconsti-tuted along gendered, ethnic, and cultural-religious lines. As a symptom of racism, racialization works in silencing the heterogeneity of identities and experiences while pointing out the intercommunal tensions among racial and cultural identities due to an uncomplicated representation within a primarily white supremacist heterosexist ideology. In current American politics, we see this most prominently in representations of people of South Asian origin in politics. The governor of Louisiana, Bob-by Jindal, is a case in point. Shunning his given Indian name, Piyush, in favor of the Americanized, "Bobby," he has been quick to distance him-self from his ethnic and multiple belongings to embrace only one ideolo-gy—white, Christian, heterosexist—with posters that project him as light-skinned as his other political buddies and champion his conservative Catholicism (Jindal was born Sikh).[3]

The subtitle of this volume, "Masks of Threat," captures the overarch-ing ways in which racialization functions to demonize minorities within dominant narratives, and the ways in which their experiences and articu-lations become disposable, dismembered, and dysfunctional, so much so that the comprehensive networks of their belongings are pathologized without an ontology or an agency. The word "mask" refers to a cover or an imposition that hides the other aspects of a racialized identity to show only the facade of an identity that is overdetermined and always already exoticised and vilified. "Masks" highlight the tendencies of racialization to diabolically generalize minority belonging while indicating the obfuscation of the realities of minority experiences in representations within hegemonic structures. Within the entrenched history of immigration and belonging in the United States, the term *Masks of Threat*, may remind one of the period of "yellow peril" that characterized American sociopolitical scrutiny initiated during the late nineteenth century resulting in changes in immigration reform and policy with the passing of the Chinese Exclusion Act of 1882, and later with the Immigration Restriction Act (1917), and the National Origins Act (1924). Yellow peril reached its peak during the attack on Pearl Harbor in 1941.

Ironically, the term now refers to racist stereotypes of threat and lack of humanity against Japanese people. Eventually, during the Cold War era, Chinese immigrants swiftly reclaimed their original perilous stature. *Good* and *Bad* Asians were defined solely on the basis of Asia's presence and impact on America's politics and economics at the time. Overall, *yellow peril* has been flexibly applied to all Asian Americans conveniently over time and according to the trajectory of historical, cultural, political, and economic events impacting America through/from (East) Asia. 1965 marked the Hart-Celler Immigration Act which started the second wave of (South) Asian Immigration to the United States but it is more closely associated with the success stories of the current generation of South Asian American professionals, primarily Hindu and Indian. The invisibility of other South Asians—along gendered, economic, religious, and political-historical lines—was internalized within this narrative of the dominant immigration success stories. Thus, throughout the spate of South Asian immigration, a monolithic identity of the immigrant was produced and disseminated. The dominant culture represented and "trusted" this simple, single category of the South Asian American. Things changed more drastically following the terrorist attacks.

Thus, *brown peril* is a racist stereotype whose trajectory follows a similar path as that associated with yellow peril, however, here, the difference in being brown in America is often conflated with religious and cultural practices that are demonized in times of crisis while remaining useful ethnic pockets of cheap labor in the global economy at other less threatening times, within structures of capitalism. Understanding the ways in which brown peril plays out in current American policies is slightly murkier than the historical contexts underlining Asian American racialization. Hence, the term *masks of threat* refers to the mainstream interpellation of the South Asian religious-cultural-ethnic identity, objectifying it into a monolithic object of danger, scrutiny, and unbelonging. The moral, political, economic panic associated with the threat from *brown peril* seamlessly connects the brown racial body to the cultural practices most commonly ascribed to those bodies. However, as mentioned above, brown hindu bodies were quick to distance and disavow themselves from "other" brown bodies, bodies that were economically on a lower rung, and/or were religiously marked as such, that is, as Muslim bodies.

Consequently, the interpellation of Muslim South Asians or South Asian Americans into subject-positions of threat- and terror-mongering agents within hegemonic spaces, disempowers them significantly in the sociocultural and economic domains. Currently, brown peril showcases the consolidation of anti-Muslim racism in the United States. Brown peril has gradually become associated with a neologism, such as, Islamophobia, where it is interesting to note that female South Asian bodies are constructed as victims within a Western, Christian narrative, while male bodies are clumped into one category of the villain: hypermasculined objects of distrust who oppress women (Maira 2009). As a result of this gendering and its perpetuation in film and culture (e.g., the 2005 film, *Syriana*), *Islamophobia* led to stereotypical constructs shaping images and public policies, while coloring mainstream discourse in America.[4] Although one may trace the history of the term with European animosity against its Muslim migrants in the late twentieth century, *Islamophobia* was revitalized in public rhetoric in the United States following the Gulf Wars in the 1990s. Disregarding the heterogeneity in the religious group called "Muslims," Islamophobia amplified the alienation and disenfranchisement of entire bodies of immigrant groups based on their physical appearance or faith.

Such a process had both internal and external dynamics, which exposed the fissures within communities. Thus, on reapplying Louis Althusser's concept of interpellation, it becomes apparent that the creation and construction of the Muslim/brown perilous subject results in a kind of complicity whereby the "good Muslim" maintains his/her distance from the "bad Muslim" while both categories are offered and opened up for alliance by the ruling rhetoric—U.S. Homeland Security and political ideology. After 9/11, the invisible and internal communal tensions within South Asian diasporic groups became prominent, with a growing distancing along the lines of "us/them" that was already in place within the South Asian Hindu and the lower-class migrant hindu laborers, and those between the Muslim South Asian and the migrant Muslim laboring community. The interreligious and classist difference reasserted itself promptly in its hostility against and disavowal from the bigger diasporic South Asian American identity. The backlash and intercommunal distinctions quickly followed after such categories of "good" and "bad" resonated in U.S. political narratives. South Asian Sikh lobbying efforts quickly pointed out that Sikh turbans were not the same as Muslim turbans ("The Turban is not a Hat" was a document in circulation among Sikhs after 9/11 for insisting airport security personnel that their turbans had to be unwrapped and not taken off like a hat and that it was different than "those other" turbans). In this defensive document of early Sikh advocacy, the Sikh identity had to reintroduce and reassert itself in American sociocultural life through their turban, which was provocatively differentiated from the Muslim turban. Ironically enough, in defending one community, another ethnic and religious identity became identified as the "real" object of threat. In trying to acknowledge Sikhism's peaceful nature, its anti-Muslim sentiment and disavowal from Islam had to be strictly pronounced (Puar 2008, 49).

This rhetoric has, without doubt, engendered a xenophobic, ethnocentric, and a homogenous restructuring of cultural and sociopolitical geographies, albeit the neoliberal logics of a globalized and transnational world. The problematic and reductive representation of race in American culture has been studied from the perspective of minority communities under scrutiny especially after 9/11, including Sikhs, Pakistanis, and other minority immigrants from South Asian countries. In their essay "Monster, Terrorist, Fag: The War on Terrorism and the Production of Docile Patriots," Jasbir Puar and Amit Rai discuss the development and reassertion of heteronormativity perpetuated by the state implicating race, and more interestingly, sexuality. Puar and Rai note the redefinition of the Sikh identity in post-9/11 identity through the turban, which became the symbol of cultural solidarity among Sikhs, remasculinizing and then, renationalizing them (Puar and Rai 2002, 137). While a feminist discourse focusing on how women's bodies have become a potent site in the workings of U.S. "antiterrorism" strategies, have long been lacking, Sunaina Maira's recent scholarship on the topic argues that this discourse simultaneously gets preoccupied with women's bodies while embedding the logic of the War on Terror "in the gendered politics of colonialism, nationalism, and liberalism" (Maira 2009, 632). Moreover, the criminalization of Muslim immigrants, especially men, is used to justify any militant action by the state under the guise of a "homeland security." Mahmood Mamdani's "Good Muslim, Bad Muslim: A Political Perspective on Culture and Terrorism" critiques the simplistic binary between "good" and "bad" Muslims, a binary that has become the de facto way of understanding Muslim psyche in the wake of 9/11 and that establishes U.S. security interests as the sole yardstick for defining Muslim political identities. While President Bush and his administration paid lip service to this binary, the current rhetoric within ongoing Presidential debates, resurrects the national body politic whereby *all* Muslim identities are characterized as monolithic and threatening.

Media representations constructed these groups as communities that mask their sinister designs of acting treacherously against the nation-state. Stable generalizations of who could be terrorist had made its rounds in U.S. Customs Service after 9/11, and contemporary profiling practices depend on "identifying" a terrorist as a composite category involving race, physical appearance ("look"), language, religion, and other public information that the state harvests. While Arab American studies was quick to focus critical attention in this direction, studies that underscored the situations of South Asian Muslims from other parts of the world other than the Middle East were fewer and far between. Junaid

Rana's *Terrifying Muslims: Race and Labor in the South Asian Diaspora* makes a significant contribution through its multidisciplinary, ethnographic field research, where Rana showcases the quotidian experiences of Pakistani Muslims in the labor diaspora in the United States. While this book makes a cogent analysis connecting the genealogies of race, religion, gender, class, and hegemony, it has more of a sociological scope in extending its argument rather than adding significantly to literary study and scholarship about the South Asian diaspora.

This volume then continues that conversation through studying literary and visual texts, film, art, and cultural artifacts underscoring the reinforcement of public stereotype against brown South Asians and Asian American Muslims while showcasing how communities reasserted themselves through these representations. The essays in this anthology explore this dynamic relationship among and within South Asian communities as they indicate the fissures in their interethnic relationship, while being simultaneously overdetermined as communities and spaces of threat and unbelonging in U.S. body politic. Essayists explore how South Asian intellectuals and writers respond to this reinforcement of cultural boundary making, using religion and race, and in mixing religion and class with sexuality and gender.

In its politics of belonging and disavowing any allegiance within a greater fraternity, the South Asian (Indian) diaspora has been quick to identify itself as a nonthreatening, unified, and consumable identity, rescripting itself through Bollywood as overwhelmingly Hindu, largely Indian, and primarily educated and upper class while distinctly excluding that identity from the immigrant labor diaspora primarily composed of Muslim South Asians who have been easily branded "the real enemy." This kind of an identity formation and assimilation to America actually predate the events of September 2001, and refer to a period in South Asian diaspora history when one community and its history were reasserted over silencing other community histories from South Asia.[5] Thus, a volume of essays that traces this kind of a violent distinction within the South Asian diaspora, while corroborating on the life experiences of South Asian Muslim Americans, is a needful and valuable addition to reclamation and reconfiguration of an inclusive historico-cultural-sociopolitical belonging to America. The essays included in this collection connect postcolonial approaches to the discourse of ethnic and cultural studies in order to reveal the various contexts of race, religion, and class that Islamophobia and its manifestation in state policy attempt to conflate. Each essay highlights the need for the visibility of a discourse that underscores the inassimilable conditions experienced by Muslim South Asian Americans or South Asians in America, disturbing the artificial yet forceful depiction of a harmonious multicultural coexistence in America.

Globalization theorists have already shown how transnationalism and identity formation in the diaspora result from pathways called *flows* which develop and affect subjectivities and desires within the fluid space of movement and migration (Grewal and Kaplan 1994; Appadurai 1996; Lowe 1996). Drawing from this earlier scholarship, each essay in this volume investigates the circuits of regional migration based on socio-economic status quos, and class indices, which inflect subjectivities while affecting desires and sociocultural practices within the transnational space. The constant state of flux of these transnational identities based on class and status quo is problematic when placed in perspective of racial formations. As an analytical category, class then becomes a marker that essays in this volume use to explore race and racialization within a wage-based economy and its relation and position within a capitalist global system based on transmission or creation of wealth. Labor diasporas in the South Asian context are always already gendered, thus, it is also masculinized in dominant sociocultural contexts. The male migrant worker having fluid subjectivity is often attached to the concept of crimi-nality or with terrorist affiliation. The complicated terrain of navigating the labor diaspora while being Muslim, male, and from South Asia illu-minates the multiplicity of the diaspora's engagement with race, class, and religion, underscoring a heterogeneous concept of identity formation for South Asian Muslims in America and elsewhere. This uneven topog-raphy of belonging that each essay in this volume charts through under-standings of race and surveillance reiterates the ways of performing South Asian and American notions of citizenship—sociopolitically and econo-culturally. By reexamining cultural and literary texts, this book illustrates how gender, race, class, and religion become imbricated in the fabric of national and political life in the United States and help reconfig-ure South Asian American identities.

In examining the contours of these evolving identities, thrust upon by the nation-state, or by performing local culture, the essays in this volume expose a complex web of interconnections that govern the boundaries of belonging and unbelonging of communities within the American polity. Therefore, each essay questions the cartographies of Americanness and South Asian Muslimness while revealing the underlying patterns of interaction, contradiction, and community formation in this minority community. This anthology centralizes the heterogeneity of Muslim American histories and identities by geopolitical and cultural location and stresses the impact of the transnational labor migration on commu-nity formation. As a volume that examines cultural and literary texts in an unfolding narrative of race and racialization of the South Asian Mus-lim identity, it makes several important contributions to the field of cul-tural studies, ethnic studies, South Asian studies, postcolonial studies, Asian American studies, gender and race studies, Diaspora studies, and transnational and global studies. Since the essays in this volume take the events of 9/11 as a departure point to discuss the concepts of belonging for South Asian Americans, it also provokes interaction within several texts in the field.

Previous studies have included understanding the role of loss and trauma in the context of 9/11. _Literature after 9/11_ (Keniston and Follanbee 2008) poignantly showcases and analyzes narratives of pain, memory, and trauma, and highlights scholars' study of the human predicament and loss associated with the events during and after 9/11. Literary and creative responses from South Asian American writers about the lived experiences within the Asian community in the context of 9/11 amid growing Islamophobia are missing from the ethical questioning that _Literature after 9/11_ promises. Literary works focused more intensely on South Asian narratives find resonance in Pei-Chen Liao's recent _'Post'-9/11 South Asian Diasporic Fiction: Uncanny Terror_ (2012). Liao studies the genre of literature after 9/11 through the concept of Freud's _unheimlich_ or the uncanny and unhomely. Other notable studies include understanding sexuality and South Asianness in popular culture (Lee and Zhou 2004), such as in film (Gopinath 2005), in literature and popular culture (Maira 2002). More recent contributions to the field have a more ethnographic thrust. For example, Khyati Joshi's _New Roots in America's Sacred Ground_ (2006) links race, religion, and ethnicity in interviews and case studies involving second-generation Indian Americans spanning in age from elementary school to adulthood. In this reexamination, Joshi underscores the ways in which race, religion, and appearance have recreated a different space for these Americans within their communities while sociocultural and political events have resulted in a backlash affecting their belonging within America, especially after 9/11. Susan Koshy and R. Radhakrishnan's edited collection _Transnational South Asians: The Making of a Neo-Diaspora_ (2008) undertakes the work of studying the "other" of the South Asian Diaspora, often misrepresented and ignored in mainstream diaspora studies and scholarship, thus, slaves, women migrants, queer desis find mention and relevance in this volume of essays. These look at political organizing and global circuits of communications, including social networking, to understand the pivotal role that South Asians play within the diaspora. While questions of race and class may not be the major focus here, they are underlying issues within a bigger discourse linking displacement, globalization, and the labor and transnational networks of South Asians within the diaspora.

Shalini Shankar's ethnographic work, _Desi Land: Teen Culture, Class, and Success in Silicon Valley_, published the same year as _Transnational South Asians_, resituates the conversation linking South Asian youth cultures in Silicon Valley and their impact on the economies and issues of belonging to the South Asian diaspora simultaneously informing terrains of consciousness involving race, class, gender, and sexuality. Vivek Bald et. al's edited collection, _The Sun Never Sets_, is also a recent ethnographic addition talking about those South Asian maritime labor migrants from the turn of the century along with those deported after 9/11, who are often unacknowledged. Bald and his colleagues reveal the contours of U.S. imperialism in shaping South Asian belonging over time, ultimately arguing for the significant role and impact that these migrant sectors and communities have fulfilled to reexamine the American public imagination and the place of the the South Asian migrant in it. Nitasha Tamar Sharma's *Hip Hop Desis* deserves a special mention since she draws the important connection between South Asian hip-hop artists and racialized and black minorities in the United States while forging a sense of their belonging to the greater South Asian communities in the United States and beyond. Through the premise of music and hip-hop artists within the desi circuit, Sharma argues that this interracial connection unfolds a youth culture ready to enable social change by being expansive in articulating an alternative space of solidarity and belonging to the greater society through the premise of music. Khyati Joshi and Jigna Desai's edited collection, *Asian Americans in Dixie* (2013) talks about incorporating an understanding of the development of the South Asian identity in the American South in mainstream scholarship mostly dealing with the binaries of black-white relations. Reexamining the supposed sociocultural isolation of the region, this volume of essays initiates the useful conversation of including South Asians within a global network across the Pacific, Caribbean, and Atlantic and in understanding their identity formation along these economic and global networks of power. Other prominent studies on South Asianness and race include Junaid Rana's *Terrifying Muslims: Race and Labor in the South Asian Diaspora* (2011), Vijay Prashad's *Uncle Swami: South Asians in America Today* (2012), and Deepa Kumar's *Islamophobia and the Politics of Empire* (2012). Kumar's work unearths the genealogy of colonial construction during the interaction between Muslims and Europeans. Kumar argues that ideological differences and the terror narrative on the Muslim were important pillars to sustain the imperial hegemony. While its sociohistoric, economic, and cultural compass cannot be undermined, Kumar's book is more of a primer in understanding the roots and routes of Islamophobia. It importantly reminds us that ethnic and minority backlash against South Asians in America following 9/11 became more pronounced and that more critical and scholarly attention is necessary to critique and expose a racist machinery while being cautious about multiracial (or post-racial) euphoria. This is where volumes like *South Asian Racialization and Belonging after 9/11: Masks of Threat* step in.

Thus, Chandrima Chakraborty's "Remembering the Air India Tragedy in an Age of Terror" analyzes the 1985 airplane bombing that led to the Canadian government's consequent reconfiguration about identity and belonging for Sikh Americans and South Asian Canadians. Chakraborty's essay then grids the events of 9/11 to trace a pattern of remembering, mourning, and equating past experiences of racial and cultural discrimination against South Asians in North America. Reading the Canadian Prime Minister, Stephen Harper's public apology in 2010 on the Air India bombing, Chakraborty takes readers down to fictional remembrances in her reading of Anita Rau Badami's *Can you Hear the Nightbird Call?* and Bharati Mukherjee's "The Management of Grief." Chakraborty explores these literary narratives to (re)examine their intersections and echoes with ongoing racialized experiences shaping South Asian subjectivities in the diaspora. Indicating the irony in the prompt call of Harper who wants to enlist racialized minorities in the war on terror by promising to "make the skies safe for travel," Chakraborty reminds readers of the positions of the narratives by Badami and Mukherjee that alert us to the conditions on the ground that critique the government's projection of a happy multicultural existence. The study of minority belonging and racialization after 9/11 within the perspective of other events in the past—such as the Air India bombing in 1985—not only puts the events of 9/11 in conversation with other such events involving terrorism and state policies, it simultaneously puts to dialogue the long history of racialization and disenfranchisement against South Asians in North America long before the events of 9/11. While expanding the compass of studying racialization of South Asians in North America and arguing that it predates 9/11, Chakraborty's essay initiates an important engagement embedding fiction, fact, and policy making, and in tracing the sociohistorical and systemic exclusion of South Asians.

Resonating Chakraborty's point, John Hutnyk's chapter "Sexy Sammy and Red Rosie?: From Burning Books to the War on Terror" examines the literary, sonic, and visual regimes that chronicle the shift from the spectacular to the "low intensity warfare" that the war on terror has become. Whereas the war on terror is usually rendered in iconic terms, denoted by phrases such as "clash of civilizations," its implementation pervades the empirical, which makes it more, rather than less, violent and makes it that much more difficult to counter. Instead of exceptionalizing 9/11, Hutnyk connects the post-9/11 discourses of race and terror to the historical events of 1989, especially the fatwa against author Salman Rushdie and the recalibration of the relation between race and religion in its aftermath. Both Chakraborty and Hutnyk show the interconnectedness of 9/11 and South Asian exclusion and prejudicial treatment based on race, class, and ethnicity, while arguing that the event cannot be studied in isolation to the systemic exclusion of South Asian immigrants in the West.

Using ethnographic research and methodology, Stanley Thangaraj, delves into the complicated terrains for defining belonging for bona fide Americans with South Asian Muslim lineage. Taking sporting practices, especially basketball, Thangaraj underscores the processes through which Pakistani Muslim American men perform their renditions of Americanness. Laying focus on its gendered and racially heteronormative ways that distances the community from the mainstream representation of the "terrorist" while structuring exclusions within their community, Thangaraj argues that by performing their own takes on basketball masculinity, young men affirm a normative masculinity that sets the parameters of belonging within their community. In the process, Muslim class respectabilities and one's relation to the "model minority" status affirm practices of belonging through cultural citizenship. This essay shows the ways Pakistani American men negotiate American popular culture to affirm and perform an Americanness that counters the racial logic involved in the "war on terror." They are not subjects who are impossible to assimilate but are rather interesting subjects who complicate and extend the boundaries of Americanness.

In dialogue with Thangaraj is a timely examination by Hasan al Zayed in "'The City's Changed': *Home Boy, The Reluctant Fundamentalist*, and the Post 9/11 Urban Experience." This chapter explores the intricacies of belonging that an urban metropolitan space forges within conditions of neoliberalism. Studying Mohsin Hamid and H. M. Naqvi's novels, the essay tracks the relation between the inhospitable city and the migrant who finds it changed in the wake of the terror attacks while being forced to reconsider his place in it. The essay hinges on the idea that in their efforts to narrate the migrant's struggle and dilemma in the post-9/11 New York City, Naqvi's and Hamid's novels also expose the vicissitudes of urban experience, bringing into focus not only the precarious nature of migrant experience but also the internal unevenness of the neoliberal, cosmopolitan urban space. Although both *Home Boy* and *The Reluctant Fundamentalist* predominantly focus on the religious-cultural components of the post-9/11 situation, their engagement with the political-economic aspects of the immigrant life remain cursory. It is these novels, which highlight the viscerality of the imperialist venture that often get obscured by the glossy rhetoric of justice and culture war. Uniting urban geography and the experiences of migration and belonging, this essay importantly continues a conversation that compels us to reexamine the contours of imperial urbanscapes in charting belonging.

As these essays provide perspectives on belonging for the South Asian within cityscapes and through sport fraternities, Lopamudra Basu and Sarah Wahab argue about interethnic animosity and complicated distancing involving South Asian racialization. Thus, Basu's chapter explores a performative distancing between Muslim and American identities while paradoxically demonstrating how denouncing one leads to reinforcing a negative association with the other. Wahab's chapter reasserts the playing of this binary and talks about the dynamics between Sikh and Arab belonging in the media, whereby one group distinguishes itself from another by the disturbing logics of "good" and "bad" racialization. Basu's "Between Performativity and Representation: Post 9/11 Muslim Masculinity in Ayad Akhtar's *Disgraced*" brings to a critical dialogue many contemporary trends in the discourse of racialization of South

Asian Muslims in post-9/11 U.S. society. The play's main character simulates a Moor-like attitude, associated with misogynistic traits, and sexual jealousy, while ironically distancing himself from his religious affiliation in keeping with the assimilatory politics to belong to secular, multicultural America. His behavior affirms the stereotype of Islamic misogyny circulating about the South Asian Muslim male in post-9/11 America. Alerting readers to the limits of performative agency, Basu's chapter critiques the prominence of a deterministic trope for South Asian Muslims essentializing their cultural and religious identities within American civic and political life.

Sarah Wahab's chapter, "'Sikhs aren't terrorists, those Arabs are:' Collective Forgetting and Resistive Remembering in Sharat Raju's *American Made*" critique the way minority racialization and difference is produced and sustained by the state for upholding the exclusivities that come with citizenship and assimilation. Focusing on the site of the Sikh turban which dissociates itself from the Muslim and Arab hat, Wahab's essay critiques the politics of division by studying a film, *American Made*, where the Sikh turban becomes an object signifying "good" or "bad" citizenship. Such a kind of dubious characterization of citizenship reinforces the State's logic of continually persecuting racialized bodies. Simultaneously erasing the histories of the violent contexts of racializations, such a mechanism, Wahab argues, unobtrusively reflects back to the exclusions that citizenship and belonging entails within a nation-state. The concluding chapter, Reshmi Dutt-Ballerstadt's, "Terror Narratives: Art, Music and the post-9/11 Surveillance Culture" argues that public responses to U.S. "domestic tensions" post 9/11 are rather benign when rendered through fiction. The essay showcases that it is indeed not imaginative literature (fiction) but provocative art and music that have captured more directly the racialized repercussions of the "war on terror." These artistic responses attempt to document the various dehumanizing efforts the war on terror have produced on the racialization of subjects deemed as the "other" by a state sponsored surveillance system post 9/11. By probing into the works of Iraqi dissident artists such as, Wafaa Bilal and his project called "Domestic Tensions," Bangladeshi artist Hasan M Elahi's exhibition called "Tracking Transience," along with jazz pianist Vijay Iyer albums *In What Language* and *Holding It Down: The Veterans' Dreams Project* (documenting the experiences of people of color at the airports, and Iraq and Afghanistan wars experienced by veterans of color), the essay maps the ways in which the culture of surveillance have terrorized the lives of the racialized other both within and beyond the United States.

Each chapter within this volume offers a premise for a conversation on race, belonging, and identity, in continuum. Highlighting the broader contexts of racialization pre- and post 9/11 and showcasing the strategic and internal communal tensions of belonging to American civic and public life, this collection renews the conversation on race and belonging.

Simultaneously, its focus avenues through art and literature bring out the deceptive disciplining of minority and immigrant identities, ultimately revealing the logics of a hegemonic neoliberal, racist, and sexist state. This highlights the significance of reevaluating the complicities of marking bodies racially—economically—by religion, both within the community that is under scrutiny, and in the wider arena where it is being reconfigured as such. While the political ethos examining the effectiveness of such a study is a matter of time, *South Asian Racialization and Belonging after 9/11: Masks of Threat* is a valuable addition in the field of South Asian, race, and cultural studies in uniting diverse voices, perspectives, and texts, and indicating the heterogeneous pivot points of arguments constructing race, religion, and class in discourses about South Asian belonging, citizenship, and in forging identity in America post 9/11.

## REFERENCES

Althusser, Louis. "Ideology and Ideological State Apparatuses." *Lenin and Philosophy, and Other Essays*. Trans. Ben Brewster. London: New Left Books. 1972. 127–188. Accessed October 17, 2014. https://www.marxists.org/reference/archive/althusser/1970/ideology.htm.

Appiah, Antony. "Race, Culture, Identity: Misunderstood Connections." *Color Conscious The Political Morality of Race*. Eds., Anthony Appiah and Amy Gutmann. Princeton: Princeton University Press. 76–80. 1996. Accessed April 1, 2014. https://204racethought.wikispaces.com/file/view/Appiah,+Amy+Gutmann+-+Color+Conscious+-+1998.pdf.

———. "Identity Against Culture: Understandings of Multiculturalism." Avenali Lecture. Ed. Christina M. Gillis. Berkeley, CA. September 12, 1994. Accessed January 23, 2015. http://townsendcenter.berkeley.edu/sites/default/files/publications/OP01_Appiah.pdf.

Appadurai, Arjun. *Modernity at Large: Cultural Dimensions of Globalization*. Minneapolis: University of Minnesota Press, 1996.

Bald, Vivek, Miabi Chatterjee, Sujani Reddy, and Manu Vimalassery. Eds. *The Sun Never Sets South Asian Migrants in an Age of U.S. Power (NYU Series in Social and Cultural Analysis)*. New York: New York University Press, 2013.

Bald, Vivek. "'Lost' in the City: Spaces and Stories of South Asian New York, 1917–1965." *South Asian Popular Culture* 5.1 (April 2007): 59–76. *Academic Search Complete*. Accessed October 17, 2014. http://web.b.ebscohost.com.proxydc.wrlc.org/ehost/pdfviewer/pdfviewer?sid=30dd3bff-47c8-4ae2-887e-bf07cf65a461%40sessionmgr102&vid=30&hid=124.

Fanon, Franz. *Black Skin, White Masks*. Trans. Charles Lam Markmann. London: Pluto Press, 1986.

Goldberg, David Theo. *The Racial State*. Cambridge: Blackwell, 2002.

———. *The Threat of Race: Reflections on Racial Neoliberalism*. Massachusetts: Wiley-Blackwell 2009.

Gopinath, Gayatri. *Impossible Desires: Queer Diasporas and South Asian Public Cultures*. Durham, NC: Duke University Press, 2005.

Grewal, Inderpal, and Caren Kaplan. Eds. *Scattered Hegemonies: Postmodernity and Transnational Feminist Practices*. Minneapolis: University of Minnesota Press, 1994.

Joshi, Khyati Y., and Jigna Desai. Eds. *Asian Americans in Dixie: Race and Migration in the South (Asian American Experience)*. Champaign: University of Illinois Press, 2013.

Joshi, Khyati Y. *New Roots in America's Sacred Ground: Religion, Race, and Ethnicity in Indian America*. New Brunswick, NJ: Rutgers University Press, 2006.

Keniston, Ann, and Jeanne Follansbee Quinn, Eds. *Literature after 9/11*. New York: Routledge, 2008.

Koshy, Susan, and R. Radhakrishnan. Eds. *Transnational South Asians: The Making of a Neo-Diaspora*. New York: Oxford University Press, 2008.

Kumar, Deepa. *Islamophobia and the Politics of Empire*. Chicago, IL: Haymarket Books, 2012.

Lee, Jennifer, and Min Zhao. Eds. *Asian American Youth: Culture, Identity and Ethnicity*. New York: Routledge, 2004.

Liao, Pei-Chen. *'Post'-9/11 South Asian Diasporic Fiction: Uncanny Terror*. New York: Palgrave Macmillan, 2012.

Lowe, Lisa. *Immigrant Acts: On Asian American Cultural Politics*. Durham, NC: Duke University Press, 1996.

Maira, Sunaina. "Good and Bad Muslim Citizens: Feminists, Terrorists, and U.S. Orientalisms." *Feminist Studies* 35.3 (Fall 2009): 631–56. *Academic Search Complete*. Accessed March 27, 2014. http://web.b.ebscohost.com.proxydc.wrlc.org/ehost/pdfviewer/pdfviewer?sid=30dd3bff-47c8-4ae2-887e-bf07cf65a461%40sessionmgr102&vid=24&hid=124.

Maira, Sunaina, Elizabeth Soep, and George Lipsitz. Eds., *Youthscapes: The Popular, the National, the Global*. Philadelphia: University of Pennsylvania Press, 2004.

———. *Desis in the House: Indian American Youth Culture in New York City*. Philadelphia: Temple University Press, 2002.

Majid, Anouar. *We Are All Moors: Ending Centuries of Crusades Against Muslims and Other Minorities*. Minneapolis: University of Minnesota Press, 2009.

Mamdani, Mahmood. "Good Muslim, Bad Muslim: A Political Perspective on Culture and Terrorism." *American Anthropologist* 104.3 (2002): 766-775. *Academic Search Complete*. Accessed January 23, 2015. http://jan.ucc.nau.edu/sj6/mamdanigoodmuslim-badmuslim.pdf.

Mufti, Aamir. *Enlightenment in the Colony: The Jewish Question and the Crisis of Postcolonial Culture*. Princeton, NJ: Princeton University Press, 2007.

Omi, Michael, and Howard Winant. *Racial Formation in the United States: from the 1960s to the 1990s*. New York: Routledge, 1994.

Ong, Aihwa. *Flexible Citizenship: The Cultural Logics of Transnationality*. Durham, NC: Duke University Press, 1999.

Prashad, Vijay. *Uncle Swami: South Asians in America Today*. New York: The New Press, 2012.

Puar, Jasbir K. "'The Turban is Not a Hat': Queer Diaspora and Practices of Profiling." *Sikh Formations: Religion, Culture, Theory* 4.1 (2008): 47–91. *Academic Search Complete*. Web. May 12, 2015. http://www.jasbirpuar.com/assets/The-Turban-is-not-a-Hat-Sikh-Formations.pdf.

Puar, Jasbir K. and, Amit S. Rai. "Monster, Terrorist, Fag: The War on Terrorism and the Production of Docile Patriots." *Social Text* 20.3 (2002): 117–148. *Project Muse*. Accessed March 27, 2014. http://web.b.ebscohost.com.proxydc.wrlc.org/ehost/pdfviewer/pdfviewer?sid=30dd3bff-47c8-4ae2-887e-bf07cf65a461%40sessionmgr102&vid=17&hid=124.

Rana, Junaid. *Terrifying Muslims: Race and Labor in the South Asian Diaspora*. Durham, NC: Duke University Press, 2011.

Shankar, Shalini. *Desi Land: Teen Culture, Class, and Success in Silicon Valley*. Durham, NC: Duke Universtiy Press, 2008.

Sharma, Nitasha Tamar. *Hip Hop Desis: South Asian Americans, Blackness, and a Global Race Consciousness (Refiguring American Music)*. Durham, NC: Duke University Press, 2010.

*Syriana*. Dir. Stephen Gaghan. Perf., George Clooney, Matt Damon, Amanda Peet. Warner Bros.: USA, 2005. DVD.

## NOTES

1. See *New York Times*, Sept. 23, 2013, "Chronicling Anti-Sikh Violence, and Now a Victim." J. David Goodman. A 18. Accessed October 12, 2014. http://www.nytimes.com/2013/09/24/nyregion/chronicling-anti-sikh-violence-and-now-a-victim.html?_r=0.

2. See White House Archives, President George W. Bush's "Address to a Joint Session of Congress and the American People" delivered Sept. 20, 2001, http://georgewbush-whitehouse.archives.gov/news/releases/2001/09/20010920-8.html.

3. Jindal is not alone in this conscious political distancing. The governor of South Carolina, Nikki Randhawa Haley, joins him in this conscious distancing from ethnic and cultural heritage to carve out an "American" belonging, while still touting the model minority card. So, brown respectability becomes problematic in political life, unless brown *becomes* a lighter shade, almost resembling white.

4. See page 6 of this volume.

5. During the early years of the South Asian immigration to parts of the United States, Punjabi settlers in the West Coast (pejoratively called "rag heads") from the first two decades of the twentieth century came in as farmhands. Their later involvement in the fledgling Indian Nationalist Movement, or in the Revolutionary activities of the Ghadar Party saw a culmination of their presence in the U.S. body politic in the legal case of Bhagat Singh Thind in 1923. By recoding South Asian membership within the citizenry of the United States, the Thind case placed South Asians in the category of "Oriental"—putting them in an already racial schema that later formed part of the Asiatic threat to America, the *yellow peril*. Even in those early years, the predominant narrative of the South Asian diaspora categorically excludes the experiences of "other" South Asian immigrants—Indian Muslim maritime workers who resettled in New York, other exiles, and students (Vivek 2007, 61). These different kinds of migrant trajectories are silenced in dominant South Asian diaspora history, while the more acceptable narratives of the immigrants from 1960s see more commendable mention.

# ONE

# Remembering Air India Flight 182 in an Age of Terror

Chandrima Chakraborty

On April 16, 2015, Narendra Modi, the first Indian prime minister to visit Canada since 1973, joined Canadian Prime Minister Stephen Harper at Humber Bay Park (Toronto) to honor the victims of the 1985 Air India bombings. Prime Minister Modi's symbolic visit to the Air India memorial is symptomatic of our anxious age, an age of terror. It illuminates how the threat of terror and the fight against terrorism dominate national politics across the globe and how the association of terror with particular bodies in the post-9/11 era has resulted in a history of anti-minority national policies being effectively covered over by a reinvigorated discourse on terrorism.

The 1985 Air India bombings are a case in point. Three hundred twenty-nine people lost their lives in a bomb explosion on June 23, 1985, on board Air India Flight 182, en route to Delhi from Montreal via Toronto. Another bomb, intended for Air India Flight 301, detonated in the baggage transfer at Narita International Airport in Tokyo, killing two baggage handlers. Although most of the passengers on board Air India Flight 182 were Canadians of Indian heritage, the Canadian government dismissed the bombing as a foreign tragedy: "A foreign carrier had crashed off foreign seas" (Blaise and Mukherjee 1987, 174).[1] However, in the aftermath of the attacks on the Twin Towers in New York City on September 11, 2001, and the United States–led "war on terror" that followed, the Canadian government revised its lengthy disavowal of the 1985 Air India bombings as a "foreign" tragedy. Public memorialization of the 1985 Air India bombings as a "Canadian tragedy" ranged from the construction of public memorials in Toronto, as well as in Vancouver, Ottawa, and Montreal, to the naming of June 23 as a National Day of Remembrance for Victims of Terrorism. Yet, in the recontextualized terrain of race and racialization in post-9/11 North America, these belated public memorializations did not prompt an engagement with the state's treatment of South Asians in the past; it helped the state to legitimize its increased surveillance of racialized minorities.

By reconceptualizing the Air India bombings and the losses they represent as "Canadian tragedy," the Canadian state sought to stake a claim to terror and to trauma for the explicit purpose of marshaling the Air India tragedy for the war on terror. In his final report of the Commission of Inquiry into the Investigation of the Bombing of Air India Flight 182 on June 17, 2010, Commissioner John C. Major concluded that a "cascading series of errors" by the Canadian government and official agencies had contributed to the Air India tragedy (Major 2010).[2] Five days later, in a commemoration ceremony at the memorial site in Toronto, Prime Minister Stephen Harper apologized on behalf of the federal government for what he called the "institutional failings of 25 years ago and the treatment of the victims' families thereafter" (Harper 2010). Delivered before and to grieving families, predominantly Canadians of Indian descent who had spent decades pressuring the government to take responsibility for its contribution to the tragedy and the mistreatment of families in its aftermath, the apology deflects attention away from structural racism, even as South Asian (and other) immigrants to Canada are made more vulnerable by post-9/11 state policies.

Through an examination of former Prime Minister Harper's "statement" or official "apology," this chapter addresses the national and political rhetoric in Canada decades after the crash, and its connection to South Asian racialization in an age of terror. It offers a critical reading of the official apology, which revises the Canadian government's initial representation of the Air India bombings as a foreign tragedy and the lengthy disavowal of the bombings and the losses as of serious significance to Canada, in relation to creative remembrances of the tragedy. I argue that the apology functions as a strategy and discourse that seeks to consolidate official multiculturalism by clarifying to families and friends of Air India victims that the state did not kill, its citizens did—and, further, that these citizens are their own (i.e., Indo-Canadians). It reminds those gathered at the commemoration ceremony that this particular violence was "conceived in Canada, executed in Canada, by Canadian citizens, and its victims were themselves mostly citizens of Canada" (Harper 2010). The intent is to hold Indo-Canadian immigrants responsible for importing "blood-feuds" (Harper 2010) from India into tolerant, multicultural Canada. Thus, while the Prime Minister's public acknowledgement of the bombing of Air India Flight 182 as a Canadian tragedy points to the state's and its majority citizens' belated acceptance of racialized minorities as citizens with rights and protections guaranteed by the state, it also presents the bombing of Air India Flight 182 as *India's* problem with *its* (Sikh) minorities, ignoring Canada's historical contributions to these racial tensions and its own failure to protect its minorities. Linking the state's conceptualization of brown bodies as potential terrorists to the Air India bombings—by, for example, naming June 23 as the National Day of Remembrance for Victims of Terrorism (in 2005)—the government, through the apology, urges Air India victims' families and friends to embrace a multicultural future by endorsing its post-9/11 anti-terrorism initiatives "to prevent another Flight 182" (Harper 2010). The implication is that the Indo-Canadian community's failure to live up to Canada's multicultural ideal in the past makes its commitment to the government's antiterrorist initiatives in the present all the more urgent.

The official apology, then, in seeking to offer redress, functions as a tool of the state to bolster its surveillance of South Asian Canadians. Reframing the Air India bombing from a non-Canadian tragedy involving non-Canadians to a terrorist attack post-9/11 effectively reduces brown bodies to potential terrorists who pose an ongoing threat to Canada. Yet, reading the apology in conjunction with two fictional remembrances of the Air India bombings, Bharati Mukherjee's 1988 short story "The Management of Grief" and Anita Rau Badami's 2006 novel *Can You Hear the Nightbird Call?*, directs the reader's gaze to the lived experiences of Indo-Canadians pre- and post-1985, interweaving the production of the ordinary (everyday racism and racial grief) with the excessive or the extraordinary (terrorist acts). These two creative texts address the implications of the politics of official apology/official multiculturalism by emphasizing "the constitutive role that grief plays in racial/ethnic subject-formation" (Cheng 2000, xi) in multicultural Canada. Whereas Harper's apology seeks to narrativize the Air India tragedy and its aftermath as an exceptional or aberrant event (or series of events) in Canadian multiculturalism, Mukherjee and Badami propose that everyday grief and racial violence need to be acknowledged and articulated publicly. In declaring the state's acceptance of its errors in the past, the apology reinstates Canada's celebrated multiculturalism—its openness and acceptance of *others*—and, in so doing, seeks to orient the Air India families away from dwelling in the past and toward looking to the future. In contrast, "The Management of Grief" and *Can You Hear the Nightbird Call?* insistently look to the past in ways that call our attention to how South Asian immigrants continue to be made vulnerable by state policy. Prime Minister Harper sought to enlist racialized minorities in the state's war on terror by promising to "make the skies safe for travel" (Harper 2010) to ensure a happy, multicultural future for Canada. The push for increased surveillance and securitization in a post-9/11 context is legitimized in the name of public good. However, "The Management of Grief" and *Can You Hear the Nightbird Call?* urge the state to actively reflect on its long history of racism against South Asians, who continue to grieve their past, thus troubling the government's projection of a happy multicultural future.

## "CANADA'S 9/11"?

Recent scholarship on the Air India tragedy points to a shift in framing from "foreign tragedy" to "Canadian tragedy" in the aftermath of the September 11, 2001 attacks in the United States.[3] Through such strategic reframings, scholars argue, Canada emerges as a victim of foreign political violence brought on by racialized immigrants, successfully obscuring the central role that systemic racism played in the Air India events. It did, after all, take the government of Canada twenty-one years to launch a public inquiry into what has been characterized post-9/11 as "the single worst act of terrorism in Canadian history" (Harper 2010), "the largest mass murder in Canadian history" (Major) and "Canada's 9/11" (MacQueen and Geddes).

In his May 1, 2006, announcement of the Commission of Inquiry, PM Harper repeatedly stated that the intention of the Inquiry was to "bring a measure of closure to those who still grieve for their loved ones." The agenda set forth for the Commission, however, was limited to "a focused and efficient inquiry" that would "provide information that will help ensure that Canada's police agencies and procedures, its airport security systems and antiterrorism laws are the most effective in the world" (Harper 2006).[4] Thus, while the Inquiry's first phase provided opportunities for victims' families to give public testimonies of their losses and of how Canadian officials, agencies, and the larger public treated them, the government's focus was limited to the prevention of future terrorist attacks.[5] The racial injuries repeatedly noted by the families in testimonies and interviews with the press were glossed over, not seen to merit the government's attention.

The lawyer representing the families commissioned University of Toronto sociology professor Sherene Razack to write a report on the Air India bombings for the Commission. In her report, Razack discusses in great detail the role that systemic racism played in the pre- and post-bombing activities and responses of Canadian officials. After studying numerous security documents, Commission reports, and trial testimonies, Razack concluded that because of "systemic racism," the potential threat to Indo-Canadians was not taken seriously. "In a nutshell," she writes, "systemic racism operates when all lives do not count the same and when those charged with protection are not inspired to do their best to ensure that no life was lost" (Razack 2007, 3). In his summative remarks that frame the final report, Commissioner Major also comments on this negligence:

A cascading series of errors contributed to the failure of our police and security forces to prevent this atrocity. The level of error, incompetence, and inattention which took place before the flight was sadly mirrored in many ways for many years, in how authorities, Governments, and institutions dealt with the aftermath of the murder of so many innocents: in the investigation, [in] the legal proceedings, and in providing information, support and comfort to the families. (Major 2010)

Yet the Commission's final report, though subtitled *A Canadian Tragedy*, fails to explore the reasons behind the Canadian official agencies' disregard of pre-bombing security briefings; the slow, apathetic response of the Canadian state in the aftermath of the bombings; and the remarkable indifference of the Canadian public to the tragic loss of lives. Razack notes in her expert witness report that "Canadians do not recall June 23, 1985. As a nation, we were not shaken, transformed and moved to change our own institutional practices for a tragedy we considered had little to do with us" (Razack 2007, 9). Indeed, her report is excluded from the Commission of Inquiry's official website, revealing the government's careful attempt to manage a reading of the Air India story suitable to its political agenda.[6] Questions raised by Razack at the Inquiry remain unanswered even today. Why did the nation and its official agencies "not care as much as when far fewer Canadians lost their lives in the World Trade Centre . . .? What can we say about successive federal governments that made no public space for inquiry into the bombings, could not bring itself to even express condolences, and was not moved to commemorate the Canadian lives lost that day until more than twenty years after?" (Razack 2007, 24).

Harper's 2010 apology to the families, even though twenty-five years late, gestures toward embracing the loss of lives on Air India Flight 182 as a *Canadian* loss. The families' grief over the loss of loved ones on Air India Flight 182, exacerbated by the indifference of the state and many of its citizens, seems to have gradually seeped into the national consciousness, for, as Harper affirms, "*Your* pain is *our* pain. As *you* grieve, so *we* grieve. And as the years have deepened *your* grief, so has the understanding of *our* country grown" (Harper 2010, emphasis added). However, this reaching out to (primarily) Indo-Canadians does not overturn the government's initial perception of the events as "theirs" rather than "ours": the binary oppositions of *your/our* and *you/we* instead perpetuate what Cassel Busse describes as a long history of national exclusion and "a narrative of Othering that is not reconciled even in the public act of 'truth and reconciliation'" (Busse 2012, 237). The families' ("your") grief does not inform the change in the understanding of their ("your") country for, according to Harper, the grief is *yours*, but the country is *ours*: "[A]s the years have deepened *your* grief, so has the understanding of *our* country grown." And, while grief is recognized and named here, the underlying structure of differentiation remains: in the ephemeral nature of the apology, delivered at a memorial site rather than in the House of Commons (like the 1998 apology for the Second World War internment of Japanese Canadians, the 2006 apology for the Chinese head tax, or the 2008 apology to First Nations and other Indigenous Canadians for the Native residential school system) and archived on the prime minister's website rather than in Hansard, and in the nonrecognition of the grief produced by the government's apathy toward and disrespect of the families. Thus, the state's marginalization of the Air India tragedy in the nation's history continues despite this public recognition of loss.

Rajeswari Sundar Rajan argues that in official apologies those admitting to guilt not only "continue to occupy, and to speak from, a position of power" (Sundar Rajan 2000, 162), but also treat wrongs as isolated events in the past, thus ignoring the ongoing implications of those events. The Air India apology for "institutional failings" is an admission of past wrongs, not of systemic racism, as Razack has argued. It does not facilitate revisiting the past or reflecting on continuing practices of racism against minorities in Canada.[7] Instead, the wrongdoer—the Canadian state—reestablishes through this public speech act, which admits that the state and its agencies contributed to the tragedy and mistreated families in its aftermath, *its own value* as a liberal democracy, a caring nation that listens to minority grievances and takes responsibility for its own (in)actions. In the same instant that the state appears to come clean before its citizens, it directs focus away from its wrongdoing by reminding the Air India families of Canada's generosity in allowing Indo-Canadians' entry into Canada. It then holds the Indo-Canadian community responsible for wreaking havoc on this purportedly peaceful, multicultural nation. The lesson that the government learned from the Air India bombings—which is clearly conveyed to those gathered at the memorial ceremony—is that it needs Indo-Canadians for the success of its post-9/11 surveillance, security, and antiterrorism initiatives. In other words, the government strategically reaches out to Indo-Canadian families who lost loved ones on Air India Flight 182 *as Canadians* in order to solicit their support in distinguishing between bad ("terrorist") minorities and good ("model") minorities in this era of deep fear and distrust of brown bodies, not to work with them toward producing an inclusive nation.

Support for this endeavour to secure the nation's future in an age of terror can be created only by eliciting fear of the faceless terrorist lurking in our midst. Thus Harper declares in his apology,

> Sadly, we have no way of knowing when, if, or how, we may once more be attacked, or by whom. We know only that terrorism is an enemy with a thousand faces, and a hatred that festers in the darkest spots of the human mind. And we fear that when we invite from around the world, those who share our aspirations for a better life, others also come, those who see in our Canada, not new bridges to a

hopeful future but only another chance to travel the old roads to the blood-feuds of the past. (Harper 2010)

Echoing a long-standing official line of argument, here Harper's apology traces the Air India bombings directly to religious hostilities in India between Hindus and Sikhs. Framing (good) immigrants as those who are "invite[d] from around the world" because they "share our [Canadian] aspirations for a better life," Harper warns about "others [who] also come"—those who should not have been allowed entry but who got in anyway because of Canada's openness (multiculturalism). Because these feared others came in along with the invited outsiders, the state now needs the invitees to look out for this "enemy with a thousand faces." It is ironic that while immigrants emerge here as fundamental to Canada's self-construction as an open and inclusive multicultural nation, the project of imagining the nation's future also insists on "foreign" others as potential threats requiring surveillance and eventual assimilation.

Harper contends as well that "it is incumbent upon us all, not to reach out to, but rather to marginalize, to carefully and systematically marginalize, those extremists who seek to import the battles of India's past here and then export them back to that great and forward-looking nation" (Harper 2010). Thus the abstract image of the "enemy with a thousand faces" now gets fleshed out in the figure of the "extremist" or "separatist" Indian Sikh or the Khalistani. This reduction of terrorist identity allows some brown faces to *pass* as safe while restricting the mobility of other brown faces by eliciting anxiety on trains and airplanes, in streets, and at gas stations. This is evident from the numerous instances of hate crimes recorded against Indian Sikhs, in particular, in the aftermath of the attacks on the Twin Towers in New York. For example, the first person arrested as a terrorist suspect after the 9/11 attacks in the United States was a Sikh man, Sher Singh, who was taken off an Amtrak train bound from Boston to New York on September 12, 2001. The first case of retaliatory killing was of another Sikh man, Balbir Singh Sodhi, who was shot in front of his gas station in Mesa, Arizona, on September 15, 2001. Such instances of state and public surveillance clearly demonstrate how a war on terror successfully reactivated the word *terrorist* and effectively attached it to Sikh male bodies in post-9/11 North America. The rhetoric of terror and counterterrorism measures in the post-9/11 era can now quickly fall back on the 1985 Air India bombings in order to justify antiterrorist initiatives in the present. In 2011, for instance, Prime Minister Harper announced the launch of the "Kanishka Project" (named after the Air India Flight 182 plane), a five-year, ten-million dollar counterterrorism initiative. Transforming racialized citizens into subjects of surveillance and reprisal thus facilitates Canada's participation in the United States–led War on Terror.

By inserting fears of homegrown terrorists into the public consciousness, the renewed state interest in the Air India tragedy also urges Canadians to look out for suspicious others (notably, brown men with turbans
or beards) in their midst. Arguably, it is official discourse like this that
enables social violence to take place by creating the conditions under
which social groups become pitted against each other in mutual fear and
hatred. Scholars note that the general failure to recognize people "who
appear to be 'Middle Eastern, Arab, or Muslim'" (Volpp 2003, 147) in
post-9/11 North America as also constituting the American or Canadian
nation suggests that there is "a new national imagining as to what bodies
are assumed to stand in for 'the citizen' and its new opposite 'the terrorist'" (Puar 2007, 159). With the war on terror turning brown immigrants
into subjects of surveillance by the state and the "patriotic populous"
(Puar 2007, 180) in a post-9/11 racial landscape, important ethical questions arise: Can Canadians of different races and religions mourn the Air
India tragedy while also being suspicious of friends and neighbours? Can
racialized subjects stake claims to Canada as home if they are continuous-
ly relegated within discourse to a non-Canadian homeland?

THE MODEL MOURNER/THE MODEL MINORITY

Harper's apology ends with this assertion: "The greatest legacy we can
leave to our loved ones is to make the skies safe for travel" (Harper 2010).
But the government's desire "to make the skies safe for travel" is not
accompanied by a similar desire to make the people on board those
flights feel at home once they disembark in Canada. Also, the apology
seeks to distinguish between racialized immigrants. Yet in Mukherjee's
"The Management of Grief" and Badami's *Can You Hear the Nightbird
Call?* we see how this "new country" (Mukherjee 1988, 193) prompts the
same immigrants, despite differences in language, food, religion, and
class, to seek out each other. Both Mukherjee and Badami note that fellow
feeling among immigrants from India results from their recognition of
the difficulties in settling in Canada. For example, Mukherjee's central
character, Shaila, describes relationships between minoritized subjects in
the years before the Air India Flight 182 bombing as "a time when we all
trusted each other in this new country, it was only the new country we
worried about" (Mukherjee 1988, 193). Similarly, Bibi-ji and Pa-ji, in Badami's novel, run "an open house. Anyone was welcome: relatives,
friends of friends, refugees, children of friends" (Badami 2006, 42), and
we see the effects delineated in detail through the intimate friendship
that develops between the North Indian Bibi-ji and the South Indian
Leela Bhat.

Mukherjee's story begins in Shaila's house, peopled with friends and
strangers who, without being asked, have gathered to offer support to

Shaila, who has lost her husband and two sons on Air India Flight 182:
"A woman I don't know is boiling tea the Indian way in my kitchen.
There are a lot of women I don't know in my kitchen, whispering and
moving tactfully. They open doors, rummage through the pantry, and try
not to ask me where things are kept" (Mukherjee 1988, 179). A house full
of immigrants from the Indo-Canadian community, who have discreetly
gathered at the narrator's home to offer solidarity and support, makes the
indifference of the Canadian public stand out. This is further clarified for
the reader when one of the men in Shaila's house complains that the
preachers on television carry on "like nothing's happened," and Shaila
thinks that it is because "we're not that important"; "*they* care about
nothing" (180, emphasis added).[8] This issue of marginalization, of the
invisibility of brown bodies, is also brought up in Badami's novel. Bibi-ji,
the "beautiful and accomplished proprietor" of a shop and the owner of
an apartment, is aware that she is "invisible" to white Canadians, who
view her as "an insignificant brown foreigner, one of the people who ran
small shops . . . or worked in the sawmills, or cleaned up in the posh
restaurants, hardly worthy of notice" (Badami 2006, 44–45). Leela took
great pride in her husband's family lineage—"the Bhats of Bangalore"
(102), "the famous family of Kunjoor Bhats" (115)—but similarly comes
to understand her position after moving to Canada as that of "a Minority
lumped together with an assortment of other minorities" (137). She
muses, "How long would she remain foreign?" (129).

The precariousness of minority existence is established in both texts:
the transition from "foreigner" to either "model minority" or "terrorist
suspect" seems to depend on official discourses. Shaila, faced with the
tragic loss of her family, feels "[n]ot peace, just a deadening quiet" (Mukherjee 180). She wishes that she "*could scream, starve, walk into Lake Onta-
rio, jump from a bridge*" (183). However, on the surface, she appears to be
unnaturally calm. This makes a young government social worker, Judith
Templeton, conclude that Shaila is "coping very well" (183). Templeton
views her as a model mourner, which, to social service agencies, means
someone who can accept the loss and move ahead with life. She suggests
that Shaila's apparent strength—"the strongest person of all" (183), according to most observers—might be of practical help to those who are
"hysterical" (i.e., mourning improperly). She asks Shaila for help as an
intermediary or cultural translator for other traumatized families. Keen
to ensure that there is "the right human touch" (183), she declares, "We
don't want to make mistakes" (183). "More mistakes, you mean" (183),
corrects Shaila, reminding Templeton that the government had failed to
protect its citizens in the first place and contributed to their deaths.

Shaila believes that she is "behaving very oddly and very badly" and
does not consider herself "a model" mourner (183). Hesitantly, she ac-
companies Templeton to meet an elderly Sikh couple who had been
brought to Canada just two weeks before their sons were killed in the

crash and who refuse Templeton's help. Shaila doubts that she will be of any assistance because, she believes, the Sikh couple "will not open up to a Hindu woman" (193). But when she identifies herself to the Sikh couple as another of the bereaved, another parent who has lost her boys, their shared grief creates (even if momentarily) a common ground, and she is able to move beyond her involuntary fear "at the sight of beards and turbans" (193), a fear arising from her knowledge that "Sikh Bomb[s]" (179) were likely responsible for the deaths of her family members.[9] We see here how grief both acts on individuals and spurs them to act. Grief that makes Shaila anxious about Sikh turbans also produces empathy for the turban-wearing Sikh parent. Shared grief allows her to reach out and connect with terrorist look-alikes, despite regional, linguistic, class, and religious differences, and despite the generalized fear and suspicion of members of the Sikh community as alleged perpetrators, supporters, or bystanders of the crime. Similarly, on hearing of Shaila's loss, the old Sikh mother's "eyes immediately fill with tears" (193), and her husband mutters, "God provides and God takes away," which to Shaila "sound[s] like a blessing" (194). We see here the potential to produce community within difference through the recognition of shared (parental) grief. While divisions are created within communities, the strangeness of strangers is replaced by an acknowledgement of loss that has altered their lives forever. Thus, a relative form of kinship remains, as victims bond over shared experiences that reach across differences.

The elderly Sikh parents' refusal to sign any of the official documents signifies to Shaila that they have not yet given up hope for their sons' lives. She observes, "In our culture, it is a parent's duty to hope" (195). She suggests to Templeton that bereaved families will employ different means to cope with the loss of loved ones: "Nothing I can do will make any difference. . . . We must all grieve in our own way" (183).[10] But the understanding that there are different modes of grieving is incomprehensible to Templeton. The government, Templeton says, wants nothing more than to help the family members "accept" loss by assisting them to enroll in college or to volunteer with cultural societies (192). For government officials, "Acceptance means you speak of your family in the past tense and you make active plans for moving ahead with your life" (192).

Templeton wants the bereaved Sikh parents to sign the official documents quickly so that she can close their file and move on to the next family or task on her list. Her push for quick closure risks depriving the grieving parents of time to grieve the loss of their children in culturally specific ways. In addition, she misreads the parents' inflexibility, their pushback against the government's insistence on closure, as an indication of their ignorance and illiteracy. "You see what I'm up against?" she tells Shaila. "I'm sure they're lovely people, but their stubbornness and ignorance are driving me crazy" (195). Templeton's exasperation embodies the Canadian government's impatience with minorities who continue to turn back or hold on to lost objects (whether homelands, cultural practices, or memories of dead sons) rather than accept the government's reconciliatory gestures of closure (whether a public inquiry, monetary compensation, or an official apology) and move on.

What might it mean, then, for the long-disavowed Air India bombings to occupy a central place in the Canadian state's discourse on terrorism in a post-9/11 era? More than a decade after Mukherjee's fictional representation of how Shaila and an array of others who lost loved ones on Air India Flight 182 find ways to live with their losses, the Canadian government issued its apology. The apology clarifies for *real* family members what the "management of grief" and "moving ahead" with one's life signifies in this era of heightened anxiety and increased securitization. The families are reminded that members of their own (Indo-Canadian) community perpetrated the crime, and to secure their future, they must now become foot soldiers for the state in its war on terror.

With the model mourner represented in Mukherjee's story merging seamlessly into the figure of the model minority enunciated in Harper's apology, the norms for "managing grief" seem to be reiterated.[11] Racialized Canadians, we are reminded, are perpetual others who need to be on their guard while displaying their emotions—their loss, pain, anger, or frustration. The model immigrant, like the model mourner, successfully suppresses his or her racial grief and grievances against the state, is compliant, displays approved public behavior, and supports the policies of the state.[12] More importantly, immigrants are reminded, they will be *tolerated* as long as they remain model mourners or model immigrants.

In "The Management of Grief," the Sikh couple, by refusing to sign the documents provided by Miss Templeton, resists closure, while beards, turbans, and, one can assume, their ethnic attire, render them hypervisible. As Sunera Thobani notes, "Multiculturalism has had the effect of constituting people of colour as possessing an excess of culture that marked them as outsiders to the nation" (Thobani 2007, 162). So cultural diversity itself becomes "a problem," "an issue for national concern, consideration, and management" (162). Writing in the post-9/11 American context, Jasbir Puar and Amit Rai similarly note that more visibly "cultured" or "ethnic" South Asians such as Sikhs and Muslims with beards or turbans are perceived as "fringe" model minorities (Puar and Rai 2004, 82). This is clearly established in post-9/11 novels such as Neesha Meminger's *Shine, Coconut Moon*, which poignantly depicts the resurgence of racial anxieties in the perception of "turban-wearing, dark-bearded, and mustached men" (Meminger 2010, 2), who are quickly associated with none other than the terrorist par excellence, Osama bin Laden.[13] Or Mohsin Hamid's *The Reluctant Fundamentalist*, whose Pakistani American protagonist, Changez, decides to grow a beard. All of a sudden, he recognizes a certain kind of nervousness around him at his workplace: he "seemed to become overnight a subject of whispers and stares" (130).

Unlike Meminger's and Hamid's novels, Badami's *Can You Hear the Nightbird Call?* is set in a pre-9/11 Canadian context. Still, the turban is a visible marker of difference. The narrator tells us of "the suspicious glances of the Europeans" in Vancouver and of Pa-ji's "fear that the look in their eyes would turn to violence" (Badami 2006, 203). The turban marks the next generation of urban Vancouver Sikhs as different, too, when Pa-ji's foster son, Jasbeer, constantly gets into trouble at school. This in turn makes Pa-ji's wife, Bibi-ji, wonder, "Was there something wrong with the school, or was it the way she and Pa-ji were bringing up this boy?" She is concerned specifically with Jasbeer's long hair: "[W]as he teased or bullied at school for the colour of his skin or because he wore his hair in a topknot like all good Sikhs? Should she ask Nimmo whether they could cut his hair—the marker of his Sikh identity—as so many other Sikh parents in their community had done for their sons, so that Jasbeer could blend in?" (197).

The turban emerges as *the* identity marker that immigrants should give up in order to embrace the state-endorsed multicultural future, so that they will not stand out in public spaces and be cast out. This is evident when the school principal summons Bibi-ji and Pa-ji because Jasbeer has brought a kitchen knife to school. As Jasbeer explains, "Jason said I was a wimp because I wore my hair in a bun like a lady, so I was showing him how brave Sikhs are" (211). During the sardonic exchange between Bibi-ji and the principal that follows, we notice Jasbeer's mounting anger: "Jasbeer kicked the leg of the principal's table. He recognized that tone of voice. It made him helplessly furious. Too young to know that the word to best describe that tone was patronizing, he was not too young to understand the thread of meaning that ran through it" (211). By calling attention to Jasbeer's suppressed anger, the narrative emphasizes how "the social and subjective formations of the so-called racialized or minority subject are intimately tied to the psychical experience of grief" (Cheng 2000, x). These everyday, unarticulated (often unarticulable) experiences of discrimination, coupled with knowledge of historical discrimination perpetuated by the Canadian state, can render racialized minorities unhappy, alienated, and aggrieved.

Badami's novel effectively captures a long history of grief and of the struggles of racialized minorities to manage such grief. We are aware from its beginning that, as a young child, Bibi-ji had heard "endless stories of a ship called the *Komagata Maru* and a voyage that ended in nothing" (Badami 2006, 5).[14] Harjot Singh's traumatic memories and experiences left an indelible mark on his young daughter's psyche. The young Bibi-ji "hated this ship . . . that had snatched his [her father's] dreams away and turned him into a barren-eyed man" (11). But her father's stories also produced in her an intense longing for the land that had refused her father entry. She has dreamed about Canada "ever since she could remember" (27). Later, as a parent, Bibi-ji recounts to Jasbeer, numerous times, the *Komagata Maru* incident and its effects on her father, followed by Pa-ji's "comment at length on the injustice of the whole episode" (198). At one point, Bibi-ji contemplates whether they had "burdened the boy with an impossible load, a feeling of grievances unresolved" (198).[15] Indeed, Jasbeer embodies the long-term effects of living with stories of pain and injustice. As Sara Ahmed reminds us, "Migration is not only felt at the level of lived embodiment. Migration is also a matter of generational acts of story-telling about prior histories of movement and dislocation" (Ahmed 2000, 90). Jasbeer's personal circumstances—alienated in urban Vancouver, with a deep grievance against his birth parents for having given him "away" (289)—are compounded by his knowledge of his grandfather's "aborted journey on the ship called the *Komagata Maru*, turned away by this very city" (198). Later, after hearing of the atrocities that the Indian state perpetrated against Sikhs, Jasbeer, who has grown up with "too *much* of a sense of history" and "[t]oo much of ancient stories of wars and warriors" (198) because of Pa-ji's attempts to foster in him "a sense of the people he belonged to, a pride in his Sikh roots" (206), joins the Khalistanis. Shaped by the remembrance of injury and the desire for justice, Jasbeer gravitates to this secessionist movement with its legends and heroes to compensate for his feelings of lack and of non-belonging in Canada, for what he characterizes as "living a meaningless life" (289). As the narrator notes, "Dr. Randhawa's diatribe of conquest and betrayal and revenge appealed to him. The older man seemed the epitome of a heroic figure lashing out against greater, darker powers" (253).

In suggesting that Jasbeer's embrace of religious extremism is the consequence of the Canadian state's historical and continuing racist practices against Indo-Canadians, *Can You Hear the Nightbird Call?* offers a serious rebuttal to the state's rhetoric of Sikh extremism in Canada as imported from elsewhere and to the state's portrayal of the Air India tragedy as an isolated wrong—an aberration—in its treatment of South Asians. The novel writes into the nation's memory a whole litany of wrongs—monumental ones such as the *Komagata Maru* and mundane ones such as the discrimination experienced by minorities in their everyday lives. Rather than see the surge in Sikh militancy as an effect of Bibi-ji's narration of the *Komagata Maru* incident to Jasbeer, we can follow Amber Dean's suggestion that we "contemplate how the derision of mostly Sikh men as 'Hindoo invaders' during and after the *Maru*'s time in the Vancouver harbor can be understood as a racializing practice that *produces* such militancy as an *effect* of the state's discriminatory policy" (Dean 2012, 207). Dean urges us to recognize how the Air India bombings are "bound to colonial histories of injustice that cross state lines and remain inseparable from the production of racialized subjects" (207). Further to these observations, I add that it is racial grief or the continuous engagement with the pain of state violence (Indian and Canadian) that, in Badami's novel, makes Jasbeer join the secessionist struggle. His knowledge of past and present persecution of Sikhs determines his present (as the persecution itself determines the transnational present).[16] Jasbeer does not successfully hide his grief from the public; he does not "manage" it like the model mourner/model minority. Instead, his grief erupts beneath a mask—masking the inexpressible, the unarticulable—as his own experiences of racism are overlaid with other memories and histories. Linking the *Komagata Maru* to the Air India bombings, grandfather to grandson, and Canada to India, the narrative exposes this hidden grief to the public eye.

Such narration of Jasbeer's story alongside Pa-ji's in *Can You Hear the Nightbird Call?* and Shaila's alongside the elderly Sikh couple's in "The Management of Grief" disallows narratives of unhappiness (racism, discrimination, alienation, and oppression) or of irreconcilable mourning of the loss of another country from retreating into the background. In this light, the government's call in the Air India apology to "systematically marginalize" and "not . . . reach out to" alienated and disgruntled Canadians appears to be profoundly shortsighted. Texts such as *Can You Hear the Nightbird Call?* urge the state to attend to the grief and grievances of those who are "othered" and to reflect on the conditions within the nation that breed anger and frustration in minoritized populations, in order to be able to work toward producing a more habitable future. The government, by treating the Air India tragedy as an anomaly in its history of accepting diverse populations (as evident from its innate or originary multiculturalism), dismisses calls for the state to address ongoing issues of racialization and discrimination that affect the lives of minorities.[17] Moreover, the government's stance positions anyone who seeks to probe the Air India story—or other national histories with alternative personal and collective histories or memories—as a threatening body that requires strict vigilance and, possibly, disciplining by the state. Erasing any possibility that dissent might have a positive value, the apology suggests that living with difference necessitates increased surveillance and policing of difference, rather than finding ways to reconnect with aggrieved communities or reach out to alienated youth to make them feel at home in *their* home.

## THE PAST IN THE PRESENT

Reading the Air India apology in conjunction with pre- and post-9/11 fictions such as Mukherjee's and Badami's works reveals how a history of racism is being effectively covered over in the present by a reinvigorated discourse on terrorism. Thus, while the pre-9/11 characters in Mukherjee's and Badami's texts lament the invisibility of racialized minorities in

Canada, the post-9/11 retroactive framing of the Air India bombings as a "Canadian tragedy" and the enforcement of new surveillance and security measures mean that it is nearly impossible now for turbaned or bearded brown men, whether Sikhs, Hindus, Muslims, Christians, or Parsis, to remain *un*marked.

In acknowledging that the Air India bombings were planned and executed in Canada, the official apology suggests that the Canadian state initially failed to recognize the "terrorists." Rather than address the reasons for this failure, though, the apology uses it to rationalize increased vigilance toward nonwhite immigrants seeking entry into Canada and toward racialized minorities who reside in Canada. The discourse of "an enemy with a thousand faces" can thus result in the minoritized Indo-Canadian male eliciting fear and evoking a sense of danger merely by inhabiting space with others. Encoded with the ostensibly "seeable" (readable) signs of "terrorist" identity—brown skin, turbans, beards, or ethnic attire—can these bodies be trusted in this age of terror? *Should* they be?, asks the official discourse. In contrast, Mukherjee's and Badami's narratives unravel a prehistory of casting immigrants from India as undesirable outsiders to an imagined national community. Thus, the new war-on-terror frame of interpreting difference that conflates "brown" with "immigrant" or "terrorist" emerges as a direct legacy of past policies of viewing racialized Canadians as "perpetual outsiders to the nation" (Jiwani 2006, 1). In revisiting the past and linking the past to the present, Mukherjee's and Badami's texts then successfully render the apology's idealized vision of an inclusive, progressive nation as a strategy for closing off any avenues through which to revisit the nation's past.

The state's assumption seems to be that if racism were preserved not in official archives but only in minority memories and consciousness, then, as Ahmed writes, "racism would 'go away' if only they would let it go away, if only they would declare it gone" (Ahmed 2010, 148). That is, the state does not need to address its past; it merely needs to convince minorities not to look in that direction. Although the premise of citizenship is that it leads to happy multiculturalism, racialized minorities must first demonstrate that they are worthy of being treated as citizens by being model mourners or model minorities. State versions of happy multiculturalism require leaving behind the old world (transnational affiliations) and the past (such as the government's mistreatment of the Air India families) and expressing willingness to adopt the state's version of the future. Yet this call to be model mourners or model minorities—that is, loyal Canadians—is not neutral, for, as Badami reveals through Jasbeer, how one deals with grief and which direction one takes are determined by one's relation to a broader history of loss and suffering.

Thus, while "a proximate 'we'" of those "who might be assumed to be 'with me' as well as 'like me' (sharing my ideals)" (Ahmed 2004, 106) is produced in the name of official multiculturalism, the post-9/11 framing of Air India Flight 182 as a *national* tragedy continues to marginalize Indo-Canadians and *their* grief through the state's tactics of differentiation. The purported need to demarcate model minorities from terrorist minorities—that is, the assumptions that immigration brings in terrorists and that those terrorists cannot be differentiated from the welcomed immigrants—already marks brown bodies as *others*. The question of difference also comes into play in the conceptualization of the Air India bombings, in which the loss is understood to be that of Air India families and friends who lost loved ones. The Air India trials, the Commission of Inquiry findings, and Prime Minister Harper's apology do not recognize the effects of the Air India bombings and their aftermath on others beyond the immediate families and friends of those killed. In contrast to the state, invested in particular practices of remembrance of Flight 182 and in narrowing forms of remembrance, the fictional texts discussed here situate the Air India tragedy within a long history of racial grief (dislocation and resettlement, in/visibility of minorities, and the psychic and corporeal effects of racialization).[18] They suggest that a commitment to multiculturalism means working to produce multiple and contested histories of different marginalized groups that can allow these groups to reflect on and share their repressed histories and personal memories of marginalization. By sharing historically significant, if silenced and forgotten legacies of racism, suffering, and loss with the next generation of readers, Mukherjee and Badami urge Canadians to look back actively instead of close off grief.

*This chapter has drawn on research supported by an Insight Grant of the Social Sciences and Humanities Research Council of Canada.*

*An earlier version of this chapter, titled, "Official Apology, Creative Remembrances, and Management of the Air India Tragedy," was published in* Studies in Canadian Literature/Études en littérature canadienne *40.1 (2015): ): 111–30.*

## REFERENCES

Ahmed, Sara. *The Cultural Politics of Emotion*. New York: Routledge, 2004.
———. *The Promise of Happiness*. Durham, NC: Duke University Press, 2010.
———. *Strange Encounters: Embodied Others in Post-Coloniality*. London: Routledge, 2000.
Badami, Anita Rau. *Can You Hear the Nightbird Call?* Toronto: Knopf, 2006.
Blaise, Clark, and Bharati Mukherjee. *The Sorrow and the Terror: The Haunting Legacy of the Air India Tragedy*. Toronto: Viking, 1987.
Busse, Cassel. "Politics of (Im)Moderation: The Production of South Asian Identities in the Canadian Apology for Air India Flight 182." *Topia: Canadian Journal of Cultural Studies* 27 (2012): 233–51.
Chakraborty, Chandrima, ed. "Air India Flight 182: A Canadian Tragedy?" *Topia: Canadian Journal of Cultural Studies* 27 (2012): 173–269.

———. "'But that was before 9/11': The Work of Memory in Neesha Meminger's *Shine, Coconut Moon.*" *Journal of Postcolonial Writing* 48.3 (2012): 278–88.

Cheng, Anne Anlin. *The Melancholy of Race: Psychoanalysis, Assimilation, and Hidden Grief.* Oxford: Oxford University Press, 2000.

Dean, Amber. "The Importance of Remembering in Relation: Juxtaposing the Air India and *Komagata Maru* Disasters." *Topia: Canadian Journal of Cultural Studies* 27 (Spring 2012): 197–214.

Failler, Angela. "Remembering the Air India Disaster: Memorial and Counter-Memorial." *Review of Education, Pedagogy, and Cultural Studies* 31 (2009): 150–76.

Government of Canada. *The Families Remember: Commission of Inquiry into the Investigation of the Bombing of Air India Flight 182, Phase I Report.* Ottawa: Ministry of Public Works and Government Services, 2008. Web.

Hamid, Mohsin. *The Reluctant Fundamentalist.* New York: Harcourt, 2007.

Harper, Stephen. "Prime Minister Harper Announces Inquiry into Air India Bombing," Government of Canada. Ottawa, ON. May 1, 2006. Accessed August 20, 2013. http://www.pm.gc.ca/eng/media.asp?id=1143.

———. "Statement by the Prime Minister of Canada at the Commemoration Ceremony for the 25th Anniversary of the Air India Flight 182 Atrocity." Government of Canada. Toronto, ON. June 23, 2010. Accessed September 11, 2013. http://pm.gc.ca/eng/media.asp?id=3471.

Jiwani, Yasmin. *Discourses of Denial: Mediations of Race, Gender, and Violence.* Vancouver: University of British Columbia Press, 2006.

MacQueen, Ken, and John Geddes. "Air India: After 22 Years, Now's the Time for Truth." *Maclean's*, May 28, 2007. Accessed October 15, 2011. http://www.macleans.ca/article.jsp?content=20070528_105308_105308.

Major, John C. "Opening Remarks by the The Honourable John C. Major, C.C., Q.C on the Release of the Report of the Commission of Inquiry into the Investigation of the Bombing of Air India Flight 182." Government of Canada. Ottawa, ON. July 23, 2010. Accessed August 10, 2012. http://epe.lac-bac.gc.ca/100/206/301/pco-bcp/commissions/air_india/2010-07-23/www.majorcomm.ca/en/reports/finalreport/commissioner-remarks.pdf.

Mawani, Renisa. "From Colonialism to Multiculturalism? Totem Poles, Tourism and National Identity in Vancouver's Stanley Park." *ARIEL: A Review of International English Literature* 35.1–2 (2004): 32–57.

Meminger, Neesha. *Shine, Coconut Moon.* New York: Margaret K. McElderry Books, 2010.

Mukherjee, Bharati. "The Management of Grief." *The Middleman and Other Stories.* New York: Grove Press, 1988. 179–97.

Puar, Jasbir K. *Terrorist Assemblages: Homonationalism in Queer Times.* Durham, NC: Duke University Press, 2007.

Puar, Jasbir K., and Amit S. Rai. "The Remaking of a Model Minority: Perverse Projectiles under the Specter of (Counter)Terrorism." *Social Text* 22.3 (2004): 75–104.

Razack, Sherene H. "The Impact of Systemic Racism on Canada's Pre-Bombing Threat Assessment and Post-Bombing Response to the Air India Bombings." Expert witness report submitted to the Commission of Inquiry into the Investigation of the Bombing of Air India Flight 182 on December 12, 2007. Unpublished.

Seshia, Maya. "From Foreign to Canadian: The Case of Air India and the Denial of Racism." *Topia: Canadian Journal of Cultural Studies* 27 (2012): 215–231. Web.

Sundar Rajan, Rajeswari. "Righting Wrongs, Rewriting History." *Interventions* 2.2 (2000): 159–70.

Thobani, Sunera. *Exalted Subjects: Studies in the Making of Race and Nation in Canada.* Toronto: University of Toronto Press, 2007.

Volpp, Letti. "The Citizen and the Terrorist." *September 11 in History: A Watershed Moment?* Ed. Mary L. Dudziak. Durham, NC: Duke University Press, 2003. 147–62.

## NOTES

1. The prolonged twenty-year investigations that followed the Air India bombings revealed that the bombings had been planned and executed in Canada. Two Sikh residents of British Columbia were put on trial, but the British Columbia Supreme Court acquitted both men, citing the mishandling of evidence by the Canadian national police force—the Royal Canadian Mounted Police (RCMP)—and the Canadian Security Intelligence Service (CSIS), along with the lack of cooperation between the two agencies. Both men were alleged to be involved with a radical Sikh separatist movement fighting for an independent Khalistan. This has strengthened the view that the bombings were an act of retaliation for the Indian state's atrocities against Sikh separatists in the 1970s and 1980s, "Operation Blue Star"—the Indian Army's storming of Sri Darbar Sahib (the Golden Temple) on June 6, 1984—and the Indian National Congress government's complicity in the anti-Sikh riots that erupted throughout India (October 31 to November 4, 1984) following the assassination of Prime Minister Indira Gandhi by two of her Sikh bodyguards (October 31, 1984). To date, only one person, a resident of British Columbia who made the bombs, has been convicted of manslaughter.

2. Prime Minister Stephen Harper announced a public inquiry into the Air India bombings and its aftermath on May 1, 2006, revising Bob Rae's report that called for an administrative inquiry on Nov. 23, 2005. The inquiry was headed by retired Supreme Court justice, John C. Major.

3. For an analysis of this shift, see Busse, Chakraborty, and Seshia in the Feature Section of *Topia* as well as Failler.

4. Commissioner Major identified the central objective of the inquiry as "recommend[ing] safeguards and systemic changes to prevent future threats to our national security and intrusions into the lives of so many innocent people."

5. See the Government of Canada's first phase of the report, *The Families Remember*, released in December 2007.

6. In her analysis of the cross-examination of Razack by Barney Brucker, counsel for the Attorney General of Canada, Angela Failler cites Brucker's concern that Razack's report "was going to form part of the public record" (159).

7. Rajeswari Sundar Rajan writes that "political apology operates only within the frame of a particular wrong around which the boundaries are drawn, so that it can ignore its implications for other times, places, actors. . . . If they have no pedagogic logic, they can have no deterrent force" (162).

8. Later on in the story, after arriving in Ireland to identify the deceased, Shaila notes the public display of emotion there. Strangers "rush" to her and give her "hugs," and some cry. "Touched" by this public recognition of the grief of family members, Shaila notes, "I cannot imagine reactions like that on the streets of Toronto" (187).

9. The turbaned Sikh father who produces fear is also affected by the fear he produces. In this context, it is interesting that Shaila notes, "My parents are progressive people; they do not blame communities for a few individuals. In Canada it is a different story now" (Mukherjee 1988, 189).

10. The story also reveals the irony of Templeton's juxtaposition of Shaila against the other mourners, whose trauma has "sprung bizzare obsessions" (Mukherjee 1988, 192), since Shaila herself is haunted by the visions and voices of her dead family members and prophetic dreams. In an abandoned temple in a tiny Himalayan village, her husband appears to her; in Queen's Park in Toronto, she hears voices of her dead family members, who direct her toward the future.

11. For critiques of the model minority, see Cheng; and Puar and Rai.

12. There are hints of how grief can transform the mourner when Shaila notes: "Once upon a time . . . our voices were shy and sweet" (Mukherjee 1988, 189).

13. In one episode in the novel, several white boys throw garbage at the turbaned Sikh American Sandeep's car, yelling, "[G]o back home, Osama! No bombs on civil-

ians here, asshole, this is America!" (Meminger 2010, 55). For a detailed analysis, see Chakraborty, "But that" (278–88).

14. On May 23, 1914, a ship called the *Komagata Maru* arrived in Vancouver with 376 predominantly Sikh Indians on board—all of them British subjects. The passengers were refused permission to leave the ship because of the continuous journey law, which required that they come via direct passage from India. The ship had departed from Hong Kong, and most passengers did not have the $200 required to enter British Columbia on hand. After two months, on July 23, the *Komagata Maru* was forced to leave Vancouver. For further details, see Dean.

15. Yet Bibi-ji never publicly expresses her grief; it is shared only within the space of the home. In fact, she advises the new immigrant Leela thus: "Forgetfulness was good. . . . A bad memory was necessary for a person wishing to settle in, to become one of the crowd, to become an invisible minority" (Badani 2006, 136–37).

16. A women at the Golden Temple tells Bibi-ji that terrorism initiated and executed by Canadians affects those living in India: "It is people like you sitting in foreign countries, far away from everything, nice and safe, who create trouble. You are the ones who give money to these terrorists, and we are the ones who suffer!" (Badani 2006, 326).

17. A number of scholars have noted the embrace of Aboriginal peoples as "our Communities" in the Canadian national imaginary in order to affirm the state's innate multiculturalism, its tolerance of diverse peoples and cultures, and in order to conceal the nation's racist past (e.g., Mawani 2004, 51). This move is one way that the nation markets itself, according to Mawani, as being absolved of "its colonial past, suggesting that we have transcended it" (52). Thobani argues that official multiculturalism enables Canada to renarrate its history and present itself "on the global stage as urbane, cosmopolitan, and at the cutting edge of promoting racial and ethnic tolerance among western nations" (Thobani 2007, 144).

18. Whereas state attempts at redress and memorialization are directed exclusively at the families of those who lost loved ones in the Air India bombings, Bibi-ji's intergenerational "memory" in *Can You Hear the Nightbird Call?* becomes transgenerational, transcultural, and transnational memory for readers of the novel.

# TWO

## Sexy Sammy and Red Rosie?

### From Burning Books to the War on Terror

### John Hutnyk

Readers in the United States may be forgiven for thinking that the war on terror began with a—grotesque—puff of dust in downtown Manhattan in late 2001, but the negative profiling of Islam of course has a longer history. What I would call the "prehistory of post-9/11" does not even start with the events in England I will relate in this chapter, but telling this story in the context of work that also provides other deeper contextualization of the propaganda war may be "salutary." My hope is that as readers recognize that the present is understood through the pictures we construe of the past, by looking at how we forget or twist the interpretation of them through the images of now, our effort to learn to read their possible recodings may teach us much. In particular, the dominant "freedom" narrative that relies upon fear and demonization of Islam after 9/11 might not always be read backward to construe earlier book-burnings as provocative in the same ways.

Almost thirty years ago, the writer Hanif Kureishi was widely criticized for two of his scripts: *My Beautiful Laundrette* (1985) and *Sammy and Rosie Get Laid* (1987). Less lyrically perhaps—and only slightly less filmic—novelist Salman Rushdie's book *The Satanic Verses* (1988) was famously set on fire in Bradford early in 1989.[1] Kureishi's film work and Rushdie's *Verses* are bound together by more than temporal proximity—one of the characters in Kureishi's later novel *The Black Album* called it: "That fatwah business" (Kureishi 1995, 140). As a commentary that warned against an emergent profiling that owed much to fascism and xenophobia, Kureishi's novels and film scripts plundered a cosmopolitan diasporic register drawn from a certain sonic "London" scene, undergoing a sexualized multicultural coming of age. While this may seem somehow antiquated today, the "antiracist desire," street riots and book burnings of that time can be, and were, taken to mark the first highly visible mobilization of a diverse and complicated British–South Asian presence in the UK. We do well to recall this as an earlier and different dispensation that, since the advent of the War on Terror, has been simplified and perhaps even erased in a significant reconfiguration of the streetscape of diaspora and multiculturalism in the years since these films and the burning of the book. Burning streets and books—not particularly good in themselves—are replaced with a more virulent racial profiling in contemporary, post-9/11 times. Without permitting every manifestation of the past to fall into the all-consuming ideological apparatus, a careful examination of early antecedents of the current conjuncture may help comprehend contemporary anxiety about and accusations against Islam and Muslims, and by extension contextualize the ways all South Asian peoples, globally, are now demonized at "home", and bombed towards "democracy" elsewhere.

More people know of *The Satanic Verses* through television news coverage and anti-Muslim profiling than through actually reading the book. Rushdie even seemed to anticipate trouble with some readers, provocatively opening with a sequence designed to puncture conservative stereotypes and the profile of the threatening immigrant. Of course to be fair, the mockery of Mohammed anticipated the future, too, but in the fall of the Asian characters Gibreel Farishta and Saladin Chamcha from an exploding plane, the terror and migration nexus is displayed in a way that is difficult not to postdate as prophetic. However, it was the perceived insult to the prophet that occasioned the banning of imports of the book to India, which led to protests in Pakistan, and inexorably occasioned the Ayatollah's fatwah,[2] and the global news controversy and public(ity) campaigns that followed—including a march in Leicester led by MP Keith Vas.[3] Tragically, book burning became synonymous in the press with the name of ex-author now-celebrity Salman Rushdie and his personal tribulations stood duty for a wider neoliberal security scare. His publishers, translators, and booksellers were threatened, with some indeed tragically murdered, including his Japanese translator Hitoshi Igarashi and others.[4] Kureishi's dramatization in *The Black Album* relocates the book burning incident to London, and as comedy, but the Bradford event—some time after protests in Pakistan and India[5]—has been construed by many commentators to mark the first public articulation and mobilization of a specifically Muslim South Asian presence on the streets of the UK (see Nawaz 2009, Malik 2009). This deserves attention precisely because of its importance to the ways in which the racialization and demonization of Islam have escaped these earlier coordinates to be framed only as "terror" and not as the street mobilization of a politically diverse multicultural compact.

There is much scholarship on this theme and the changes it brought: Gayatri Chakravorty Spivak long ago pointed out how "the Rushdie affair has been coded as Freedom of Speech versus Terrorism" (Spivak 1993, 237). Kureishi fictionalizes the burning in the context of a staged conflict between offended narrow-scope believers and a few arrogantly liberal defenders of liberalism (Kureishi 1995, 180). With a long history, the public burning of books of course agitated the sensitivities of a great many of the commentariat, some of whom were later all in favor of the bombing of Baghdad, including, presumably the destruction of various libraries, museums, and bookshops (for example, Christopher Hitchins in the "Religion Kills" chapter of *God is Not Great*). This is never to excuse death threats upon novelists, nor do I want to enter too far into the debates about censorship or appropriate handling of Islamic sensitivities—having the wives of the Prophet as prostitutes was always going to get Rushdie into trouble, planned or not, the offense was predictable, as sales publicists no doubt knew, but horribly underestimated. Rushdie himself insists he did not intend to offend, as we shall see. Kureishi was less subtle in mocking the liberal feminists who "select only Black and Asian lovers now" for political reasons (Kureishi 1995, 190). In this chapter I want to think through the reconfiguration of the South Asian streetscape, and the transformations of desire, diaspora, and the image of terror that the Rushdie book burning achieved. Or rather, to examine how the incendiary street politics of the late 1980s prefigures, and yet is rather different from, the street politics and fear, not desire, that prevails in a rather different and more bluntly racialized frame today. The book burning "stunt" has subsequently and strangely lost its innocence. That is, if it ever can have mere innocence, since book burning is almost always linked to geopolitical aspirations, and today more than ever in the context of global militarization. Rushdie himself tells of Hitchens offering a citation of a famous passage from Heinrich Heine on book burning, though Rushdie extrapolates exponentially:

> [Hitchens] quoted Heine to me. Where they burn books they will afterwards burn people. (And reminded me, with his profound sense of irony, that Heine's line, in his play Almansor, had referred to the burning of the Qur'an.) And on September 11, 2001, he, and all of us, understood that what began with a book-burning in Bradford, Yorkshire, had now burst upon the whole world's consciousness in the form of those tragically burning buildings (Rushdie, "Christopher Hitchins")

The first part of this quotation is repeated almost word for word in Rushdie's memoir, on that fatwah business, the autobiographical *Joseph Anton* (Rushdie 2012, 129). In that retelling, there is no mention of Hitchins, nor how in the *Vanity Fair* version, Bradford led inexorably to the war in Iraq.

The revisionism firmly in place, as Rushdie offers some comments about remembering Nazi book burnings and then character assassinations of British MPs Jack Straw and Max Madden, who had both supported the Muslim communities' right to protest. Whatever the merits of the debate then, and whether Bradford or Bolton or India or Pakistan were "first" to protest, the book burning is now remembered as a terrorist outrage and has a prophetic character as it reconfigures and then changes shape—as Rushdie's own characters also do—in the furnace of geopolitical intrigue. The right to protest is erased in what we might see is a morphing of an identity politics, now dated. What a change since that time—looking back at a street scene of relatively "harmless" public protest, it seems that quite some effort has been deployed to retrospectively invest those characters and issues with far darker sentiments. The opening plane explosion of *The Satanic Verses* is now played out, albeit still largely unread, as emblem of a narrowed suburban and celebrity paranoia, where urban metropolitan anxiety and geopolitical militarization dominate under cover of a race war.

I think it is useful to think about these issues through the prism of the two film "texts" also from Kureishi, since they are almost contemporary to, but slightly predate, Rusdhie's satanic versifying. The films *My Beautiful Laundrette* (dir. Stephen Frears, 1985) and *Sammy and Rosie Get Laid* (dir. Stephen Frears, 1987), both published as separate screenplays by Kureishi, invoke street politics in South London—where we will see burning cars and demonstrators fighting the police, riots, tenements in flames—perhaps documentary, but also prophetic scenes. An American photojournalist in the film is already documenting street rioting in culture industry style, grafting punk poses onto background images of blacks fighting the police in another kind of prophetic anticipation—think of magazines like *Vice* and *Juxtapoz*. The street here has what turns out to be a more than suitable allegorical purchase on how we think of terror and security in present times, where terror is continually called to attention by reported "incidents," avoided incidents—due to suitably intrepid investigations by the authorities—and anniversaries of incidents, that each in turn occasion the rollout of stock footage of scenes of conflagration. Every anniversary, and as examples we can expect any presidential speech commemorating 9/11, that lasts longer than three minutes, will include cutaways to the repertoire of "freedom" imagery, such that it is as if we must constantly be pummelled by the promise of terror, even in quiet times. This iconography ensures a persistent and everyday anxiety about alerts, threats to life, and racial profiling prevails in our surveillance state.

We should remember that this ideological complex has a longer history. Where Spivak attends to a geographic and linguistic "really existing" Asia, reaching from Southeast to Northeast (Philippines, North Korea) and Northwest to Middle East (Afghanistan, Palestine), that has now become the major location for the sharp end of the war on terror, we must recognize that this is an Asia as if filtered through U.S. foreign policy. It should not be imagined *only* as a theater of war. Spivak's effort is to "provide exercises for imagining pluralized Asias" (Spivak 2008, 2). Alongside these Asias, insofar as there are several already, there can also be the multiple and varied globalized versions that will extend possibilities and their most significant iterations, mapped out in literature and films like that of Rushdie's *Verses* and Kureishi's *Sammy and Rosie*. The trouble is that being Asian in Britain, or on the streets of the world's other big cities, like New York, morphs over time, and in the political context of the present has lost the very plurality that some had once had fought so hard to establish—and which in other circumstances would be by now the "normal" plurality of settlement. Instead, we have had almost fifteen years of the war at home, Homeland Security, UK Border Agency, Model Minority, Moderate Muslims, etc., and this has managed to transmute multiplicity back into stereotype. Spivak's work is a warning to resist the ways Asia, and Asians can become fixed in the popular imagination through ignorance and fear. My take on this makes it possible to read against these stereotypes. Here I have in mind the work of Biju Mathew, Vijay Prashad, Amitava Kumar, and Gayatri Gopinath as useful in a way that, I suggest, can return us to the films of Kureishi and Frears, and "that" novel by Rushdie, with sufficient nuance to be able to reclaim and deploy the critiques of stereotyping as a necessary patient corrective to the current reaction.

Unfortunately, in pluralizing South Asias, we must talk of an expanded, reconfigured diasporic Global South Asia insofar as it is host for another nongeographical theater of the same war of terror that codifies, and bombards, really-existing South Asia as a site of crisis in the global imaginary. Global South Asia as a war zone becomes a matter of everyday low-intensity violence in some parts, and disproportionate carpet bombing and drone assassination from the sky in others. The point is to note that urban/street conflict, in locations like London, Manchester, Bradford, Birmingham, and New York, etc., is part and parcel, along with Kabul, Helmand, Peshewar, Mumbai, and along with Sydney, Bali, Madrid and Istanbul—all in the same warfare across Global South Asia. Another argument of this essay then is that as we move away in time and outlook from the difficult multivarious ambiguity of Rushdie's fatwah business and Kureishi's cinema we are in danger of losing sight of the convoluted, complicated, and *unequivocally ambiguous* engagement and contestation of identity. This contestation was fought out on the streets of those texts, but now recedes to a past Thatcher-era London in favor of a different, and still more violent, version of the neoliberal reaction. In the new dispensation, diasporic British-Asia,[6] and the visibility of "British-Asians," loses depth and focus, even as it gains a perverse specificity through being embodied globally in the figure of the threatening Muslim:

the people of the book have become book burners and *Jihadis*, and do duty for all Asians in a trembling popular imagination that cowers in voluntary darkness or in the shadow of the two towers.

Kureishi's films, as also, then, Rushdie's book, evoked an opposition to Thatcherite conservatism and a part of this was the new times convergence of "we are here because you were there" antiracist, anti-imperialist sloganeering. How the many different sentiments that were gathered under that multiculti pageant—as expressed in the multiplicity of the Samba and circus performance of *Sammy and Rosie*—then became *only* the antecedent of a perceived militant and fanatical Islam is the work of considerable revisionist effort. Various commentators do not seem to agree on how this came to pass or what should be the response—here are far too many suggestions that have simply escalated the crisis—but clearly there are also multiple and varied globalized versionings of so-called terror and multiple ways to resist that should be open for discussion. The specificities should not be erased just because the offerings of a military-inflected propaganda tabloid newspaper television have displaced once importance nuances of critical literature and cinema. Rushdie's subsequent celebrity pages endorsement of each and every "threat" to freedom of speech, such as his widely reported tweeted criticism of Peter Carey and others' refusal to support an American PEN award to the satirical, and racist, French publication *Charlie Hebdo*, would be a case in point. That tweets serve the cause of ideological simplification should come as no surprise, just as the difficult conversations of how to combat reaction and chauvinism are not easily conveyed in headlines.

## ON WASHING OF DIRTY LAUNDRY IN PUBLIC

What is there new to say about the old controversies? Seen from "here" and "now," *My Beautiful Laundrette* and *Sammy and Rosie Get Laid*, with their self-consciously "postcolonial" politics, are inextricably mired in an "identity debate," which they perhaps could or should have outgrown. Like Rushdie's *Satanic Verses*, these films cannot be read without reference to the difficult politics of South Asians and Islam in Britain. The problem with such reading would be when attempts are made to reorder the events of these contexts in ways that ignore their political ramifications. In the recodification process witnessed since 9/11, the position of Kureishi as defender of a complicated multivariant position seems at odds with the fortunes of the one who was subject to a transformative house arrest in response to the fatwah. Of course such "tendencies" will be read backwards to identify them in already published antecedents, but in Rushdie's late work spin is added to emphasize and confirm subsequent posturing.

Rushdie's book *Joseph Anton* largely disregards explicit articulation of the issues I am concerned with here in favor of a tit-for-tat point scoring more suitable for a gossip column apologist than the more engaged, and engaging, author that Rushdie was before his seclusion. Like a newly minted *Munshi*, Rushdie documents the complicities and frustrations of his kept status followed by his well-rewarded and well-publicized high society, thrice-married, coming out. Reading the book as nostalgia as well as revisionism, we could still wonder if there is a way to reach back to the sensibilities of those times, when everything Asian in Britain was up for grabs and literary—pre-fatwah, pre-9/11—an urban multicultural exuberance found its metaphoric muscle in the gymnastic lyrical punning of "Ellowen Deeowen" (Rushdie 2012, 37). Perhaps in the to-be-restored archive of British-Asian cinema,[7] these films and texts so often seen as superseded—might instead be assessed as touch papers for the recent, more brutal, times, even, and perhaps exactly, where today they could seem dated. The point is to recall these early antecedents and see how the differences of *that* time are recoded *now* as a part of coding as such—the necessary reworkings of the past to suit the investments of the present war show up as convolutions and contortions. The certitudes of "I told you so" judgements become less plausible if close attention is paid to the particularities of these texts. In an early scene in *Sammy and Rosie Get Laid*, Sammy and his father Rafi are returning home after witnessing street rioting, petrol bombings, conflagration, and chaos in the inner city. Sammy turns a corner a little ahead of his father and begins to shout: "For fucks fucking fucks sake fuck it." His father worries about his son's language and bad education—"that I paid through my arse to get you"—but Sammy is more concerned that the street rebels have overturned and burnt his car. Sammy's pompously knowing discourse on urban vitality is doused in personal commodity dispossession, mediated by sexual expletive. We will see more of this scene, which layers a kind of comedy over a kind of violence, and is interestingly reworked and unacknowledged cultural reference by Hugh "fuckity-fuck" Grant at the start of the hit British rom-com film *Four Weddings and A Funeral* (1994, dir. Mike Newell). If the character Sammy can learn from the compromised Rafi that his complicity in Thatcherite urban consumerism with a veneer of leftist credential is so easily punctured, what then for the present self-assured *Guardian*-reading sophisticate who mixes glossed narrations of fanatical Islam with touristic exoticist cultural appreciation and lament for the ravages of "development" on pristine idylls? Both Rushdie's publicly recorded erotic conquests and the less often examined sexual charge that belongs to an opposition fascination with *jihadis*, are in need of a long kitchen table discussion, as portrayed in both *Sammy and Rosie* and in *Joseph Anton*, even if in the latter the conversations around the table are with Rushdie's police detail minders.

It will be no surprise to say the sexual politics of Kureishi's fiction stresses ambiguity. In her important book on queer Asian diasporic cultural production and politics, *Impossible Desires*, Gayatri Gopinath begins with the scene from Kureishi's earlier film. In *My Beautiful Laundrette*, Johnny and Omar's back-room caress "unbuttons" an "erotics of power." For Johnny, "sex with Omar is a way of tacitly acknowledging and erasing" a racist past, but for Omar, "queer desire is precisely what allows him to remember" rather than "succumb" and give in "to the historical amnesia that wipes out the legacies of Britain's racist past" (Gopinath 2005, 2). In 1985 and throughout the 1990s this scene continued to raise problems among the left, in addition to the homophobic right, since some found it difficult to reconcile Kureshi's up-front—shirt-front, brown shirt, national front—provocation with recognition of the "barely submerged" histories of colonialism and racism that the film also depicts. "We did not fuck fascists, we fucked them up" insists one activist friend, with somewhat surprising aggression. My feeling is that the sort of provocation Kureishi achieves in *Laundrette* is far less provocative today—indeed, in Kureishi's 2008 novel *Something to Tell You* (159), Omar reappears as a Blair-appointed Lord of Parliament, drunk and on his knees in the toilet of a working class pub (more below). Of course there are always fascists caught in their own vicious contradictions who find guilty pleasures through which to articulate their incoherence, and they found willing partners in the likes of Omar, with motives and desires all too neatly beyond censure.[8] But even if the flash point of this debate has past, the suggestion Gopinath makes about memory deserves attention: "Queer desire does not transcend or remain peripheral to these histories [of colonialism and racism] but instead it becomes central to their telling and remembering" (Gopinath 2005, 2). Omar interrupts Johnny's caress to remember, remind, and accuse him of his racist connections, of his having been seen marching in the street with the National Front. At this point Kureishi is also asking the question of Omar, and fucking fascists is not all that is at stake. Once again I am taken with how far the nuance of Kureishi's cinema script is contemporary with Rushdie's sexual politics, yet Rushdie is the one who has been more robustly associated with freedom of speech, while Kureishi and his questioning of Omar's later hypocrisy is lost.

One problem that emerges alongside Gopinath's otherwise important arguments is that the rendering of diaspora is perhaps overplayed as a "conservative imaginary" with a "peculiar" and "backward-looking" "relation to the past" (Gopinath 2005, 3). The reference here is to Stuart Hall, but Hall does not tarnish all those in diaspora with the same conservative brush. It is worth adding a caution when Gopinath asserts that "in the queer diasporic texts" she examines, "queer desire reorients the traditionally backward-looking glance of diaspora" (Gopinath 2005, 3). Certainly her work evokes a useful contrast to those who present "myths of purity and origin that seamlessly lend themselves to nationalist projects" and to those who support Hindutva and Hindu nationalism abroad, and of course it is true that a complicit diaspora can articulate quite well with "processes of transnational capitalism and globalization" (Gopinath 2005, 7). The caution to introduce here would be that attributing reorientations to "queer desire" allows a slippage that can be sustained only if the radical antiracist, anti-imperialist, and communist progressive "parts" of diaspora, historically quite important, are also gathered under the label "queer." I would be sympathetic to this idea (Kureishi as queer is plausible, Rushdie less so—four hetero orthodox marriages if you count the one before the fatwah), but complicity has a variety of forms. A further problem with an extension of the terminology of queer to include all parts of a radical diasporic sensibility would be that not all of those so gathered together would necessarily want to march, for example, in the India Day parade in New York today, or at least not without considerable debate over the idea of nation thus celebrated.

And it must be debated. To march or not to march—a politics of ambiguity of course can offer all manner of justifications and rationalizations on many sides—that is why it has political purchase. The conservative politics of model minority South Asians in the United States is a peculiarly pernicious thing—not much understood in the UK context, but perhaps emergent as we watch Asian business leaders jockey for favor in the House of Lords and so forth, and Tony Blair or David Cameron fawning over the two hundred most influential British Asian businessmen and the like, despite Cameron being on record for dislike of "Indian dancing" (Press Association). In relation to Gopinath, I am not saying that queer Asians should not make a statement on Republic Parade day— but how much more would we like it if they did so carrying the internationalist banners of the Indian Workers Association? I am not at all dismissing Gopinath's work, but only suggesting that we might also consider other more militant dynamics of expression on the part of the South Asian migrant laboring classes, as explored for example in Vivek Bald's fantastic study of the history of Bengali-U.S. merchant traders in *Bengali Harlem* or by those whom Biju Mathew writes about in his engaging book *Taxi*, where he makes the point that in present day New York City the "politics of community representation evolved out of the basic symbolic material of social justice activists." The universalism of the civil rights struggle morphed dialectically over time into "the particular right to mark difference" in the "framework of multiculturalism," even as that was itself breaking down into a "separation of communities," with "each" producing its own institutions, priorities, and campaigns (Mathew 2005, 192). This is called and "inward-looking, self dividing politics" (Mathew 2005, 193), but the burden of Mathew's book is rather to note, or insist, that alliances across differences are still very much a part of the politics of diaspora today. The taxi workers strike, build solidarity and militancy, work with other groups for an expansive left movement towards justice. Similarly, Vivek Bald's work on history and migration to New York would also stress a more convoluted notion of diasporic cultures, drawing on maritime, restaurant, and neighborhood block narratives to bring out "a different set of stories" (Bald 2007, 59; 2013). Vijay Prashad's outstanding work *Everybody Was Kung Fu Fighting: Afro-Asian Connections and the Myth of Cultural Purity* adds several other transnational left dimensions in reporting the "council" meeting of Marcus Garvey with the Gandhian Haridas T. Mazumdar and a certain Nguyễn Ái Quốc, later known as Ho Chi Minh (Prashad 2001, 267; Prashad 2000, 173). Prashad argues that 'polyculturalist' claims of cultural belonging offer "solace," but implicitly acknowledge a defensive trap that is "able only to garner crumbs from the racist table" (Prashad 2001, 68). Instead, a broad antiracist platform that retains the idea of cultural difference, does "not abdicate the right to adjudicate between different practices in struggle," and fights to "dismantle and redistribute unequal resources and racist structures" (Prashad 2001, 69).

Certainly the grounds of wider, intersectional, alliance are present with Gopinath in an opposition to what she condemns as "an imaginary homeland frozen in an idyllic moment outside history" and where the "violences of multiple uprootings, displacements and exiles" are remembered in her focus on the queer body (Gopinath 2005, 4). Yet, it is important that contestation and transformation of racist and colonial histories occurs through a range of very present, diverse, but often also submerged, alternative practices of diaspora and the varieties of opposition, intervention, reorientation, and resistance should not be left unacknowledged or displaced by the urgency of other necessary recognitions. As counters to the revisionism that erases complicated South Asian histories post-9/11, the works of Mathew, Bald, and Prashad establish lines of inquiry that can be extended—for example, South Asian communists in Britain also have a long and proud tradition of antiracist, anti-imperialist struggle that is neither conservative nor backward-looking, nor can studies of this important tradition be dismissed with vague repetition of a refrain that suggests Marxist analyses inevitably "run the risk of replicating" a totalizing framework (Gopinath 2005, 38). There is no total schema, but to use fear of one to erase communist antiracist history would be an error that belongs to an early period of demonization—of the House Un-American Activities Commission, rather than Homeland Security—and to recover and extend the multiplicity of oppositional movements is always a worthwhile project, undertaken critically.

In terms of the complications of opposition, the extensively detailed study of South Asian women in Britain by the always excellent scholar Amrit Wilson is worth noting. Wilson reports that there was both "an ever-present undercurrent of resistance from women" against patriarchal oppression within South Asian families and within the wider society, but also "a plethora of superstitions, fears and taboos [that] served to stig-matise female sexuality" (Wilson 2006, 11). She rounds upon attitudes to sexuality and staple controversies like izzat, arranged marriages, illicit and "mixed" relationships, parental discipline, the hijab, work, and relig-ion to present a considered and convoluted, even dialectical, picture of the ways women in Britain are neither fully free of patriarchy, nor simply "victims" without a strong tradition of struggle, including against the colonialism, imperialism, and capitalism which has "shaped and re-shaped" (Wilson 2006) social relations. In relation to the dialogue that Wilson's sociology can have with Kureishi, and inded Gopinath, there is space for discussion and debate. Any portrayal of Muslim's in this con-text must acknowledge a spectrum of positions, interpretation, and con-testation—the very multiplicity and uncertainty that was once possible and indeed plausible in identity discussion.

This is where Gopinath's reading of the disappearance of Tania at the end of *My Beautiful Laundrette* is an insightful critique of the limits of Kureishi's "filmic universe." That we do not know if Tania throws herself onto the tracks, or leaves on the train "to seek a presumably freer else-where," provocatively suggests the potentials of moving beyond the nor-mative female diasporic subjectivity figured as "vanishing point" (Gopi-nath 2005, 4). Victimhood and flight are not the only options, as we might glean from another scene from Kureishi's late 1980s work. Two years after *Laundrette*, we find the lesbian characters Vivia and Rani performing for the male gaze of the patriarchal father, Rafi, in *Sammy and Rosie Get Laid*. It might be argued, in identitarian terms, that these two do not move very far beyond the ambiguous marking of Tania, even with their aggres-sive, performative, queer visibility designed to shock Sammy's father. Yet a critical leftist reading will observe that they are all-important as har-bingers of Rafi's doom. Spivak notes that this is "not a subplot, their function is crucial" (Spivak 1993, 249) as their researched political inter-vention offers a more nuanced and informed, and bilingual, characteriza-tion of Rafi's impotently faded power as returned corrupt former govern-ment despot. Here the ghosting of torture and terror in the postcolonial elite's betrayal of the promise of independence struggles says much more than Kureishi's (bad-)boy's-own view of black lesbian display, even as it does not displace the cliché of the clinch. Of course a scenario like this could plausibly happen, despite denials, but that it happens in the film in just this "controversial" way says as much about stereotypes of sexuality as it does anything necessary to the plot. Dutifully acknowledged, the plot thickens to celebrate the urban licence of promiscuous multicultural-ism when Rosie's sexual experiments with cross-dressing Victoria mani-fest alongside the colonial era romance of Rafi and Alice, and the loft-living liaison of Sammy and Anna are portrayed in the justifiably famous Bollywood-style triple-horizontal-split-screen sex shot.

## THE TRIPLE-FUCK TRICK MAKES
## THE VERTICAL LIE HORIZONTAL

What strikes me as strange now, watching that sequence so many years after the Twin Towers were flattened, is how well the horizontal frame of the screen suits the old filmic version of life lived enthusiastically despite the bludgeoning, oppressive atmosphere of Thatcherite London. Flat, low-rise, oppressive London. Yet, even under the weight of the overpass that covers the community squatter camp where Victoria lives, and which is bulldozed even flatter by the end, the film invoked the optimism of resistance. The leveling of space in the face of this oppression was also one of the framing moves of the film, where street rioting and flames decorate the opening sections. Rows of houses burning in the riot torn streets of Brixton, Peckham, Lewisham, and New Cross are glossed in *Sammy and Rosie* as if they merely offered a panoramic backdrop to the entertaining explanation Sammy offers to his father about being a Londoner. Yet the film had begun with a tribute to the police or immigration squad persecution of settled Londoners and the death of a woman who had been protecting her son from arrest. Kureishi was writing after the deaths of Cherry Groce and Cynthia Jarret, killed by police (see the film *Injustice* dir. Ken Fero and Tariq Mehmood 2001 for a commentary on deaths in custody[9] ). There are vigils, protests, and escalating tension. The street contestation as presented in this perspective is also horizontal; the police enter from the right, the protesters surge from the left. A fire engine is attacked, a fancy dress group of busker musicians move in colourful single file among the crowds. The riot is not a riot but a carnival, the police retreat. Choreographed street fighting is perhaps not always the first perspective that contemporary sociology would bring to bear on a city like London. While I think the presentation owes a great deal to Kureishi's sentimental, and participatory, attachment to the metropolis of his birth, many years later the riots and the Thatcherite ambience—intentionally flat, dreary, and grim, stiff upper lip—looks like the repetition and farce that we are so often trained to identify and repeat as tragedy.

An emergent vertical view of London is prefigured by Rushdie in the opening pages of *The Satanic Verses*, where the Gibreel Farishta and Saladin Chamcha enter British airspace in an inspired performative allegory of perceived—swamping—South Asian arrival. The British-Asian, Asian-British mixed-up, muddled-up, transformed and hybridized characters are always-already complicating things, and after a bomb goes off on their plane, Farishta and Chamcha fall from the sky in a mockery of migration and terror. Plane explosions will forever be associated with immigrant news stories, prefiguring 9/11 with horror reports of unfortunate frozen stowaways dropped over London as the wheel housings into which they had climbed were lowered in preparation for landing. Amitava Kumar, in his book *Bombay-London-New York*, links this imagery to both the Rushdie *Verses* narrative and the bodies that fell from the World Trade Center in the hours after the planes hit, but before they collapsed — and again I notice now how the images are framed vertically, in striking contrast with Kureishi's 1980s London. Kumar describes the earlier trage-dy:

> According to a July 2001 report in *The Guardian*, a body was discovered in a parking lot of a department store in West London. A workman in nearby Heathrow airport had seen a figure in jeans and a black t-shirt suddenly "plummet from the sky like a stone" . . . The report said the man who had fallen to earth was Mohammed Ayaz, a twenty-one year old stowaway (Kumar 2002, 230)

Against this vertical trauma, Kureishi has Sammy and Anna, Rosie and Victoria, Rafi and Alice all lie together in cross-race, but hetero-norma-tive, embrace. This triumvirate of the missionary position was much dis-cussed upon the film's release, for many viewers the first eruption of Hindi film aesthetics into popular British cinema. Now, the major cinema chains regularly feature Bollywood screenings (see Kaur and Sinha, 2005) and books on Bollywood and other South Asian cinemas are widely available if you look (see Prasad, *Ideology of the Hindi Film* and *Cini-Film: Film Stars and Political Existence in South India*; Rajagopal *Politics After Television*; Dudrah *Bollywood: Sociology Goes to the Movies* and *Bollywood Travels*; Rai *Untimely Bollywood*; Rajadhyaksha *India in the Time of Cellu-loid*). But look first at the sexy screen: in his informative book on Kureishi, Bart Moore-Gilbert says the author "anatomizes the quasi-colonial atti-tudes, institutional structures and social hierarchies which subordinate minorities within contemporary British society" (Moore-Gilbert 2001, 3). It is also possible to feel that the split-screen sex scene flattens what might have been a radical orientation to urban living. A racial radicalism mas-querades as shock in a predictable algebraic formation, even as *Sammy and Rosie* raises the specter of postcolonial violence alongside, or perhaps exaggerating, the only then emergent flat-out opportunism of neoliberal Thatcherism's de-industrializing, little-colonial-racist, God-save-the-queen, chauvinistic-jingoistic, union-jack boot Britain.

Rafi's complicit nostalgia for Britain's colonial grandeur runs to hav-ing his toast all buttery and "cunty fingers". Just what this is remains obscure enough to leave at least one innocent colonial migrant in the dark. A kind of a crumpet perhaps? Rushdie has the same obsessive, almost prurient, longing for the language and promiscuity of Hobson-Jobson.[10] The point is that Rafi's England of yore is not prim and proper, but embraces Alice in a wonderland plateau of nostalgic desire. As Moore-Gilbert reminds us, "some critics have followed Spivak's lead" in ascribing a "multi-perspectival point of view" in the "triple-fuck" scene to "Kureishi's desire . . . to produce a more 'collective' mode of representation, in which the polyphony of narrative points of view reflect the film's pluralistic and democratic social vision" (Moore-Gilbert 2001, 95). I am *inclined* to agree.[11]

The American journalist Anna in *Sammy and Rosie* takes a great number of photographs during the rioting. It is with her in mind that Gopinath's queer warnings can be taken as a corrective supplement to the stark anti-Thatcherism of the film and not just a sectarian insistence that "my issue is the main issue." The salient point being that it might also be good to try today—as Kureishi perhaps does in *Sammy and Rosie*—to reorient the perspectives that frame multicultural *encounters* in the city, so to speak. This is to locate the settler in the city, already involved, even if American. The assumption with which to break here, the complacency that needs to be challenged, is the idea that at ground level there is chaos. The photographer takes still shots and gets actors to pose among the rubble. Windows are smashed, there are flames in the upper stories of the houses, sirens wail, but there is a degree of intentionality, and community. Everyone knows when to run. The street photographer is as much at home among the ambiguities of the urban as any of the other characters, as any of the Londoners. Then, at least. Sadly, perhaps no longer with the same strategic optimism.

## STREET WRITING SCREENED INTO GLOBAL VIOLENCE

The narrative of *Sammy and Rosie* takes us through the streetscape menagerie of Sammy and Rosie's social acquaintances, some of whom are sexual partners, some of whom are more interesting and colourful. In one scene Rosie explains her thesis study on the varieties of kissing—a kind of cod-anthropology humour on Kureishi's part, again referencing his peculiarly conflicted concerns about intimacy. Rosie was described by Gayatri Spivak as "dramatizing the confrontation between radicalism" and "simple ethics" (Spivak 1993, 247–48), as having "no final determination" (245) but being both a kind of occluded cipher for the failure to think neocolonialism and "the best hope"[12] we have. I agree, but . . .

In *Sammy and Rosie* the street riots are described, by Sammy quoting Rosie, as "an affirmation of the human spirit." Rafi scoffs. Rey Chow suggests that we need to rethink the culture of protest and its relation to a work ethic that belongs to modern secular capitalism (Chow 2002, viii). The game of street protest as representational politics, vying for a space on the spectacular news hour, forcing a minister to comment is something like a chore or a vocation—not necessarily in the most righteous sense. Do those who protest by-the-numbers—like the two million who marched against the Blair/Bush doctrine in February 2003—do so with the reflective critical awareness of what might be the best strategic response to the coercive and co-opting powers of capital, or is this also

complicity? A to B marches over and over again and the political contain-
ment of the protesters between the marked barriers and in the park at the
end for a tame rally of the same old trades union moderate media-friend-
ly speakers. All of this scripted again, visible as part of a drama. Any
deviation from the hierarchical into horizontal street protest, drifting
from the agreed route, spontaneous targeting of symbolic enemies, or
bloc diversified tactics is met with rapid response suppression, water
cannons, and/or Jenkels. The kind of street protests characterized as disorder in the press play as victory, or at least sustain encouragement,
among the protesters – and so attract all the more hostility from the
police and media, always designating uncontrolled protest as "rioting."

Perhaps with Rosie in mind, Chow writes:

> As long as minorities' rights to speak and to be are derived from and
> vested in the enabling power of liberalism, and as long as these minor-
> ities are clearly subordinate to their white sponsors, things tend to
> remain unproblematic for the latter. Should the reality of this power
> relation be exposed and its hierarchical structure be questioned, how-
> ever, violence of one kind or another usually erupts, and naked forms
> of white racist backlash quickly reassert themselves (Chow 2002, ix).

Yet Rosie is never obviously troubled by the violence on the streets. Her
pathos is in the death of the old white man in his bath in the council flats.
The arrival of Sammy's father Rafi, which both offers and threatens to
transform Sammy's previously inconsequential existence into one that
promises money and power (however corrupt) also changes the comfortable dynamic over which Rosie rules. She goes out and seduces Victoria,
demanding Sammy accept their polyamorous arrangement. Sammy, at
least not insisting on monogamy, still enacts a fantasy of retribution in
the loft with Anna. Liberalism here is the syncopated flip side of white
supremacy, as a propertied ownership of representational space. Rosie is
writing a thesis, Sammy is an accountant, writing the ledgers of commerce. Liberalism implicates well-intentioned "progressive" politics in
an everyday violence that references and is underpinned by racism, economic privilege, and brute force. The bulldozers move the alternative
squatter-musician camp from beneath the flyover—under the modernist
overpass—and yet Rosie continues to be lauded as center of her world.
That there are other political options in this scenario must be seen as a
matter of urgency. Those who center the world in their own privileged
experience are nearly always ideological participants in a much wider
project towards which they seem determinedly myopic.

Thirty years after the Miners' Strikes, Thatcherism, and the advent of
neoliberalism, it might now read as, sadly, normal that *Sammy and Rosie*
evidences a surprising absence of Reds. No communists and not even
socialists of the newspaper-wielding Trotskyite variety have any major
role. At best, an anti–National Front poster. Rosie's "politics" blatantly

stand in for that gap, erasing much in terms of British left history, including South Asian participation in Communist Party of Great Britain organizing—its first elected parliamentarian and the editor of its journal for three decades were both prominent South Asian figures (see Hutnyk 2005). Yet, it would not do to retrofit the context of these almost thirty-year-old texts so as to render Kureishi and Frears as card-carrying Party members, they were not explicitly pointing to the absence of the left in their films. It remains the case that communist histories are effectively erased even by those who remember a time when such ideas were more prominent. That the Communist South Asian heritage of Sammy is forgotten, and only rendered drunk and bedridden in *Laundrette*, is something that then permits approval of Rosie as "the best hope." Anticipating the narrow spectrum of Gopinath's political actors, we should understand this as a scarlet exclusion of deep significance.

Nevertheless, Spivak notes Rosie is in a "beleaguered position" and says "you cannot really be against Rosie . . . she loves all the right people. She's a white heterosexual woman who loves lesbians, loves blacks, is in an interracial marriage, etc, etc." This is perhaps almost what Kureishi had said, in more blunt language. But Rosie has "no final determination" (Spivak 1993, 245). Thus, while she is the most tolerant of all characters, and her guidance is love, or at least erotic pleasure, she somehow cannot be left unresolved and unredeemed. Of course, I also want to approve of her as part of the more openly sexualized multiculturalism of a generation now past, but I am chastened by Chow who reminds us that "tolerance remains cathected to advantage" (Chow 2002, 13), such that the notion of "neo-racism" (Balibar 1991, 21) manifests in "anthropological culturalism" as "inherent" to an "expansionist logic" and accelerating "racial and ethnicist violence" (Chow 2002, 14). I am again reminded of how Sammy is cathected to his car as its destruction undoes his allegiance to the street protests, and cements instead his filial investment in his father's dubious wealth. On the other hand, Rosie is something like the other-loving anthropologist who, despite the very best intentions and declarations of fidelity to, at least, ideals of diversity and equality, still manages to have her chocolate cake and eat it too. There is little good to be said for what Chow calls "well intentioned disaffiliations from overt racist practices" if professions of concern by those who scrupulously will not "speak for others" (for example, by leaving postcolonial theory to people of color) coincide with the claims of those who would help in a charitable hidden vanguardist role. These moves "often end up reconstituting and reinvesting racism in a different guise" (Chow 2002, 17).

In *Outside in the Teaching Machine*, Spivak identified the postcolonial figure of Rafi as the one who betrayed anticolonial struggles in the crucible of a new elite real-politik and neocolonial restitution of global power. This film from long ago can give us materials to think through problems and inform us of historical contexts—the role models in *Sammy and*

*Rosie* are themselves mediators of entire sociopolitical networks—Rosie (white guilt, best we can hope for), Sammy (identitarian narcissism), Victoria (sexual ambiguity/narcissism), Anna (display as photographer, with two Ws tattooed on her buttocks), Rafi (postcolonial betrayal, exposed), Vivia and Rani (activist lesbian commitment and "fact-finding" [Spivak 1993, 249]), while the taxi driver (as damaged Naxalite—the betrayal of the progressive politics) seems the key critical—and significantly ghostly, haunting–vector of the film. I do not want to lament a lost complexity, but perhaps these characters open up possibilities for discussion of political diagnostics of the present time. Sammy in particular: To his father's question as they negotiate the burning streets: "Why do you live in a war zone?," Sammy replies, with an assertion of urban pride: "We're not British, we are Londoners" and asserts that Leonardo da Vinci "would have lived in the inner city." Spivak finds the Londoners comment so significant she cites it four times (Spivak 1993, 250, 252) a "last ditch precariousness" (250) that as a refrain offers something like having a dream.

Even if this is a family drama, it is an educational one. We do live in a war zone. It is the faulty father who fails to lead the anticolonial struggle beyond its initial gains, an even worse father than drunken Papa in *My Beautiful Laundrette*. The son finds solace only in an accommodation with materialism that must also fail, to be comforted in the end by a cross-race, cross-generation community, but one that is being destroyed by Thatcherism, paving the way in due course for Blair and "New Labor." Neoliberal bulldozers crush both music and community. Rafi dies. The story is a painful one, the prognosis as bleak as the urban squalor of the time. Intellectual leadership fails—as it often does in films of the time, as with the faulty father in *Apocalypse Now* (dir. Francis Ford Coppola 1978), Colonel Kurtz (Marlon Brando), who cannot lead, despite all his learning (see below). Rosie with her thesis tends towards the sensational, and tragic events transpire despite her efforts—we should assume nonetheless she will get her MA, and then continue on as benevolent social worker. Is this so different to those who took the funding offered after the Scarman Inquiry into the Brixton riots,[13] in a collusion with political expediency—an identity—after the destructive end of *Sammy and Rosie*. It is these "types," portrayed by Kureishi, disavowed by Rushdie, who in some cases have become parodies of the committed intellectual, hopelessly weeping and defeated at the end. No wonder many are inclined not to trust the leadership pretensions of the Rosie type, but in the film we have not been in the presence of an organized left. Hardly at fault for the decline of radical politics, Rosie was a different sort of party girl than the Party capable of winning against the neoliberal wave.

Viewing the film today, it looks like a rehearsal in period costume. The performance of street protests—on the anniversaries of the New Cross Fire,[14] the Battle of Lewisham,[15] Brixton SUS[16]—are made more poignant and have to be evaluated in the context of pressing neoimperial crises that again evoke the co-constitution of Empire and metropole. List: the United States and Britain with the Iraq war and Afghanistan, the NATO intervention in Mali and Libya, the end of civil liberties and the Green Zone security of military Governance; the street violence of the Arab Spring and its counterrevolutionary Sting, the limits of Occupy and the London Riots (see Henri and Hutnyk 2012), the Indigados and the horror of conflict in Syria, in almost each scene both here and there new racist neoliberal horror is brought together in an intimate, almost porno-graphic, embrace—and this is perhaps just as Kureishi's *Sammy and Rosie* joyously foretold.

## BURNING BOOKS AS ANTECEDENT TO THE PRESENT

The moment when celluloid burns in the projector holds a certain fascina-tion. *Cinema Paradiso* (dir. Giuseppe Tornatore 1988) and so many other films use this scene to great effect. In *Sammy and Rosie*, the curtains burn as Rafi sleeps, but we could also imagine this as a direct commentary by Kureishi on the burning book that allegedly started the New Cross fire in 1981. A potent and relevant tragic moment of terror and destruction: a phone book forced through the letterbox opening of a three-story house, thirteen dead, nothing said. Clearly I also have Rushdie in mind.

There is much to consider here, I also would want to link the atrocity of book burning to the emotional charge that comes from book learning as enlightenment. Adorno and Horkheimer are close here, but not yet. I have in mind my favorite version of this: a Somerset Maugham's 1949 short story, "The Razors Edge," made into a great film of the same name starring Bill Murray, whose quest for knowledge leads him down mines and up mountains, cooking for the monks at a Tibetan monastery. We see him freezing cold in a hut where he has been sent by a holy man to contemplate, he runs out of firewood and finally burns his texts to sur-vive—cue uplifting music and *satori*-enlightenment inducing break of the sun through clouds over the Himalayas (1984 dir. Byrum). Tyrone Power in the 1942 film of the same name is also good, though the clunky sets there, and the strutting peacock, and Greco-Roman columns of Shangri-La, are, well, of the time. Bill Murray's enlightenment is sublime howev-er, and his book-burning moment throws me forward to the final se-quence from *Apocalypse Now*, where we see a ritualized working through of the father-son relationship between Colonel Kurtz and Willard (Martin Sheen), where Kurtz in turn throws a book at Denis Hopper's character to shut him up. In that last scene Kurz is reading Sir James Frazer's *The Golden Bough*. There has to be a book, according to the script, but we might wonder at the knowing conceit of choosing just *that* book. It was a shipping book in Conrad's original tale; the *Golden Bough* references an entire series of fire rituals. The horror, the horror . . .

Urban guerrilla-style struggle on the streets is something that we may think belongs to the past, to the 1960s and 1970s, to the Algerian Revolution (Gillo Pontecorvo's film *The Battle of Algiers*), *Calcutta 71* (dir. Mrinal Sen), or the Red Army Faction struggles in Germany, the years of lead in Italy, and perhaps the England of the early 1980s—Brixton, Peckham, Lewisham, as above. Aside from the occasional flare up in the northern cities, and bad news from remote sites in Asia or the Middle East, the contemporary relevance of such struggles seems historical or theatrical (for the cameras). Mogadishu, Gaza, Fallujah, should have changed this but now that London, New York, and Madrid sweat in the same war, it perhaps might pay off to reexamine some of the street scenes from earlier times. Notting Hill, Brixton, Toxteth, Manningham, Oldham, Bradford— one set of responses. Stop-and-search, custody deaths, profiling, detention—scaled up internationally on TV as live news, but with special rendition. Kidnapping and remote-controlled drone death, inserted in between the routine bureaucratic arabesques of finance, health, education, workplace, and housing scandals. At the high-profile ends of hypocrisy we have the pomp and circumstance of Westminster, and the bad faith of humanitarian bombing campaigns.

Of course, the burning of books has its own charged and charred history: degenerate art and texts burned in Nazi Germany, as Rushdie of course noted in his *Joseph Anton* "memoir" (Rushdie 2012, 129); McCarthy-era removal of "communist" books from U.S. libraries—they were burned (as reported in Fried 1990, 136). Umberto Eco's burning library in *The Name of the Rose*, echoing of course the famous, disputed (Báez 2008, 51–52), destruction of the Alexandria library, and, as Georges Bataille recounts in *Literature and Evil*, Franz Kafka left instructions that all his books and papers be burned upon his death. Of course he told this to "the one friend who had already informed him that he would never do so" (Bataille 1985, 151). Sir Richard Francis Burton's diaries, letters, and papers, and a "superior" translation of the erotic Arabic text *The Perfumed Garden*, were torched by his wife at his death (Báez 2008, 155), and so many more. Burning books is the premise of Bradbury's *Fahrenheit 451* (1953), and there are many others. Although the Rushdie controversy starts in India, commentators keep on locating it in Bradford because that burning-book image was so evocative, and the dots keep on joining up, as we too often see . . .

Which probably raises the question as to why the streets of London are not burning today? They were in Manningham and Oldham in 2001—with resultant police crackdown,[17] they did for three days in London in August 2011, but the next summer there was only the Olympics. What I would suggest is that the complexities of Rushdie and Kureishi's texts belong to a "back then" and that now in the present, due to the changed geopolitical dispensation, globally, all South Asians in Britain, and elsewhere, are rendered more simply as *terrorists* or *moderates*, so they cannot risk and are no longer allowed any more "ambiguous" articulation. Rather than a "backward looking," "conservative imaginary" (Gopinath 2005, 53), I think we can learn something of the future present from these now somehow "earlier" media texts. While for some, the British-Asian condition has been glossed over as harmless fun through comedy shows and Bollywood fashions, many Britons of South Asian provenance have suddenly been repackaged in an unrecognizably one-dimensional stereotype and retrofitted for extra-judicial deportation or detention. The police crackdown has a photo-fit profile that is simplified but is not simply a security scare, but a systematic ideological distraction that saturates our screens with the perverse alternative of either terror reports/docudramas or celebrity/real estate/personal make-over reality TV shows. Burning the streets, overturning cars, burning books even, is for sure all a bit macho: a posturing that no longer has the counterpoint context of left-leaning Rosie and her friends to affirm its validity as political expression of resistance—"affirmation of human spirit." Instead, the jingoistic Olympics of anodyne sporting success, including some "multicultural" heroes—Mo Farah, Usain Bolt—running interference for a political repression that means street struggles today lose all ambiguity and all legitimacy—to be rendered merely "terror" in the press without critical commentary or comprehension of grievances. This rapidly became as if a scene in an old movie. Global South Asian diasporic production meant screens were quickly filled with reruns of "Goodness Gracious Me" (1998), "The Kumars at Number 42" (2001), *Bend it Like Beckham* (dir. Gurinder Chadha 2002) and *Bride and Prejudice* (dir. Gurinder Chadha 2004). However edifying in terms of bright color and happy endings, there was—in the contrast everyone felt in everyday experience—no respite from entertainment vacuity and ideological heartburn.

Those who might once have joined street demonstrations and offered a militant antiracism that had—however difficult—a relation, and relationship, to a left critique of capital are now demonized. South Asian Britons who protest are cast as threatening—only moderate and cowed "community members" are, at best, tolerated in the new security compact. What the years between Bradford/Brixton and the "post-9/11" period have brought us is a narrowing and even erasure of political expression.

There are those who would attempt a more convoluted explanation of this impasse, of the emptied out terrain—comedy Asians on the one side, bearded terrorists on the other—and attempt a political diagnostic. Kenan Malik, for example, offers a heady amalgam of antiracist activist history and condemnation of "the multiculturalist" tendency in the British context, a failure of the "left." Malik's antiracist history owes much to, but does not fully acknowledge, the work of Sivinandan and the Institute of Race Relations, but on multiculturalism he only sees misguided tolerant liberalism paving a path for reaction. What happened around Rushdie's book? A celebrated, televized, burning of the book in Bradford by those who, according to Malik, acted in large part

> because of disenchantment with the secular left, on the one hand, and the institutionalisation of multicultural policies, on the other. The disintegration of the left in the 1980s, the abandonment by leftwing organisations of the politics of universalism in favour of ethnic particularism, and the wider shift from the politics of ideology to the politics of identity, pushed many young, secular Asians towards Islamism as an alternative worldview.[18]

The critique of ethnicity, identity, and multiculturalism misfires, however, where Malik insists on universalism as if it were the only and antithetical inverse of identity and ethnicity. Caught in a complementary logic, Malik's scorched-earth policy burns his own antiracist credentials and repeats the obvious and automatic reaction—endorsing an integration model for Britain today, at a time which also sees a resurgent ultra-right in the British National Party and the center-right drift of all the established parliamentary players (some could call this drift more or less a firesale or bonfire of older principles). Agreement with some of Malik's points is possible, and the case can be, and has been, made that "ethnic funding" elevated culturalist "community leaders" as a complicit "bulwark" with which to undermine militant antiracist alliances, but to then diagnose the problem as culture and insist on its overcoming in some naïve secular French Republic post-9/11 type model is a deeply conservative, even nationalist, error.

More interesting is Spivak's essay on *The Satanic Verses*, where she uses the occasion of Rushdie to consider other cases written out of the record. Her example of the internationalist feminist reading of the "sati" Shahbano, made a "figure" in a contest over votes, is exemplary (Spivak 1993, 240). She reflects on the position of Southall Black Sisters in relation to the "controversy" as crisis, to then in this context think about "freedom of expression" talk and the "uses to which the spectacular rational abstractions of democracy can sometimes be put" (Spivak 1993, 241). Rushdie, himself accused of complicity with the West's imperialist "crusade" against Islam by Ayatollahs and others, surely did not know or intend the extent to which his little fiction would offend, even as he aimed to offend indeed: as he had oftentimes done—*Midnights' Children* and *Shame* both also banned. More recently of course Rushdie has been forced into many, even far too many, "explanations" of his work of fiction: "I never set out to insult anybody." He says he offered "an extremely sympathetic portrait of a Muslim, and non-Muslim South Asian, community wrestling with the consequences of transnational migration" (Rushdie 2009, 139).

The ideal high-society dinner companion would be Gibreel Farishta, movie star. Second choice, Rushdie himself.

It is still the case, so many years later, that it is worth remembering that *The Satanic Verses*, as literature, went unread. Mazzarella notes that "liberals, of course, often complain—in India, as elsewhere—that those who seek bans on books or films often have not read or watched the items to which thy so vociferously object" (Mazzarella 2013, 103). At the time, something of a "rumor" (Spivak 1993, 228) spread that Rushdie had engaged in "gossip" about the prophet, that he had blasphemed against the Quran. Of course it is almost bad taste now to think of Rushdie's book in terms of the theoretical interests or fashions of its time of writing: when the death of the author thematic was hip, signed under the proper names of Roland Barthes and Michel Foucault, alongside celebrations of the schizoid self, and a rampant mixture and hybridity that itself celebrated difference and punning. The rumour of promiscuity, a *tamasha* in language and more, was welcome then. But author-(and bookseller-) death did not make for easy jokes about the fatwah. These controversies have a different context now, one that cannot ignore the U.S. occupation of Iraq and Afghanistan, NATO in Libya and Mali, and threatening escalations across the globe. Then, Iran was central in a different way, and the Ayatollah railed against America.

Notwithstanding, there is still something to be recalled for today in the literary political analysis of before. Spivak pointed out in her 1993 essay that critics of her reading of *The Satanic Verses* could complain that she "gives resistance no speaking part" in Rushdie's text (Spivak1993, 226). But if the book does not enact resistance as a character, perhaps we can agree with Spivak that to "state the problem" [of the hybrid, shapeshifting, complicit postcolonial migrant and the ossified, clerical, conservative] is not bad politics. She continues: "In fact, it might be poor judgement to consider academy or novel as straight blueprint for action on the street" (227). I do not find this far from Adorno's critique of an introspective protest against order that is indifferent to, and so ultimately compatible with, that order (Adorno 1970, 116). Adorno is worth quoting at length here as his commentary underpins my critique of what has happened subsequent to Rushdie/Kureishi:

> [There now is a] witch hunt against expression. . . . Although inwardness, even in Kant, implied a protest against the social order heteronomously imposed upon its subjects, it was from the beginning marked by an indifference to this order, a readiness to leave things as they are and obey. This accorded with the origin of inwardness in the labor process: Inwardness served to cultivate an anthropological type that would dutifully, quasi-voluntarily, perform the wage labour required by the new mode of production necessitated by the relations of production. With the growing powerlessness of the autonomous subject, inwardness consequently became completely ideological, the mirage of

an inner kingdom where the silent majority are indemnified for what is denied them socially (Adorno 1970, 116).

More directly relevant, and perhaps more succinctly: "Immediately back of the mimetic taboo stands a sexual one: Nothing should be moist; art becomes hygenic" (Adorno 1970, 116). Rushdie's book might indeed need to be defended on these grounds precisely where it explores blasphemy and ambiguity within Islam—a complication neither trenchant defenders of the Holy Book, nor those who attack Islam, and desecrate the book in prisons like Bagram, Abu-Ghraib, or Guantanamo, can assimilate. But the situation is different now, as Evangelical U.S. preachers and English Defence League "associates" burn the Koran simply to provoke.[19] A belligerent white supremacism fueled by international weapons commerce, detention and private security army regimentation, out and out invasion and geopolitics, has emerged into the vacuum where critical thinking once prevailed. This vacuum is a consequence, if not of the burning of Rushdie's book, it at least in some sense follows on from a retreat from the politics of "stating the problem," where the problem requires a fight against stereotypes and their vicious consequences. I do not think that burning a book today would make one iota of difference here—entire libraries have been destroyed and we see only a mild outrage in the staged statecraft of those who have responsibility for these things. The books are not sacred, of course, but to burn them misses the point.

Spivak writes of Adorno's article, badly translated in English as "Commitment," and reports that he says Brecht's use of montage "simply turns a political problem into a joke." *Sammy and Rosie* is genuinely funny in parts, but Spivak likes it for different reasons:

> One hopes that Kureishi's montage technique would have satisfied Adorno. It is much more concerned with negotiating a certain kind of unease, a laughter tinged with unease and bafflement. That comes through in the montage particularly well as the film moves away from realism and the ghostly figure of the torture victim becomes more prominent (1993, 254).

Is it the case that *Sammy and Rosie* also offered a multiperspectival and collective mode of storytelling, as Moore-Gilbert, lining up alongside Spivak, would have us believe? In the three-step unfolding of these scenes, it is the figure of Rosie in the middle (well, Rosie and Victoria) that is interesting because here cultural politics and sexual play has helped occlude an older engagement that was first displaced by identity concerns, and is now overwritten with narrow sinister consequences.

## WHAT NEXT FOR SAMMY?

The identitarian mode of address itself seems to have been suppressed in the constant barrage of station announcements, security alerts, low-level anxiety about security and surveillance—and the suspicion that your bearded neighbor is no longer a friend called Sammy—but instead a more sinister Salman. The tropes have changed, Farishta has morphed again—this is a diagnostic of the times, or rather, can be brought forward to do different duty for our times, even as we recognize the dangerous diminution of the ways in which storytelling as a mediation of multiple points of view, and varied sexualities, identities, politics, exceeds any easy calculation or ascription of the "proper" and correct interpretive framework (contra Gopinath). Farishta now is a monstrous hybrid realized as an allegation—the mask grown to stand in not as critique of cultural certitude, but its congealed profile form and "bad" character in the narrow dynamic of the war of terror. What Kureishi's difficult cinema supplied in terms of a critique that complicated South Asian presence, is lost if the public view of Asians in the metropole ignores the richness of the work of Bald, Mathew, Prashad, and Kumar, let along the "queer" diasporas of Gopinath and the potentials of pluralizing Asians of Spivak. The complications cannot be magically, but rather must be actively restored. The *Black Album* book burning, the "fatwa business" and the fascist-fucking, as well as the triple-fuck scene, was once a welcome articulation of a diverse and unsettling settlement. The vehicles of mediation, the pathways for making intentional illustrative juxtapositions or montaged, alliterative, associative points are now reduced to no more than a single image and the homeland security jingoistic narrative iteration of the next next next constant enemy: EurAsia, EastAsia, Oceania—any enemy will do Brother Orwell. This stacked-up ambiguity was important, to lose it is to lose the war.

It is still perhaps an unresolved question—for Sammy, Rafi, Rosie, and for us all in our necessary debates about the post-9/11 configuration—whether old literary and cinematic controversies can rise again as prompts for debate. At present they seem damped down under a stark reaction and the global dominant. The quietening of a critical, sexually and intellectually rampant, and promiscuous radical tradition in popular culture—that both Kureishi and Rushdie once wrote for, in some sense—means that efforts to restore the politics of a "ruthless critique of everything that exists" (Marx, 1843[20]) must be more than a shrill voice in the flames. Without Marx *and* queer, without Spivak's Rosie *and* Sammy, without rethinking how threats are masks, and masks can reveal the manipulations of threat, there is no play of perspective, no multiplicity, no community, and the books become ashes we cannot read.

*Thanks to Joel McKim and the reviewers of* Space and Culture *for comments. This chapter first appeared in a shorter form there, redeployed here with permission. This new version owes much to the editorial advice of Aparajita De.*

## REFERENCES

Adorno, Theodor W. *Aesthetic Theory*. Minneapolis: University of Minnesota Press, 1970.
Ali, Nasreen, Virinder S Kalra, Salman Sayyid. *A Postcolonial People: South Asians in Britain*. London: Hurst, 2006.
*Apocalypse Now Redux*. Dir. Francis Ford Coppola. Miramax Home Entertainment; Buena Vista, 2006.
Báez, Fernando. *A Universal History of the Destruction of Books*. New York: Atlas and Co., 2008.
Bald, Vivek. *Bengali Harlem and the Lost Histories of South Asian America*. Cambridge, MA: Harvard University Press, 2013.
———. "'Lost' in the city. Spaces and stories of South Asian New York, 1917–1965" *South Asian Popular Culture* 5.1 (2007): 59–76.
Balibar, Étienne. *Race, Nation, Class: Ambiguous Identities*. London: Verso, 1991.
Bataille, Georges. *Literature and Evil*. London: Calder and Boyars , 1985.
BBC News. "Scarman Q&A." 27 April 2004. *BBC News*. 10 July 2010 http://news.bbc.co.uk/1/hi/programmes/bbc_parliament/3631579.stm.
*Bend It like Beckham*. Dir. Gurinder Chadha. By Gurinder Chadha. 2002.
*Bride & Prejudice*. Dir. Gurinder Chadha. Roadshow, 2005.
Bradbury, Ray. *Fahrenheit 451*. New York: Ballantine Books, 1953.
Bunting, Imogen. "Rationality, Legitimacy and the "Folk Devils" of May." 2003. Accessed March 29, 2010. http://www.leftcurve.org/LC27WebPages/.
*Calcutta 71*. Dir. Mrinal Sen. D.S.Pictures, 1971.
Campo, Juan Eduardo. *Encyclopedia of Islam*. New York: Facts on File, 2009.
Chow, Rey. *The Protestant Ethnic and the Spirit of Capitalism*. New York: Columbia University Press, 2002.
*Cinema Paradiso*. Dir. Giuseppe Tornatore. Laurenfilm, 1988.
Dudrah, Rajinder. *Bollywood Travels: Culture, Diaspora and Border Crossings in Popular Hindi Cinema*. London: Routledge, 2012.
———. *Bollywood: Sociology Goes to the Movies*. London: Sage, 2006.
Eco, Umberto. *The Name of the Rose*. London: Harcourt, 1983.
*Ek Din Pratadik*. Dir. Mrinal Sen. Mrinal Sen Productions, 1979.
*Four Weddings and a Funeral*. Dir. Mike Newell. PolyGram Filmed Entertainment, 1994.
Fried, Richard. *Nightmare in Red: the McCarthy Era in Perspective*. Oxford: Oxford University Press, 1990.
*Goodness Gracious Me*. Bhaskar, Sanjeev, Meera Syal, and Anil Gupta. BBC. 12 Jan. 1998. *IMDb*. Accessed January 30, 2015. http://www.imdb.com/title/tt0137305/.
Gopinath, Gayatri. *Impossible Desires: Queer Diasporas and South Asian Public Cultures*. Durham, NC: Duke University Press, 2005.
Henri, Tom and John Hutnyk. "Contexts for Distraction." *Journal for Cultural Research* 17.2 (2012): 199–215.
History Commons. "Profile: English Defense League (EDL)." December 12, 2010. *History Commons*. Accessed January 4, 2014. http://www.historycommons.org/entity.jsp?entity=english_defense_league_1.
Hitchins, Christopher. *God Is Not Great: the Case against Religion*. London: Atlantic Books, 2007.
Horkheimer, Max und Theodor Adorno. *Dialektik der Aufklärung*. Amsterdam: Querido, 1947. Print.

Hutnyk, John. *Critique of Exotica: Music, Politics and the Culture Industry*. London: Pluto Press, 2000.

———. *Pantomime Terror: Music and Politics*. London: Zero, 2014.

———. "'The Dialectic of Here and There: Anthropology 'at Home' and British Asian Communism." *Social Identities* 11.4 (2005): 345–61.

Index on Censorship. "'The Satanic Verses: A Chronology'" *Index on Censorship* 37.4 (2008): 144–47.

*Injustice*. Dir. Ken Fero and Tariq Mehmood. Migrant Media, 2001.

Kaur, Raminder and Ajay J Sinha. *Bollyworld: Popular Cinema Through a Transnational Lens*. New Delhi: Sage, 2005.

Kaur, Raminder and Virinder S. Kalra. "New Paths for South Asian Identity and Musical Creativity." Sharma, Sanjay, John Hutnyk, and Ash Sharma (eds). *Dis-Orienting Rhythms: the Politics of the New Asian Dance Music*. London: Zed, 1996. 217–31.

Kumar, Amitava. *Bombay-London-New York*. New York: Routledge, 2002.

———. *Passport Photos*. Berkeley: University of California Press , 2000.

Kureishi, Hanif. *My Beautiful Laundrette and Other Writings*. London: Faber and Faber, 1996.

———. *Sammy and Rosie Get Laid*. London: Faber and Faber, 1988.

———. *Something To Tell You*. London: Faber and Faber, 2008.

———. *The Black Album*. London: Faber and Faber, 1995.

Malik, Kenan. *From Fatwa to Jihad: The Rushdie Affair and Its Legacy*. London: Atlantic Books, 2009.

Mann, Harveen Sachdeva. "Being Borne across: Translation and Salman Rushdie's 'The Satanic Verses.'" 1995. *Criticism: Vol. 37: Iss. 2, Article 5*. Accessed July 20, 2015 http://digitalcommons.wayne.edu/criticism/vol37/iss2/5.

Marx, Karl. "Letter to Arnold Ruge." September 1843. *Marxists.Org*. Deutsch-Französische Jahrbücher. Accessed July 20, 2011 http://www.marxists.org/archive/marx/works/1843/letters/43_09.htm.

Mathew, Biju. *Taxi! Cabs and Capitalism in New York City*. New York: New Press, 2005.

Maugham, Somerset W. *The Razor's Edge*. London: Heinemann, 1949.

Mazzarella, William. *Censorium: Cinema and the Open Edge of Mass Publicity*. Durham, NC: Duke University Press, 2013.

Mitta, Manoj. "Reading 'Satanic Verses' Legal." January 25, 2012. *The Times of India*. Accessed June 23, 2015. http://timesofindia.indiatimes.com/india/Reading-Satanic-Verses-legal/articleshow/11622048.cms?referral=PM.

Moore-Gilbert, Bart. *Hanif Kureishi*. Manchester: Manchester University Press, 2001.

*My Beautiful Laundrette*. Dir. Stephen Frears. Minerva, 1985.

Nawaz, Aki. "What Happened to the Book Burners." 13 February 2009. *BBC News Magazine*. June 23, 2015. http://news.bbc.co.uk/2/hi/uk_news/magazine/7883308.stm.

Prasad, M. Madhava. *Cini-Film: Film Stars and Political Existence in South India*. Delhi: Orient BlackSwan, 2013.

———. *Ideology of the Hindi Film: A Historical Construction*. Delhi: Orient BlackSwan, 1998.

Prashad, Vijay. *The Karma of Brown Folk*. Minneapolis: University of Minnesota Press, 2000.

Prashad, Vijay. *Everybody was Kung Fu fighting: Afro-Asian Connections and the Myth of Cultural Purity*. Boston: Beacon Press, 2001.

———. *The Darker Nations: A People's History of the Third World*. New York: New Press, 2007.

Press Association. "David Cameron: school sports targets result in 'Indian dance' classes." 10 August 2012. *The Guardian*. Accessed December 12, 2012. http://www.theguardian.com/education/2012/aug/10/david-cameron-school-sports-targets.

Rai, Amit S. *Untimely Bollywood: Globalization and India's New Media Assemblage.* Durham, NC: Duke University Press, 2009.

Rajadhyaksha, Ashish. *India in the Time of Celluloid: From Bollywood to the Emergency.* Delhi: Tulika Books, 2009.

Rajagopal, Arvind. *Politics After Television: Hindu Nationalism and the Reshaping of the Public in India.* Cambridge: Cambridge University Press, 2001.

Rushdie, Salman. "A Response." Herwitz, Daniel, and Varshney Ashutosh. *Midnight's Diaspora.* Delhi: Penguin Books, 2009. 136–40.

———. "Christopher Hitchens." February 2012. *Vanity Fair.* December 12, 2012. http://salmanrushdie1.tumblr.com/post/15369634397/christopher-hitchens-vanity-fair-feb-2012.

———. *Joseph Anton.* London: Random House, 2012.

———. *The Satanic Verses.* London: Random House, 1988.

*Sammy and Rosie Get Laid.* Dir. Stephen Frears. Cinecom/Film Four, 1987.

Shama, Sanjay. *Multicultural Encounters.* London: Palgrave Macmillan, 2006.

Sharma, Sanjay, John Hutnyk, and Ash Sharma. *Dis-Orienting Rhythms: the Politics of the New Asian Dance Music.* London: Zed Books, 1996.

Spivak, Gayatri Chakravorty. *Other Asias.* Malden: Blackwell, 2008.

———. *Outside in the Teaching Machine.* New York: Routledge, 1993.

*The Battle of Algiers.* Dir. Gillo Pontecorvo. Prod. Antonio Musu and Yacef Saadi. By Franco Solinas and Gillo Pontecorvo. Perf. Brahim Haggiag and Yacef Saadi. Allied Artists Corporation, 1969.

*The Kumars at No 42.* Sanjeev Bhaskar, Meera Syal, Indira Joshi, Vincent Ebrahim, BBC, 2001. *IMDb.* Accessed January 30, 2015. http://www.imdb.com/title/tt0300792/.

*The Razor's Edge.* Dir. John Byrum. Twentieth Century-Fox Film Corp., 1984.

Ventura, Marco. *From Your Gods to Our Gods: A History of Religion in Indian, South African, and British Courts.* Eugene, OR: Cascade Books, 2014.

*Wild West.* Dir. David Attwood. 1992. Film.

Wilson, Amrit. *Finding a Voice: Asian Women in Britain.* London: Vintage, 2006.

# NOTES

1. Less famously, the book is reported to have been first burned in Bolton on December 2, 1988 (Ventura, 42). For more on chronology, see note 6.

2. The fatwah was declared on February 14, 1989, perhaps a mischievous Valentines Day card, initially perceived as a bit of Khomeini theatrics ten years after the Iranian hostage drama, which in turn had its part to play in the U.S. change of president—enter Ronald Reagan, former film actor (grim chuckle). Khomeini had been voted *Time Magazine* Man of the Year in 1979.

3. The Rajiv Gandhi government banned import of the book in 1988 after author Kushwant Singh advised Penguin India that a local edition "might offend the religious sensibilities of Muslims" (Mitta 2012). Vaz has been a long-standing Labour MP and may or may not be the basis of characters in Kureishi's novels.

4. Thirty-seven Alevi poets, artists, and others died in a hotel fire in Turkey after a mob attacked the presumed location of Rushdie's Turkish publisher. Also a large number of persons died in protests against the book, though these are harder to document: for example six in Pakistan on February 12, 1989, and twelve shot by police at a protest in Bombay on January 25, 1989 (Amir Hussein in Campo 2009, 595).

5. A chronology prepared by *Index on Censorship* in 2008 names Syed Shahabuddin as the instigator of the first campaigns against the book in India in mid-September 1988, while Faiyazuddin Ahmad of the Islamic Foundation of Leicester is credited with contacting British Muslim Organisations in October of 1988, and soon after the Islamic Conference Organisation (ICO) in Saudi Arabia (Index on Censorship, 144)

6. There are immense problems with the terms here, but it is useful to keep them difficult. I favor the uncomfortable and slightly awkward neologism "Br-Asian" (Kaur

and Kalra 1996) used in *Dis-Orienting Rhythms* (Sharma et al. 1996) and *A Postcolonial People* (Ali et al. 2006). I don't use it in this particular essay because the commentary is about the projection of allegedly "not-quite" Britishness, and the "ish" is erased in Br-Asian (though of course on purpose).

7. For the Br-Asian section of Global South Asian film and television studies I am keen on Kureishi, the pre-*Bhaji* work of Gurinder Chadha—who also has made some surprisingly snarky assertions about Kureishi's introspection being a consequence of his British-Asian "mix"—the excellent *Wild West* (dir. David Attwood 1992), written by Harwant Bains, and critiques like that of *East is East* by Sanjay Sharma in his 2006 book *Multicultural Encounters*.

8. No less a "firing squad" than the Chilcot Iraq Inquiry soft peddled the war crimes and encouragements to reaction given by bleeding heart prime ministers of dubious reputation—documentation here: http://www.iraqinquiry.org.uk/ (accessed March 10, 2010).

9. *Injustice* deals with the stories of families and friends fighting for justice in the cases of police custody deaths in the UK. A report on this film, and the controversy surrounding its screening, can be found in Imogen Bunting's 2003 article, "Rationality, Legitimacy and the 'Folk Devils' of May" (*Left Curve*)

10. Hobson-Jobson was, or is, the dictionary of Anglo-English colonial slang and colloquial loan words, like umbrella, thug, pajama, bungalow, and other pukka formulations.

11. I found Harveen Sachdeva Mann's essay too late for it to influence this chapter, which was mostly written in 2012, revised 2014, but she confirms this with her comments—with much well-observed detail, for example noticing the developer forcing through the evictions of the squatter troupe's caravans is Alice's son—"A pivotal scene in *Sammy and Rosie Get Laid*, three quarters of the way through the film, is the horizontal, triple split screenshot of the three couples—Sammy and Anna, Rosie and Danny, and Rafi and Alice—having sex" (Mann 1995, 491).

12. Comment by Gayatri Spivak in discussion of this text with the author in a 1995 workshop at Keele University.

13. Lord Scarman was head of the Government Inquiry into the Brixton riots of 1981 (BBC News).

14. The New Cross fire occurred in 1981 and involved the tragic loss of thirteen young lives in an incident many thought was a case of arson on the part of fascists against local youth.

15. Battle of Lewisham in 1977 was a day of running protest against the National Front.

16. Stop under Suspicion laws allowed police to disproportionately harass black citizens of London, fueling tensions.

17. The street protests in the North of England during the summer of 2001 were not unanticipated, and in some quarters were quite a conflagration. That Mosque leaders and families subsequently "shopped" wayward sons to the police was problematic enough, but that the lag between these events and the court cases for these youth meant that September 11, 2001, became a backstory and the sentences handed down for minor misdemeanors and first offenses were unconscionably severe. This was replicated again with the 2010 London student protests and more severely in the 2011 London "riots" aka "uprising" (see Henri and Hutnyk 2012).

18. http://www.kenanmalik.com/lectures/rushdie_boi.html accessed June 6, 2009

19. An article appeared on the English Defence League website imploring the leadership not to burn the Koran, though the article was soon taken down. Stories of such burnings proliferate following Florida pastor Terry Jones's calls for the same, and his 2010 invitation by the EDL to speak in Britain, though his visa was refused (History Commons).

20. "it is all the more clear what we have to accomplish at present: I am referring to ruthless criticism of all that exists, ruthless both in the sense of not being afraid of the results it arrives at and in the sense of being just as little afraid of conflict with the powers that be" (Marx).

# THREE

# Managing Race, Class, and Gender

*Atlanta's South Asian American Muslims and the*
*Localized Management of the "Global War on Terror"*

Stanley Thangaraj

*During my research on South Asian American basketball communities in Atlan-*
*ta, Ali[1] was one of my key interlocutors. He is a Muslim Pakistani American. It*
*was August 10, 2009, and I had Ali and his wife, Susan (a white Catholic), over*
*for dinner. The conversation turned to many things including the recent eco-*
*nomic crisis, their newly married life, Susan's pregnancy, and basketball. Since*
*August 14 and August 15 were around the corner, I asked a question that made*
*sense to me, "Ali, what are you doing for Independence Day?" He replied con-*
*fused, "Huh? What?" I repeated myself, "What are you doing for Independence*
*Day?" Ali was now clearly confused, "What are you talking about? Indepen-*
*dence Day? That was last month." Now I was confused, "Two months ago? I am*
*talking about August 14." As I slowly made this connection, Ali laughed, "Man,*
*I was talking about July 4." He considered July 4 Independence Day while I had*
*assumed that he and his family celebrated Pakistani Independence Day on Au-*
*gust 14.*

Ali's celebration of July 4 and consequent identification of that date as
meaningful represents one set of practices of cultural citizenship. For him
and his South Asian American peers, their quotidian performances of self
were woven into renditions of Americanness. They did not doubt their
Americanness. However, South Asians Americans are often commonly
understood as "perpetual foreigners" (Lowe 1996) without the requisite
cultural attributes, ability, or bodily constitution for U.S. citizenship.
Since the September 11, 2001 terrorist attacks on U.S. soil, this community

has faced the brunt of racial hysteria, Islamophobia, and heightened state surveillance and detention (Rana 2011; Maira 2009; Afzal 2014; Thangaraj 2015). They have been marked simultaneously in expansive categories as terrorists and as terror that is ongoing. Such racial significations of South Asians outside of the U.S. national fabric is not new, the indexicality of "terror" however is.

In the late 1800s and early 1900s, the "racial formation" (Omi and Winant 1994) of South Asians as "Hindoos" through immigration laws and policies projected these Punjabi Sikhs and Muslims as unsuitable for citizenship because of their outward makeup, their cultural practices, their relation to white men, their relation to white women, and their "lewd" tendencies (see Haney-Lopez 1994; Koshy 2007; Puar 2007). As agrarian workers, their lower-class status and their racialization as non-normative men prevented social mobility as well as access to key resources—such as owning land. Increasing nativist sentiment stemmed immigration from South Asia until the 1965 Immigration Act that opened U.S. borders to South Asian professionals in an attempt to combat the U.S.S.R. at the height of the Cold War (see Bhatia 2007; George 2005; Prashad 2000). The professionals were interpellated as the "model minority" who were seen as culturally proficient and endowed with the work ethic to succeed. Such a racialized moniker positioned these South Asians, as well as other Asian Americans, as good minorities in contrast to African Americans and Latinas/os who, at the height of the civil rights movement, were feminized because they were deemed as depending on governmental aid. Even though these professionals were brought in to supplement the U.S. imperial machinery, the "model minority" discourse did not grant absolute entry into Americanness as they were seen as failing to achieve normative white masculinity. Using the term "model minority" was still a projection of abjection while constituting white masculinity as normative American masculinity/subjectivity.

In the contemporary period, Muslim Pakistani American men, like Ali, are represented by the U.S. state and mainstream media as recalcitrant masculinities—the racial formation of "Muslim looking" (Ahmad 2004)—who cannot be assimilated into American citizenship. South Asian Americans, especially Muslim Pakistani American communities, are cast as "terrorists" while whites and acceptable racial Others are reaffirmed as patriots (see Afzal 2014, 2009; Maira 2009; Rana 2011; Puar and Rai 2004; Thangaraj 2015). The U.S. public envisions Muslims as always committed to their homeland and bent on destroying the foundational fabric of the American nation. They are, thus, brought into essentialized subjectivity as "terrorists" and "nerds" in contradictory ways (Thangaraj 2015). However, the vignette above offers a counternarrative to mainstream racializations where Muslim South Asian Americans, like Ali, embody Americanness through a variety of cultural practices. One such practice was Ali's embodiment of Independence Day that grounded his

American identity with certain Muslim Pakistani cultural practices (such as the events and rituals for his wedding) but with little affiliation with the nation of Pakistan. On July 4, he would have friends over for an all-American cookout where he grilled burgers, hot dogs, and other items. Similarly, the key organizer, Daniel (Catholic Malayalee American finance professional), of pickup basketball in Atlanta would also host a major July 4 cookout at his house. Whereas U.S. Independence Day celebrations take place only once a year, Ali and Daniel also performed their Americanness through quotidian encounters with basketball. Basketball, as a quintessentially American sport, presents a realm where young Muslim South Asian American men reconfigure the racial, gendered, and classed dimensions of national "belonging."

## POPULAR CULTURE/SPORT AS CULTURAL CITIZENSHIP

The racialized discourses of South Asian American men dislocate them from the American imagination by fixing their bodies outside the racial, gendered, classed, and sexual realm of Americanness. By assuming that South Asian Americans consume Bollywood and cricket as the main cultural forms for negotiating identity, it fixes them in symbolic and physical territories of South Asianness. Members of Atlanta's South Asian American community, especially the young men playing in South Asian American basketball leagues and mostly South Asian basketball recreational venues, take part in various forms of popular culture that collapsed Americanness and South Asianness into South Asian Americanness (see Thangaraj 2015, 2010a, 2010b). Although some South Asian Americans did take to South Asian cultural forms like cricket and Bollywood cinema, Ali and his basketball peers chose to participate in basketball as positions of "counter-identification" (Medina 2013; 2003) from cricket players. There is a large cricket community in Atlanta composed of Indian, Pakistani, Bangladeshi, West Indian/Caribbean, English, and Australian players. Most of the South Asian cricket players in 2009 were international students and recent immigrants to the United States. West Indian cricket great Desmond Lewis, who lives in Atlanta, gave me a window into the local history of cricket. He explained that the early league games contained heterogeneous South Asian teams that congregated regardless of religion, ethnicity, or nation of origin. However, in the following years preceding and following the 1996 Olympics, Atlanta became a key destination city for South Asian Americans; the population boomed. As a result, the heterogeneous South Asian teams dismantled and reassembled under particular national and religious contours. Desmond Lewis informed me that the Muslim-Hindu and Pakistan-Indian binary caused much internal strife in the cricket league. As a result, Caribbean teams did not want to play into those dichotomous logics and thus exited the league. Those types of strife are not common within the basketball communities I ethnographically charted.

During one of the car rides to an Asian American tournament with Muslim Pakistani American players on team *Atlanta Rat Pack*, Imran (team organizer and point guard) pointed to an American football field at Georgia Tech right alongside the gymnasium where the basketball games were held. Imran, a player on the *Atlanta Rat Pack* basketball team pointed out that, "FOBs play cricket. They play every weekend at Georgia Tech [Georgia Institute of Technology]." FOB stood for "Fresh Off the Boat," a pejorative term used by second-generation South Asians in the U.S. to solidify "foreignness" and un-American masculinity through cricket onto the bodies of recent male immigrants, mostly international students. By depicting them as "fresh off the boat," it was also a classed judgment of masculinity. Cricket players were represented as immigrants without the class resources or cultural knowledge to buy into "American basketball cool." It is not to say that South Asian American men cannot play cricket and identify as American, rather basketball players engage in "intra-ethnic Othering" (Abelmann 2009) by positioning cricket players as less capable, less manly subjects. Even the team names for the Atlanta Cricket League were initially names, in 2009, that conjured up British and middle-class sensibilities. Some names included Indus Sports Club while others were Stockbridge CC (cricket club) and some had common European soccer names like United. However, recently, these cricket team names involve evoking more common U.S. popular cultural names such as Panthers and Predators. The first set of names were a reflection of consumption of British and Indian sporting popular culture whereas the basketball team names were a result of consumptive practices of U.S. popular cultural forms like hip-hop, Hollywood, and mainstream sporting cultures.

South Asian American basketball players felt the urge to counteridentify with cricket since many non-South Asians, mostly whites, conflated South Asianness and cricket. Whites, some players told me, frequently asked, "Don't you guys play cricket?" The reference to cricket distends these U.S. ethnic subjects back to South Asia. Accordingly, these young men are pictured as not having the racial ability or the masculine prowess to play basketball. Furthermore, the realm of cricket is fairly alien and can be part of the cultural repertoire for representing South Asians as always foreign, dangerous, and terroristic. In addition, when playing cricket, the terrorist and model minority stereotypes mix in complicated ways. They are seen as having bodies suited for an upper-class, colonial gentlemen's game that is not as rough or aggressive as basketball.[2]

South Asian American basketball players displaced the racializations of South Asians in the United States onto cricket players whom they imagined to be new immigrants who failed to shed their foreign layers and adapt to the masculine norms of U.S. sport. With the popularity of basketball, the ease with which to organize basketball games, and the ways in which basketball communicated ideas about race and masculinity (Cole and King 1998; Brooks 2009; Thangaraj 2010a), the young men actively partook of basketball play and corresponding social interactions. Some participated in ethnically and religiously exclusive leagues such as Indo-Pak Basketball (South Asian American),[3] Asian American leagues,[4] and Muslim tournaments. Within these ethno-religious spaces, the South Asian American players could express their versions of Americanness and masculinity—they performed "cultural citizenship" (Maira 2009) that went beyond the legal norms of citizenship. Practices of cultural citizenship, such as playing basketball, extended the limits of American citizenship onto South Asian American bodies and South Asian American places. By playing basketball, they could invert and dismantle the racialization of religion and ethnicity that posits them as the American terror.

## MASJIDS AS SITES OF AMERICANNESS

Contrary to popular belief and mainstream media depictions in the United States, Muslim South Asian American centers of worship were not sites of latent "terror cells" (Rana 2011). Both racializations, of the "terrorist" and "model minority" fix Muslim South Asian American men as failing bodies without the ability to perform or maintain the normative boundaries of American citizenship. As such, these racializations were a judgment on their masculinity. For my informants, sport participation was a "racial project" (Carrington 2010; Omi and Winant 1994) that contested mainstream racializations of Muslim South Asian Americans as nerdy or terroristic masculinities. Sport participation served to invert racial belonging predicated on a black-white binary (see Yep 2012, 2009; Thangaraj 2012) thereby securing performances of citizenship for those apart such a racial logic. As part of citizenship in the U.S. is predicated on legibility within the black-white racial dichotomy, consumptive practices of basketball by these racial subjects reconfigures the boundaries of belonging. In addition, by inverting that racial binary, Muslim South Asian American men could simultaneously lay claim to Americanness while reconfiguring the relationship between "race and ability" (Maram 2006). By reconfiguring the relationship between race and ability, South Asian American men, especially Muslims, could enter the fabric and discourse of Americanness other than as terrorists.

From the early construction and to the early years of Al-Farooq Masjid (the first mainstream, international mosque in Atlanta), sports were central to the spiritual training of Muslim men within the arena of Americanness. While many of the newly arriving immigrants played cricket, Muslim South Asian American men who were born or grew up in the U.S.

socialized into American masculinity through their social interactions on the masjid basketball court. When Al-Farooq Masjid came into existence in 1980, it was through the financial support and resources of the Muslim South Asians who came through the post-1965 wave of professionals. These early Muslim communities were comprised of international students at Georgia Tech and professional doctors, engineers, and scientists. The elders wanted to include a basketball court as a means to assimilate their children (sons) into U.S. society. Sport, Islam, and Americanness existed on the same plane of masculinity formation. Like many churches throughout Atlanta, the mosques contained a basketball component. During my research into the heterogeneous North American South Asian American basketball community, South Asian American men all stated vehemently that their places of worship were one of the instrumental sites where they encountered sport and assimilated into U.S. society. Many of the athletes iterated that their early intimate and affective encounters with basketball took place at their local Gurdwara (Sikh place of worship), Mandir (Hindu temple), church, or mosque.

With their financial standing as high-level professionals, the elders in the Muslim South Asian American community were able to integrate several sporting events as part of Muslim Americanness. The Muslim community hosted several coreligious basketball tournaments. On August 15, 2009, India's Independence Day, Angul, an organization for Muslim youth, structured a 3-on-3 basketball tournament in a Gwinnett County public gym. Gwinnett County is one of the counties of metro Atlanta with one of the fastest growing South Asian American communities in the U.S. (Thangaraj 2012). This 3-on-3 tournament was gender segregated in that only men could play while women were allowed in as spectators. At the tournament, there was what anthropologist Ahmed Afzal (2014, 2010) terms as "Muslim heritage economy" where Muslims from various national and ethnic backgrounds congregated under an open concept of the "ummah" (Muslim community).[5] African Muslims, South Asian American Muslims, Middle Eastern American Muslims, white Muslims, African American Muslims, and Latino Muslims played. During the break for lunch, two Muslim community elders came out and preached about the links between sport, Muslim masculinity, and Muslim respectability. A basketball event such as this interjected different cultural forms, racial bodies, and ways of being into Americanness. A few South Asian Muslims played wearing their *kurtas* (long, flowing outfits seen as respectable garb for Muslim men). Each basketball movement integrated Muslim respectability, masculinity, and citizenship. Instead of celebrating Indian or Pakistani Independence Day on August 15 and 14 respectively, these young men chose to play basketball and form a sense of community through these sporting practices. Part of playing basketball was also a site for practicing, performing, and learning the connections between Islam, masculinity, and American identity.

South Asian American men arrived at the tournament with great enthusiasm to reconnect with their co-ethnic peers. In other parts of Atlanta, the Pakistani and Indian communities celebrated Pakistani and Indian independence. The *Atlanta Journal Constitution*, the major newspaper in Atlanta, covered events in South Asian American communities in ways that manufactured monolithic representations of them, minus the work by journalist John Blake. Whereas celebrating Indian and Pakistani Independence Day parades and local South Asian eateries is important for some people in the community, this is a form of multiculturalism that does not account for the multiplicities and contradictions within South Asian American identity formation. For some, participation in these parades is one expression of cultural citizenship and American belonging; this was not, however, the case with the basketball players. It is because of singular media coverage, I propose, that this community is interpellated as "foreign," which can lead to the racialization as "terrorist." The focus on these Independence Day celebrations alone projects the young men outside the national and racial logic of American citizenship. The disregard of these young South Asian American men for the South Asian festivities was their own way of assembling their gender, racial, class, and national identity. Partaking of basketball—both at major tournaments and in their everyday lives—was routine and part of the fabric of South Asian American masculinity. Participation in basketball was part and parcel of an Americanness that Muslim American players never questioned. It was the larger U.S. public that doubted the Americanness of Muslim men. Dr. Abdul emphasized, "Muslims are 80 percent more patriotic to the U.S. than non-Muslims in this country. We love this country." He added,

> This [post-9/11 racial hysteria] has awakened Muslims to the need to interact with the community at large and explain the teachings of Islam instead of having radicals explain Islam. We are extra vigilant with our own behavior and stay away from all forms of extremism and violence and actions to strengthen the fabric of this society . . . we as Muslims [must be] perceived as an asset to society.

Even one of the key South Asian American basketball players, Mustafa, mentioned this distance from extremist beliefs. He told me that the International Islamic Congress was taking place in Atlanta in 2011 and that it was a great thing. Mustafa hoped that young men would go to it. When I asked why, he responded, "They need to attend. They need to go so that they [young South Asian American Muslims] don't get it [Islam] twisted." His vernacular injunction of "twisted" refers to the corrupt and extreme versions of Islam that are often seen as the norm (see Abu-Lughod 2013). Mustafa sees Islam and its teachings as a way to create respectable masculinities, not terror cells or enemy combatants.

At this 3-on-3 tournament, Muslims from various backgrounds contested the monolithic, essentialized construction of Muslimness in the larger public as anti-American and un-American (see Karim 2009). The tournament provided a safe space to perform one's rendition of masculinity, Muslim, and Americanness that countered the racial formation of "Muslim looking." In the safety of this exclusive space, these young men partook of physical, aggressive, and rough play. Each shot was contested. When the basketball was in the air, players tussled and wrestled for position. In this Muslim-only space, the young men could safely perform the multiplicity of Americanness, weaved through different ethnic and national registers, and basketball masculinity. The fouls were grueling in an attempt to prevent opponents from taking an easy shot. Roughness and aggressiveness of this sort was not read as terroristic nor was it seen as outside the logic of normative sporting masculinity. Participants could enjoy competitive basketball, even with inferior levels of play, without compromising their manhood. Only by closing basketball off to the general public and by purchasing this gym could they articulate the masculine and racial contours of Americanness.

*Playing through Americanness in the Asian Ballers League*

On the same day of the Angul tournament, a few other Muslim South Asian American players, including Imran and Ali whom we discussed earlier, played in a different ethnic basketball league playoff tournament. Ali and his Muslim Pakistani American peers chose to partake in a much more competitive basketball circuit, known as the Asian Ballers League (a pan-Asian American league)[6] than the Angul tournament. He played with a team of mostly Sikh Americans called Hit Squad. His brother, Mustafa, played with a team of Muslim Pakistani Americans called Atlanta Rat Pack. Participation in sport opened up space to provide political critiques that their own communities were afraid to make. Soon after the September 11, 2001, terrorist attacks, the consequent racial hysteria collapsed ethnicity, religion, location, phenotype, and cultural practices into the racial terrorist category. As a result, Latinos, Arabs, Middle Easterners, South Asians, African Americans, and Muslims were targeted at disproportional rates. The Department of Homeland Security conducted high levels of surveillance at Al-Farooq Masjid and the other neighborhood mosques. Basketball was one space to address Muslim heterogeneity while contesting the common racial classifications of South Asian American men. However, it is important to note that not all South Asian Americans experienced the post-9/11 racial hysteria equally. The finance professionals and middle-class South Asian Americans playing in the weekly pickup games (Thangaraj 2015), did not see 9/11 and the subsequent U.S. state response as an attack on their communities or part of the larger fabric of marginalization of minoritized masculinities. When I asked these professionals what they thought of 9/11 and the events that followed afterword, their responses included:

> *"A very tragic day."*
> *"It meant a change of reflection on how vulnerable we are."*
> *"I think we all realize that it was a day that ended our feelings of security/ safety from foreign attacks. Everything is not in our control, and sometimes life-altering events can happen without any prior action by any of us. As for me, I at first felt like it may be the event that defines my generation; or at least the event that took the innocence out of my generation."*
> *"It was a tragic event in the country's history, but I didn't feel like it necessarily directly impacted myself or my family. It did change my perspective on how Americans are viewed by the rest of the world, however."*
> *"To me it meant an opportunity for the country to become one again."*

As some Hindu Americans have preached Hindutva (Hindu fundamentalism with links to the Bharatiya Janata Party in India)[7] as a way aligning with whiteness and distancing themselves from Muslims, this has meant that Hindu American communities in Atlanta did not always experience 9/11 equivocally as other South Asian American communities. For some, their professional and middle-class status further acted as a buffer against racializations as the "terror." Thus, some of these professional Hindu Americans did not feel the violence, deaths, and fear experienced by the working poor (who were targeted for deportation and detention) and religious Others (Sikhs and Muslims had members of their community killed and places of worship vandalized). Muslim and Sikh South Asian Americans did not share the same sentiment concerning 9/11 and post-9/11 life as their Hindu professional peers:

> *"Very saddening. Also, since I am a turban wearing Sikh, I did expect ignorance and hatred comments from many Americans."*
> *"Devastating, Confusion, Fear, Embarrassment, Hard to put into words, Still choke up thinking about that day."*

Sikh and Muslim American teams use basketball as a space to offer social critique of the Judeo-Christian foundations of social life and the marginalizations in U.S. society. Playing basketball becomes one way to perform citizenship and challenge mainstream stereotypes.

One interesting realm of contestation involved team formation and its corresponding symbolic manipulations. The South Asian American teams, with a majority of Muslims, formed through heterogeneous categories that highlighted shared experiences of racialization for Middle Eastern, Arab, Sikh, Hindu, Muslim, and other South Asian men.

Kashif previously played for team Atlanta Rat Pack but was dissatisfied with the minimal playing time. He decided to form his own team— Sand Brothaz. By strategically using the name Sand Brothaz, he added

several elements of "cool pose" (Majors 2001) through black aesthetics—
the "az" instead of "ers"—and a tough black masculinity (see Kelley
1997). The team name also addressed social bonding for men of color via
the paradigm of *brotherhood*. Two Sikh Americans, Riad (Arab American),
and several Muslim South Asian Americans made up this team. When I
asked Kashif about the reasons for team name, he responded, "I wanted
the team name to be something funny, ethnically describing us, and
something related to brotherhood or team chemistry-like. So I first
thought of *Sand Niggaz*, ha, ha, out of joke only, but of course that word
wouldn't work then I thought of Muslim Brotherhood but not all the
guys were Muslim. At the end, I combined it to make Sand Brothaz." By
referring to an initial comical choice of Sand Niggaz, Kashif simultaneously intimates the racial, gendered processes of sameness and difference. The pejorative term, *sand n*****, is used to conflate Arab, Middle
Eastern, Muslim, South Asian, and other brown communities. Yet,
"sand" stood for the foreignness, an abnormal masculinity, in positions
of difference from black masculinity. The assertion of "sand" differen-
tiates between communities of color whereby the black subject stands in
as the emblematic non-normative, queer[8] masculinity in relation to white
masculinity. The African American subject is consolidated at the bottom
of the racial hierarchy while South Asian Americans exist in an ambiguous racial category outside of but always conversant with the black-white
racial logic. By inserting "sand," it is a practice of American racialized
vernacular that creates ideological, cultural, symbolic, and corporeal difference between black and brown bodies.

Despite the distance from blackness, the team name Sand Brothaz
symbolizes a brotherhood among the Muslim South Asian American,
Muslim Lebanese American, and Sikh American players. They use black
cultural forms and vernacular as the means to assert their Americanness
and reconfigure the boundaries of their sporting, masculine community.
Using "brothaz" allows for a sense of community for the players whose
communities have similar/shared experiences with the post-9/11 racial
hysteria and the subsequent War on Terror. Instead of accentuating one's
religious, geographic, and ethnic histories as points of difference from a
normative American masculinity, these young men expand the meanings
of Americanness that is inclusive of ethnic and religious heterogeneity.
Kashif, other Muslim South Asian Americans, Riad, and the Sikh
American players, through their team socialities, create a sense of community that incorporates those subjects produced as "terrorists" in the
American imagination (see Jamal and Naber 2008).

## DISRUPTING SOUTH ASIAN AMERICAN
## MASCULINITY THROUGH CLASS

The markers of class identity and access to resources surfaced within the basketball circuit as well. We find this evident detailed above where finance professionals did not feel the intimate wrath of post-9/11 racial hysteria as their Sikh and Muslim and lower-class brethren. Basketball players played through their class positions which reinforced class differences within this basketball community. In this case, class is not something people possess but rather their relationship to power (Collins 2008; Davis 1985). As many of the members of these various teams showcase the complex relationship to citizenship, masculinity, race, and sport, their classed position—as professionals or children of the post-1965 waves of professionals—makes their pleasures of sport not easily available to all. Class is an important category that disrupts the uniformity of Muslim South Asian America. Some of my interlocutors, like Ali and Mustafa, stem from the post-1980 wave of immigrants whose parents united with respective professional siblings already established in the United States. Some of the children of the post-1980 Muslim Pakistani immigrants, such as Mustafa, Ahmed, and Mahmoud, had a different relationship to South Asian American identity, the "model minority" moniker, and to basketball. They all could not sufficiently, with time or money, manage basketball into their quotidian performance of race, masculinity, and Americanness. Ahmed, Mahmoud, and Mustafa did not attend a four-year college and did not possess the same social mobility as their professional coethnic peers. Although Mahmoud boasted about "making bank" (vernacular used to describe monetary affluence), he did not have the luxury of time to partake of basketball. He owned and managed several gas stations so as to secure financial stability and provide the financial resources for his younger brother, Atif, to attend college and graduate school. Unlike his younger brother, Mahmoud and his lower-class status peers were at the mercy of U.S. state, both at the federal and local levels, through heightened post-9/11 surveillance. This was also similarly the case with some Bangladeshi Americans I met in Atlanta. They owned and worked at several gas stations across Atlanta. They recruited family members to work them. In addition, they also took part in underground markets to eke out a living.

In addition to deportations, these young men are in a precarious situation where they encounter a greater threat of detention. Emerging private detention centers in the U.S. South are affiliated with the U.S. Immigrations and Customs Enforcement (ICE) office which is affiliated with Department of Homeland Security.[9] Furthermore, other governmental task forces have used the September 11, 2001, hysteria to partake in other aspects of racial profiling that have directly affected the South Asian American—especially the Muslim—community. As a result, young men like Mahmoud live under precarious conditions. One such governmental project, "Operation Meth Merchant," was put in place in January 2004 and lasted until June 2005,[10] which resulted in a surprising number of indictments. The July 19, 2007, issue of the *Atlanta Journal Constitution* states "While 80 percent of stores in the area of 'Operation Meth Merchant' were owned by whites or other ethnic groups, 23 of the 24 stores targeted were owned by South Asians, claimed the ACLU." Players working service jobs and performing nonprofessional labor did not have the financial and temporal luxury to play basketball as freely as their professional co-ethnic peers. In addition, post-1965 children of professionals considered such work, as that done by Mahmoud, as lower class and used the term "ghetto," which is itself a racialized term, to reference such labor (see Jones 2010). Such labor fell outside the boundaries of normative citizenship and Mahmoud, Mustafa, and Ahmed were not read as performing the classed, "model minority," contours of Americanness.

Ahmed sulked with envy when he spoke with Mustafa before an Asian Ballers League game, "Man, I wish I could come out and play with you guys. Why didn't you let me know?" Unlike the members of Atlanta Rat Pack who were in four-year colleges and in finance professions, Ahmed attended a community college and worked during his free time at an electronics store. In addition, the Asian Ballers League games were held in the southwestern part of DeKalb County and quite far from his parent's home in Gwinnett County.

When Ahmed asked why he was not invited to play with Atlanta Rat Pack, the relationship between class and Muslim respectability also became apparent. The main players and captains of team Sand Brothaz, Camel Jockeys, and Atlanta Rat Pack were the children of professionals who structured specific classed ideas of Muslim masculinity that paralleled middle-class, Sunni (a dominant branch of Islam) Muslim respectability. As a result, young men like Mahmoud and Ahmed were not invited to play on their teams. Ali did not receive an invitation to play on Rat Pack alongside his older brother Mustafa. His intensity on the court was deemed by members of Rat Pack as out of the bounds of respectability. One of the players, Mohammed, explained, "He is out of control. Ali shouts at the refs. He gets in trouble with the refs and the refs then give us bad calls." Mustafa provided an alternate explanation, "They [Rat Pack] don't pick him up to play because they think he smokes [marijuana] too much." Ali's bodily comportment and behavior stood in contrast to the classed expectations of Mohammed and his peers. As a result of the intersections of race, gender, and class, Muslim South Asian American men have differential resources to claim spaces and perform cultural citizenship.

However, young men like Ali do encounter Mohammed and his peers in some of the leagues. For Ali, he finds opportunities to play basketball and dominate his professional co-ethnic opponents. When team Hit Squad defeated Rat Pack, Ali's skill was on display. This victory gave him satisfaction as his opponents were slightly emasculated with the loss. The basketball court then becomes the realm where Americanness is expressed through contestations of race, gender, and class. Although he cannot play as frequently as Mohammed and Imran, he tried to maximize each encounter by dominating his co-ethnic peers. With each victory Ali was able to claim a tough, skilled, sporting masculinity that was made possible by one-upping his opponents. By scoring prolifically on his opponents, by dribbling past them, and weaving difficult passes to his teammates for easy shots, he was able to position himself in a symbolically elevated position that challenged the hegemony of the "model minority."

## CONCLUSION

Basketball play, both in religious centers and ethnic minority leagues, allows South Asian American men to create social networks, partake in the pleasures of homosocial athletic competition, and express the contours of their Americanness. Through the active work of creating safe spaces for co-ethnic sporting participation, Muslim South Asian Americans now had safe spaces to perform masculinity and cultural citizenship that incorporated basketball, Islam, and Americanness. The expressive practices and embodiments of basketball masculinity in co-ethnic sporting venues could not so easily take place for Muslim men in other social venues. As South Asian American men oscillate in the U.S. imagination between "model minority/nerd" and "terrorist" (Puar and Rai 2004), their acts of basketball toughness and aggression in the public sphere would be read as outside the boundaries of normative masculinity. But in multiracial leagues, South Asian American men were racialized outside the boundaries of acceptable sporting masculinities but they could exhibit Americanness only through ethnically and religiously, exclusive basketball formats. In multiracial and public sporting circuits, the specter of "terrorist" and "terror" continued to haunt them.

*I want to thank Surbhi Malik, Aparajita De, Kimberly Hoang, and Kemi Balogun for their insightful comments.*

*A version of this chapter was previously published in "Atlanta's Muslim South Asian Americans and cultural citizenship." Routledge International Handbook of Race, Class, and Gender (2014).*

## REFERENCES

Abelmann, Nancy. 2009. *The Intimate University*. Durham, NC: Duke University Press.

Abu-Lughod, Lila. 2013. *Do Muslim Women Need Saving?* Cambridge, MA: Harvard University Press.

Afzal, Ahmed. 2014. *Lone Star Muslims*. New York: New York University Press.

———. 2010. "From an Informal To a Transnational Muslim Heritage Economy: Transformations in the Pakistani Ethnic Economy in Houston, Texas." *Urban Anthropology* 39(4).

———. 2009 "'It is Allah's Will That I Am Here': State Surveillance and Pakistani Immigrant Experience in Texas Following 9/11," In M. Viteri and A. Tobler (eds.) *Shifting Positionalities: The Local and International Geo-Politics of Surveillance and Policing*. Boston: Cambridge Scholars Publishing.

Ahmad, Muneer. 2004. "A Rage Shared by Law: Post September 11th Racial Violence As Crimes of Passion." *California Law Review* 92(5): 1259–330.

Bhatia, Sunil. 2007. *American Karma*. New York: New York University Press.

Brooks, Scott. 2009. *Black Men Can't Shoot*. Chicago: University of Chicago Press.

Carrington, Ben. 2010. *Race, Sport and Politics: The Sporting Black Diaspora*. London: Sage Publications.

Cole, Cheryl L., and Samantha King. 1998. "Representing black masculinity and urban possibilities: Racism, realism, and Hoop Dreams." *Sport and Postmodern Times*: 49–86.

Collins, Patricia Hill. 2008. *Black Feminist Thought*. New York: Routledge.

Davis, Angela. 1985. *Women, Culture, Politics*. New York: Vintage Books.

Espana-Maram, Linda. 2006. *Creating Masculinity in Los Angeles's Little Manila*. New York: Columbia University Press.

George, Sheba. 2005. *When Women Come First*. Berkeley: University of California Press.

Haney-Lopez, Ian. 1994. *White by Law*. New York: New York University Press.

Jamal, Almaney, and Nadine Naber. 2008. *Race and Arab Americans Before and After 9/11*. Syracuse, NY: Syracuse University Press.

Jones, Nikki. 2010. *Between Good and Ghetto*. New Brunswick, NJ: Rutgers University Press.

Karim, Jamillah. 2009. *The American Ummah*. New York: New York University Press.

Kelley, Robin D. H. 1997. *Yo Mama's Dysfunktional!* Boston: Beacon Press.

Khandelwal, Madhulika. 2002. *Becoming American, Being Indian*. Ithaca, NY: Cornell University Press

Koshy, Susan. 2007. *Sexual Naturalization*. Palo Alto, CA: Stanford University Press.

Lowe, Lisa. 1996. *Immigrant Acts*. Durham, NC: Duke University Press.

Maira, Sunaina. 2009. *Missing*. Durham, NC: Duke University Press.

Majors, Richard. 2001. "Cool Pose: Black Masculinity and Sports." In S. Whitehead and F. Barrett (eds.) *The Masculinities Reader*. Cambridge, MA: Polity Press.

Manalansan, Martin. 2003. *Global Divas*. Durham, NC: Duke University Press.

Medina, Jose. 2013. *The Epistemology of Resistance: Gender and Racial Oppression, Epistemic Injustice, and Resistant Imaginations*. Oxford: Oxford University Press.

———. 2003. "Identity Trouble: Disidentification and the Problem of Difference." *Philosophy and Social Criticism* 29(6): 655–680.

Omi, Michael, and Howard Winnant. 1994. *Racial Formation in the United States*. New York: Routledge.

Prashad, Vijay. 2000. *The Karma of Brown Folk*. Minneapolis: University of Minnesota Press.

Puar, Jasbir, and Amit Rai. 2004. "The Remaking of a Model Minority." *Social Text* 22(3): 75–104.

Puar, Jasbir. 2007. *Terrorist Assemblages*. Durham, NC: Duke University Press.

Rana, Junaid. 2011. *Terrifying Muslims*. Durham, NC: Duke University Press.

Thangaraj, Stanley. 2015. *Desi Hoop Dreams: Pickup Basketball and the Making of Asian American Masculinity*. New York: New York University Press.

———. October 2013. "Competing Masculinities: Ethnic Sport Leagues and South Asian American Masculinity." *South Asian Popular Culture* 11(3)

———. June 2012. "Playing through Difference: The Black-White Racial Logic and Interrogating South Asian American Identity." *Journal of Ethnic and Racial Studies* 35(6).

———. 2010b. "Liting it Up: Popular Culture, Indo-Pak Basketball, and South Asian American Institutions." *Cosmopolitan Civil Societies: An Interdisciplinary Journal 2(2).*

———. September 2010a. "Ballin' Indo-Pak Style: Pleasures, Desires, and Expressive Practices of 'South Asian American' Masculinity." *International Review for the Sociology of Sport* 45(3).

Yep, Kathleen. 2012. "Peddling Sport: Liberal Multiculturalism and the Racial Triangulation of Blackness, Chineseness and Native American-ness in Professional Basketball." *Ethnic and Racial Studies* 35(6).

———. 2009. *Outside the Paint*. Philadelphia, PA: Temple University Press.

## NOTES

1. I use pseudonyms for all individuals to maintain their confidentiality; I also provided informed consent forms to all respondents.

2. For scholarship on cricket, see Carrington (2010).

3. See Thangaraj (2010a).

4. See Thangaraj (2013).

5. See also Karim (2009).

6. For more information on South Asian American participation in the Asian Ballers League, see Thangaraj (forthcoming).

7. See Prashad (2000).

8. Like Manalansan (2003), I use "queer" as a non-normative category and an anti-normative signifier.

9. See http://www.ice.gov/pi/dro/facilities/stewart.htm for more information. See also www.businessofdetention.com and http://theleastofthese-film.com/

10. See *Atlanta Journal Constitution* July 19, 2007, October 13, 2005, as well as various articles on the ACLU website concerning civil rights issues concerning the operation and conduction of "Operation Meth Merchant."

# FOUR

# "The City's Changed"

*Home Boy, The Reluctant Fundamentalist,* and the
Post-9/11 Urban Experience

## Hasan al Zayed

Mohsin Hamid's *The Reluctant Fundamentalist* (2007) and H. M. Naqvi's *Home Boy* (2009) are both novels of return. Changez, the protagonist of Hamid's second work, travels to the United States for a better life. A bright young man from Lahore, he easily makes it to the upper echelons of Princeton's undergraduate population despite his financial stress. Changez devotes a significant part of his time working part time. Eventually, his Princeton degree and sharp analytical ability helps him get a position in a small but very efficient and high-wage evaluation firm named Underwood Samson where he begins his career as an analyst and he continues to excel. His success is, however, offset by the New York City terror attacks, which destabilize his apparently harmonious relations to the city. Transformation of his adopted home—New York City—affects Changez deeply and personally. Unable to negotiate his raging anger against American imperialism on the one hand and his ambivalence toward the changed city on the other, Changez finally leaves Underwood Samson and returns to Lahore, the city where he grew up.

An almost identical thematization of return can be noticed in H. M. Naqvi's fiction as. His debut novel *Home Boy* tells the story of three young men of Pakistani ancestry—Chuck (Shezad), Jimbo (Jamshed), and AC (Ali)—whose blithe misadventure to find a missing friend turns into a solemn tragedy when they get arrested and are brought into a detention center. Self-proclaimed "renaissance men" who think they have their fin-

gers on "the great global dialectic" (Naqvi 2009, 1), these three young
men revel in the cosmopolitan life offered by New York City. It is only
when they are arrested do they realize that their right to navigate the city
undeterred has come to an abrupt end. In the changed climate of growing
antipathy Shezad and his friends find themselves reduced to beings without right to citizenship—rightless people or *homo sacers*,[1] to travesty
Georgio Agamben. Shezad's apprehension of this reality induces him to
abandon his dream of seeking permanent residency in New York City.
Like Changez, the protagonist of Hamid's *The Reluctant Fundamentalist*,
Shehzad also returns to his native city of Karachi, putting an end to the
pursuit of immigrant dreams.

Changez and Shezad's returns stand in contrast to many South Asian
fictions about arrival. Naipaul's *The Mystic Masseur* and *Mimic Men*, Mon-
ica Ali's *Brick Lane*, Jhumpa Lahiri's *The Namesake*—all seem to stage allegories of arrival in the metropolis. *Home Boy* and *The Reluctant Fundamentalist* tell us the other, less frequently narrated story of immigrants: how,
having found the resplendent metropolis uninhabitable, the migrant returns to her own nation-state to begin afresh. Although both novels powerfully question us on the role of the nation-state, it is, ultimately, the city
that emerges as the privileged site of exchange and struggle. The entire
monologue—the entire narrative of *The Reluctant Fundamentalist*—takes
place in a marketplace in Lahore, albeit the story that Changez tells mostly contains reminiscences about his New York City life. Likewise, it will
be difficult to ignore *Home Boy*'s cosmopolitan urban sensibility; *Home
Boy*'s geography and language are unmistakably urban, evocative of the
kind of narrative to which New York City's educated immigrant youth is
often attached. The cosmopolitan global metropolis, thus, remains central
to the thematic organization of these two novels, not only because the city
is the locus of experience and activity but also because the city's abandonment embodies trauma and loss.

Although the relationship between the city space and aesthetic production has been explored in numerous studies, it still remains a productive site for understanding aesthetic imagination of society and the body
politic.[2] It is also possible to tease out, from fictional representation of the
city, the deep structures that underlie and mediate relations among beings, for, to echo David Harvey, "the question of what kind of city we
want is not divorced from what kinds of social ties, relationship to nature, lifestyles, technologies and aesthetic values we desire" (Harvey
2008, 23). Cities, therefore, are both material spaces and relationships,
sites that mediate and are in turn mediated by numerous other sites and
relationships existing in society. Harvey's insistence on the cognitive re-
ception of spaces through the frames of multiple dialectical relationships
is perhaps equally appropriate for cities which are not only human creations emitting cultural signs but also human habitats imbued with personal attachments and memories. It is because of such complex and, of-

ten, contradictory tendencies and characteristics that Harvey proposes to read cities dialectically through the grids of representations, lived experiences, productive relations, and distributor networks. When, for instance, Harvey contends that "[t]he meaning of a place, both individual and collective, is both powerfully present (absolute) and unstable (relational), dependent on the context in which the place and the human agents are situated," (Harvey 2009b, 177) he is not merely suggesting that places (cities) are both relational and absolute but foregrounding the idea that a particular place's representation is determined and mediated by a whole host of concepts and relationalities that are solidly grounded in everyday life and people's consciousness.

In *The Reluctant Fundamentalist* and *Home Boy*, New York City attains profound complexity because the narrators' mental concepts of the city comes to collide with their traumatic encounter with the metropolis. Both novels successfully explore the chasm between the representation of the city—the city of images and imagination whose story attains mythical stature in popular imaginary—and lived experience that seems to be in deep tension with the mythologized representation of it. The New York of Changez and Chuck's imagination is a place edified by popular imagination; it is habitable in a very specific sense: "you could . . . spend ten years in Britain and not feel British, but after spending ten months in New York, you were a New Yorker, an original settler" (Naqvi 2009, 19). It is this New York of imagination that Changez reminisces about in the busy market of Lahore: "I was, in four and a half years, never an American; I was immediately a New Yorker" (Hamid 2007, 33). Yet, as Chuck and Changez's return to Pakistan suggests, such conviction about the city becomes untenable in the aftermath of 9/11; after the 9/11 attacks, New York City, like the rest of America, changes to become narcissistic, acutely nationalist, and inhospitable: "America was gripped by a growing and self-righteous rage in those weeks of September and October," Changez tells his American interlocutor (94). It is in this environment of heightened antipathy that Changez hears strangers calling him "a fucking Arab" and Shezad and his friends are thrown out of a New York City bar. Chuck and Changez eventually discover, through their numerous encounters with the changed reality, that their mental image of the city barely maps onto their lived experience.

In this chapter, I seek to read the phenomenon of return not only as the narrators' apprehension of their precariousness[3] but also as their deliberate attempts to affirm discontent against conditions within whose perimeters precarity is normalized and given the form of law. In what follows, I discuss how *The Reluctant Fundamentalist* and *Home Boy* symptomatically represent the vicissitudes of post-9/11 urban experience, bringing into purview the juridical and political processes through which precarity is distributed. I examine the neoliberal economic structure which mediates the production and distribution of precarity along racial,

gender, religious, and ethnic lines. Distribution of precarity and disciplining of migrant labor, I argue, are woven into the same network of the
capitalist accumulation process. It is for this reason that I propose to
stretch beyond the biopolitical veneer of precariousness to understand
the dialectical relationship between "differential allocation of precarity"
(Butler 2009, 3) and neoliberal accumulation strategies.

If New York City appears, to the two young narrators in their early
twenties, as spaces of freedom and habitability, it is because their class
position does not allow for a clear insight into various forms of oppres-
sions and exclusions the New York City's migrant underclass has been
subjected to. The post-9/11 political and social reality simply redistributes
precarity along ethnic and religious lines to bring within its fold middle-
class and upper middle-class Muslim populations. The abandonment of
New York City thus symbolically represents the abandonment of the
Muslim middle class's utopian vision of the cosmopolitan metropolitan
cities and its acknowledgement of the limits of first world cosmopolitan
utopia. It is in this context that the two narrators' returns strike as a
deliberate act of defiance: by abandoning the city they question, first of
all, the mythical status of the first-world metropolitan city and, secondly,
the neoliberal ordering of daily life that allows no insight into the subject's participation in the process of imperialist exploitation. Yet, as I also
argue in the concluding section, paradoxically both the narrators remain
trapped in the same ritualistic neoliberal-cosmopolitan forms they pas-
sionately seek to abandon. Their cosmopolitan, urban consciousness fails
to find a viable alternative outside the ones presented by the status quo.

## HOME BOY AND THE URBAN EXPERIENCE

*Home Boy* narrates, in a language that is reminiscent of slam poetry, the
experiences of Chuck (Shehzad), Jimbo, and AC whose fast metropolitan
lives come to a halt when FBI agents arrest them on terrorism charges.
The crisis is sparked as much by the changing circumstances of the post-
9/11 New York City reality as by the revelation that they have become
pariahs in the city that embraced them as its own, the same city that has
historically paraded its cosmopolitan social order and liberal cultural mi-
lieu. Two moments specifically stand out as emblematic of the narrator's
bafflement. The opening sentences of *Home Boy* express the narrator's
disappointment and qualm in the following manner: "We have become
Japs, Jews, Niggers. We weren't before" (Naqvi 2009, 1); the inconsolable
gap between becoming "Japs, Jews, Niggers" and living as "boulevar-
diers, raconteurs, renaissance men" is the locus of difference that separates the former from the latter. The "Metrostani" "boulevardier" (1) lifestyle that Chuck and his friends take as a talisman against the persecuto-
ry mechanism of the state apparatus is leveled off by the sweeping cultu-

ral and religious homogenization in the post-9/11 United States. As "self-invented" and "self-made" metrosexuals who have their "fingers on the pulse of the great global dialectic" (1), they hope to be recognized as such—as global citizens with their deep roots in cosmopolitan intellectual make up. The long list of their quotidian activities exemplified by extremely eclectic reading and listening habits in the first passage—Russian and postcolonial literature reading, cocktail drinking, cocaine snorting, pornography watching and pork avoiding "gansta rap" connoisseurs whose daily life is distinguished by their investments in multicultural urbane lifestyle—is indeed a rationale provided by the narrator as a signpost of difference. By their conscious and unconscious choices they want to make a statement against the objectifying mechanisms of the culture they live in. Yet, as the first sentence also suggests, the sweeping generalizations of the cultural and state apparatuses ironically reduce their difference with the attackers and lump them together with all other Muslims who must be disciplined and brought under the control of the neoliberal state. Neither the FBI agents who arrest them nor the brawlers who assault them take note of their cultural and intellectual outsidedness. America's lack of interest in their difference and narrative is compellingly presented in the penultimate chapter of the novel. After reading in a newspaper the obituary for his missing friend Mohammed Shah (Shaman) the narrator caustically remarks: "There was no mention of the ship jumping, gas pumping, porn watching, cigarette running . . . and there was no mention of us" (214). Shezad's reminder that the state-sponsored rhetoric of divisiveness subsumes him and his friends' narratives, is evocative of the polarized schema of popular imagination. It is no coincidence that Shezad and his friends listen to George W. Bush's speech on TV at Mohammed Shah's residence in Connecticut when they break into the house to find out about his long absence.

One needs put Shezad's claim about the city's metamorphosis within the broader context of state sponsored ordering of the social and cultural sphere and, racial, cultural, and religious distribution of precariousness. Judith Butler posits precariousness as a conceptual frame through which political distribution of vulnerability can be apprehended. Such an apprehension, Butler cautiously notes, can lead toward further violence and antipathy, for the cognizance of the other's physical and social vulnerability may induce in the subject the desire to destroy the other. Yet, framing others' precariousness has the potential to lead one to stand in solidarity with the other (Butler 2009, 2). Butler's call for a "new bodily ontology" is thus premised on the ethical obligation to protect the life that is socially and politically marked for death, and the first step towards that end is the apprehension of the other as living. Apprehension of precariousness, then, not only presupposes the apprehension of bare life but also a recognition of life's loss—that what is apprehended as living may be injured or lost in certain given circumstances (13). Since precariousness is the very norm of apprehending a being as living (or not), questions about a being's precariousness cannot lead one to understand under what normative conditions a being attains the status of personhood and is apprehended as living; the more productive way of apprehending life is asking questions about its precarity, whether or not "the social conditions of persistence and flourishing are . . . possible" (Butler 2009, 19–20). Butler's emphasis on normative conditioning of precariousness leaves space for understanding Shezad's musings on the absence of his narrative as apprehension of his own precarity. In a rhetorical universe divided between "us" and "them" that only recognizes United States' precariousness and injurability against an assaulting Muslim population seeking to inflict pain and injury to its western other, Shezad and Mohammed Shah must remain unrecognized, and thus, not living. Mohammed Shah, who finally attains recognition of a lost life, achieves so by relinquishing his distinction with his American friends. The obituary claims he was "like us" who "worked hard, played hard" (Naqvi 2009, 213). It is this loss of identity that allows for the apprehension of his life as a lost life (grieveable life)—one who lived and played hard and died in the World Trade Center like those who are incorporated in the normative category "us."

Butler's concept thus provides a theoretical tool for understanding Shezad's recognition of himself as an ungrieveable life: the absence of his narrative in the post-9/11 New York City is suggestive of his absence from the normative category of the living. Nevertheless, Shezad's precarity is more a consequence of the changing reality than a permanent condition; New York City's underclass remains carefully hidden from Shezad, only occasionally making vicarious appearances through characters like Gator, whose cursory remark summons into existence the city's invisible population: "There are still crack whores in Bushwick who will give you a blow job for *five smackers*" (Naqvi 2009, 37). One needs to, therefore, read Shezad's claim about the city's transformation as a subjective and individualistic apprehension of precarity. It is not that the violent attacks of 9/11 transformed a benevolent New York City into a hostile city; what changes, however, is that at the wake of the attacks the city's distribution of precariousness extends to include the previously excluded South Asian upper echelon made up of educated middle-class and relatively well-off Muslims living in the city.

In the thick of the city's changing demography, there have been several communities and races who have been collectively subjected to oppression and violence. Both Irish and Italian communities faced acute discriminations at turn of the twentieth century. African Americans have always found themselves at the receiving end of the city's most oppressive disciplinary mechanisms. *Home Boy*'s first sentence indeed captures the phenomenon of racial and ethnic distribution of precariousness, while the novel remains largely silent about some of the most violent repressions carried out against African Americans and the immigrant population throughout the 1990s, suggesting its narrator's incognizance of New York City's neoliberal makeover and the history of systemic expulsion of immigrants and poor inhabitants from Manhattan and other boroughs. As such, the iconographic representation of the city as a hospitable space becomes emblematic of the narrator's entrapment in neoliberal ideology which often operates through spatial essentialism: New York appears to attain the status of the sanctuary for the ethnic migrant, obliterating the city's history of violence against and expulsion of racial and ethnic minorities. In *A Brief History of Neoliberalism* (2005), David Harvey recounts how the neoliberal reconstruction of the city was achieved through brute force and mass incarceration. He writes:

> Working-class and ethnic-immigrant New York was thrust back into the shadows, to be ravaged by racism and crack cocaine epidemic of epic proportions in the 1980s that left many young people either dead, incarcerated, or homeless, only to be bludgeoned again by the AIDS epidemic that carried over into the 1990s. Redistribution through criminal violence became one of the few serious options for the poor, and the authorities responded by criminalizing whole communities of impoverished and marginalized populations (48).

The figure of the "crack whore" carries the burden of this history. In Shezad's narrative that locates in September 11 a sudden rupture or disruption of a rather smooth cohabitation with the welcoming city, the figure of the "crack whore" remains disembodied, deprived of a narrative, and her life remains unaccounted for.

## EXPLORING THE "PROCRUSTEAN MACHINERY"

Although precariousness appears as the dominant reason behind Shezad's departure from New York, lack of employment opportunities also plays a significant role in cornering him. One of Shezad's biggest disappointments comes from his dismissal from the Wall Street investment bank. After joining the bank he works "fourteen, fifteen-hour days, including most weekends." Despite his role in "multimillion-dollar mergers, acquisitions and debt and equity issues" (Naqvi 2009, 29) his labor remains ghastly and invisible. Nevertheless, trained in the humanities, Shehzad seems well aware of his status as a wage laborer. The sly irony of him being a part of a competitive firm that he considers as "a procrustean machine," is both poignant and symptomatic. The narrator's caricature of Wall Street as a homogenizing, value-producing, "intricate" tool allows for an understanding of the ruthlessness of neoliberal capitalism itself. Although he participates in it, he only vaguely feels a part of it. His is, indeed, a "slave's" vision of the master's system (29).

The heartlessness of the "procrustean machinery" is not fully revealed to him until he is fired from his job. After a year of overwork and dedication, he is laid off unceremoniously when the market hits a crisis. In Shehzad's parlance, his axing was "quick and efficient" (30). The objective ruthlessness, which was distant and abstract, he soon discovers, is now a subjective reality, throwing him out of work, showing no remorse at his removal. The objective ruthlessness is further solidified by the VP's interjection: "you know it's not personal, right?" (30). Their mutual recognition of the process as an objective and necessary measure for the effective functioning of the system erases the systemic brutality that Chuck brings into visibility. The view that is accorded here not only exposes the systemic ruthlessness of capitalism but also lays bare the ideologies that teach people to accept the systemic violence as a quotidian reality. What remains veiled under the VP's rhetorical humanity is Shezad's labour. Thus, in response to the VP's professional sympathy, when Shehzad silently notes "I suppose I did; it had to do with the bottom line, the Invisible Hand" (30). Although the full import of Shezad's thought is irrecoverable, his travestying of Adam Smith's phrase does indeed conjure up the vision of the free market procrastination whose class logic remains invisible, well hidden behind its rhetorical empathy.

Following his departure from the investment bank, which was then followed up by a short period of inactivity and surviving on savings, Chuck devotes himself to becoming a cab driver. During his training, he meets other trainees mostly from Asia and Africa. The constellation of incumbent drivers stage world systems theory in its miniscule: third-world labor meets first-world capital in a cab-driving world dominated by large fleet-owning companies. It is here that the ethnic and racial division of labor becomes flagrantly present. In Chuck's description:

> There were nineteen of us, none of whom was Pakistani (although I learned that South Asians comprised a third of the New York cabbie population, distributed almost equally among Pakistanis, Bangladeshis and Indians). A bony Indian from Patna, a wide-eyed Bangladeshi, a square-faced Egyptian . . . the rest hailed from the Dark Continent (37).

This multinational crew of the cab-driving force form the bottom quarter of New York City's population, occupying jobs that are both low paying and labor intensive.[4]

If Chuck's critique of neoliberalism remains tacit and masked, available only to attentive eyes, Changez's engagement with the same remains predominantly explicit and forthright. Although the apparent simplicity of *The Reluctant Fundamentalist* can lead one to hastily dismiss it as a novel lacking aesthetic innovation and profound theme, one needs to cautiously look into the narrative to understand how in its apparent simplicity the narration mirrors the narrator's uncomplicated and somewhat idealistic understanding of the world. Although himself a product of corporate America—"a very satisfied instrument of the American capitalist machine," (Hamid 2007, 70) as Rajini Srikanth calls him—Changez is wary that corporate efficiency mongering comes at the expense of workers who must be thrown out of work so as to make the firm profitable. On a number of occasions the narrator of Hamid's novel expresses his concern about the ruthless trimming of workforces. A few days after America's assault on Afghanistan begins, Changez is sent to New Jersey to evaluate a cable company that is struggling to make profit. When he expresses his alarm at the prospect of firing workers who were elderly, possibly with children of his age, he is reprimanded. "Focus on the fundamentals," Wainwright, his colleague and friend, advises him. Focusing on fundamentals, Changez reveals, has been the "guiding principle" of Underwood Samson, mandating "single minded attention to financial detail" (98). What is brought under scrutiny here is the other, less discussed, fundamentalism—market fundamentalism—whose global production marks off the pioneering moments of neoliberalism. Srikanth is both perceptive and categorical in identifying this other form of fundamentalism: "The fundamentalism to which the title refers and which Changez eventually disavows is not religious fundamentalism but economic fundamentalism, à la free market enterprise" (70).

## *THE RELUCTANT FUNDAMENTALIST* AND THE NEOLIBERAL AMERICAN EMPIRE

In her elegant discussion on Mohsin Hamid's *The Reluctant Fundamentalist*, Rajini Srikanth contends that Changez's monologue—the entire novel is written in monologic form in which the narrator tells his story to an unnamed American who is most probably a CIA agent—is a counterdiscourse, the objective of which is to bring an end to the "dominance of the U.S. voice on the global stage" about matters related to terrorism. In Hamid's well-crafted novel, a U.S. agent is reduced to the role of the silent listener, forced to listen to the story of one of those who his state has branded as an enemy. Srikanth, then, goes farther and claims that Changez's is a voluntary transformation stirred by genuine "empathy" for the victims of U.S. imperialism. She notes:

> In Changez, we have an individual who moves voluntarily from being enthralled with the economic culture of the United States to adopting a position of deliberate dissatisfaction. Only when he assumes these perspectives does he become aware of the seduction that have overcome him and prevented him from recognizing the depredations of the lives of others. His empathy is now channeled toward those countries that are caught in the web of the imperialist and capitalist ambitions of the United States (Srikanth 2012, 72).

Srikanth's characterization of Changez's discontent as "deliberate dissatisfaction" valorizes the idea that his is a conscious disengagement with America. Yet, the trajectory from voluntary servitude to intentional distancing is not a linear development. Erica, whose love Changez seeks and who symbolically represents America, both disrupts and hastens Changez's antipathy towards American empire. Srikanth traces the beginning of Changez's transformation way back in his first business trip to Manila. Sitting in a limousine with his colleagues in Manila's thick traffic, Changez feels the heat of the "undisguised hostility" of a jeepney driver's gaze, wondering what might have induced such resentment. Although Changez is unable to understand the rationale behind the driver's "obvious, intimate" dislike (Hamid 2007, 67), he gradually mounts up enough understanding of capitalist accumulation process and American imperialism to critically look into his own contribution to both. Although Changez reveals that he has "always resented the manner in which America conducted itself in the world" (156), his awareness about his own complicity does not fully emerge until he is confronted by the Chilean book publisher Juan-Bautista. Already troubled by America's indiscriminant bombing of Afghanistan and arm twisting of Pakistan, Changez starts neglecting work when he is sent to Chile for evaluating a book publishing company. Juan-Bautista, the chief of the company whose understanding of books runs much deeper than those evaluating his business, is both irate and troubled because of the intrusion of the valuation firm. Convinced that Changez is different from the rest of his firm, the old book publisher takes him out for lunch. "Does it trouble you," he asks Changez, "to make your living by disrupting the lives of others?" (151). Unconvinced by his young companion's answer that Underwood Samson is only an evaluation firm, Juan-Bautista asks if Changez has heard of the janissaries. In response to Changez's baffled "no," the veteran publisher says:

> They [janissaries] were Christian boys . . . captured by the Ottomans and trained to be soldiers in a Muslim army, at that time the greatest army of the world. They were ferocious and utterly loyal: they had fought to erase their own civilizations, so they had nothing else to turn to (151).

Changez later recounts how Juan-Bautista's historical chronicle "plunges" him into "a deep bout of introspection," inducing in him the awareness that he was "a servant of the American empire" (152). The essential irony of situation lies not so much in Changez's realization that he is working against the interest of his own nation but, rather, that his cosmopolitan life in Princeton and New York City accords him no insight into his own reality. It is the outside—the spaces that have already experienced U.S. imperialism—that must warm him up to the idea that he has been the empire's mercenary. Nevertheless, Changez is no soldier, shooting at random with his gun; his job at Underwood Samson requires him to evaluate malfunctioning businesses. Still, as Juan-Bautista correctly points out to Changez, the effect of his action has real consequences. The ingenuity of this episode resides in its suggestiveness: it slyly points toward the nexus between American imperialism and finance. In a deeply fascinating paragraph where Changez tells his American audience that his country's "constant interference in the affairs of others was insufferable," he also asserts that "finance is [sic] the primary means by which the American empire exercised its power" (156). Changez's gesture toward the financial empire draws attention to the United States's role in imposing neoliberal economic policies around the globe, especially through imperialist means and strategies, enforcing austerity measures and disciplining labor through layoffs.

In a paper titled "Creative Destruction and Narrative Renovation: Neoliberalism and the Aesthetic Dimension in the Fiction of Arvind Adiga and Mohsin Hamid," Weihsin Gui contends that Hamid's third novel, *How to Get Filthy Rich in Rising Asia*, offers "an immanent critique of neoliberalism and globalization" (Gui 2014, 174). While Gui's description of Hamid's third novel is both insightful and accurate because it operates at multiple levels critiquing and parodying not only the trope of the "rising Asia" but also the ubiquitous figure of the rural entrepreneur making his fortune in the city, his perception can be easily extended to *The Reluctant Fundamentalist* as well, which mocks and critiques neoliberal ideology and strategies. Indeed, compared to *How to Get Filthy Rich* where the critique of neoliberalism is tropologized and masked, in *The Reluctant Fundamentalist* such critiques appear forthrightly, in the mode of saeva indignatio.

An immanent critique of neoliberalism seems to echo in the novel's imagination of the city space as well. Matthew Hart and Jim Hansen contend that *The Reluctant Fundamentalist* exposes the "limits of cosmopolitan space" (Hart and Hansen 2008, 507). Hamid's novel does indeed impressionistically capture the whispering South Asians in the Pak-Punjab Deli discussing police brutality, indiscriminant arrests, and Muslim men's disappearance into detention centers (Hamid 2007, 94); New York City's ultranationalistic makeover; and the city's implosion into a xenophobic world. Yet, as Megha Anwer brilliantly notices, one of the real achievements of the novel is its contrapuntal navigation through the streets of Lahore and New York—a move that not only puts these two cities into relation but also juxtaposes the lives that are lived in them. Anwer, in the vein of Hart and Hansen, reads *The Reluctant Fundamentalist*'s representation of New York City as a counterdiscursive strategy that exposes the limits of uber-busy, orchestrated life of New York City dominated by neoliberal, cosmopolitan values. In her brilliant analysis Lahore's Anarkali Bazaar emerges as a space of languid, alternative life—a countersite in which the acutely competitive, individualistic metropolitan life appears bizarrely out of place.[5]

## CONCLUSION

If *Home Boy* and *The Reluctant Fundamentalist* are both novels of return, convention requires that we look deeply into this unusual phenomenon and ask: what is the symbolic and political import of this gesture? I have already pointed out in the first section of this chapter that these returns are deeply symptomatic for a number of reasons; the manner in which they stage a desire to return to the national space or shed light on the precariousness of certain peoples or bring into purview the processes of surplus labor production and so on—all are important in today's context. However, amid all the critical discussions on these novels, especially in case of the discussions about these novels' ability to make available experiences of precariousness and imperialism, what remains almost unexplored is these novels' entrapment in postmodern aesthetic forms and fetishisms. Neither Hamid's *The Reluctant Fundamentalist* nor Naqvi's *Home Boy* aesthetically challenges the postmodern novelistic conventions that are in currency today. Much more limiting than that, none of these novels seem able to trace, within daily life and social practices, the existence of an alternative mode of being with emancipatory possibilities. Changez and Shezad's baffling responses to post-9/11 situation, parade their helpless surrender to a de rigueur response to violence and oppression. Changez's response to the changing reality is recourse to religion and nationalism, whereas Shezad's is his resignation and pacifism. It is in their response to the intolerable present reality that one is able to track the residues of the neoliberal ideology of an eternal capitalist present. The complete absence of any discussion of an alternative outside religious nationalism and cosmopolitan globalism thus gestures toward one of the grand fetishisms of neoliberal capitalism, giving currency to the idea that there is no alternative, that our capitalist present is also our future.

In his discussion of Marx's concept of time in *Capital Volume One*, Fredric Jameson contends that *Capital* makes visible two definitive characters of capitalism's response to its own history and temporality. One of the typical responses of capitalism towards its own violent history is to erase all traces of violence, thus concealing its past. The other typical response is to block the future by forcing upon consciousness the idea of an eternal present—a process which, after Marx, Jameson calls "eternal virginity of the capitalist present" (Jameson 2011, 104). In a world devoid of a strong left opposition, neoliberalism's assault on capitalism's past and its future seems both rigorous and unanswerable. The operative neoliberal ideology deftly conceals capitalism's essential reality. It is because of this that despite gaining an insight into his own place in the great

"procrustean machine" Shezad accepts his fate supinely; convinced surrender to fate is the only logical response to economic violence. It is here
that one of the grand fetishisms of the neoliberal era reveals itself with
utmost clarity. In order to further clarify our understanding of the somewhat slippery concept of fetishism, we can perhaps recourse to Karl
Marx. For Marx, fetishism is neither entirely irrational (religious) venera-
tion nor excessive desire; it is, first and foremost, concealment. Commodities circulating in the market for exchange are fetishistic because they
conceal the relations of production and the labor that have gone into
producing them (Marx 1990, 165-66). Commodity's appearance, its bodily
form and sensual character, makes it difficult to see through it and discover its social character and the forms of abstractions that have turned it
into an exchange value or object of exchange in the first place. I use the
term *fetishism* to imply that a structure of concealment is in place—one
that covers over the possibilities existing in nascent form.

There is no after story in Naqvi's *Home Boy*—no follow up of what
happens after Chuck (Shehzad) leaves the United States. A crestfallen,
dejected Chuck departs from New York City leaving AC in the detention
center. Before his departure he meets Amna, Jimbo's college-going sister
who likes Chuck and possibly wants to marry him. The last few days of
Chuck's New York life are very economically described, with little clue as
to what his thoughts are. Since Chuck's is a deeply personal story, it ends
in a personal note, with his first arrival to New York City. The chapter
before that, which describes Chuck's departure from the city, holds clues
to what the novel is trying to press through. Right before leaving his
apartment Chuck notices a newspaper with an obituary for his missing
friend Shaman (Mohammed Shah) who died while attending a conference in the World Trade Center. The obituary describes Shaman as an
unusual Muslim, one who was more like "us": "Everybody thinks all
Muslims are fundamentalists . . . Mohammed wasn't like that. He was
like us. . . . He worked hard, played hard" (Naqvi 2009, 270). Changez
correctly notices that there is no mention of the likes of him and his
friends in the Manichean post-9/11 narrative; the likes of him have suddenly become unrepresentable:

> It was the oddest obituary. Perhaps all obituaries are fundamentally
> odd. There was no mention of the ship jumping, gas pumping, porn
> watching, cigarette running—*de mortuis nil nisi bonum*—and there was
> no mention of us. The story was simple, black and white: the man was
> a Muslim, not a terrorist (270).

What Chuck wants, it appears, is recognition of the existence of his
kind—a narrative that accords a space to cosmopolitan South Asian Muslims whose stories get lost in the charged, patriotic environment of the
post-9/11 America. Unlike Changez, who is willing to force his story on
his American counterpart, Chuck accepts his condition passively and

moves quietly out of New York after saying his prayers for his dead friend.

Changez, the narrator of Hamid's *The Reluctant Fundamentalist*, on the other hand, goes back to Lahore to become a lecturer of finance. Now convinced that U.S. imperialism is deeply detrimental to Pakistan's independence, he professes "disengagement" from the United States for "greater independence in Pakistan's domestic and international affairs" (Hamid 2007, 179). Although his students mostly include "bright, idealistic scholars" who he addresses as "comrades" implying his left-leaning politics, the alternative that he suggests involves demonstrations against the bully of the United States. The book's final paragraph, however, renders Changez's entire narrative unreliable and it is possible to read his narrative as a fictitious story constructed to allure the American agent into the dragnet. Since the last passage also blurs the distinction between Changez being a left-leaning university professor and him being an assassin, no determinate answer as to what constitutes Changez's resistance is possible. What is indeed possible is an account of whether or not Changez's return looks into an alternative outside capitalism. Having identified finance capital as the fundamental impetus behind American imperialism, the narrator of Hamid's novel has no other alternative but to recede back to the nationalist quasi-religious struggle.[6] It is not that Changez does not know the shape of the beast; it is, rather, that having understood it all, he has to channel his resistance through the nation/religion space because the existing reality conceals the other alternatives. The returns embody hopes for an alternative mode of existence but the novels, having failed to find traces of that possibility in existing reality, remain trapped in what exists and what is dominant.

## REFERENCES

Alter, Robert. *Imagined Cities: Urban Experience and the Language of the Novel*. New Haven, CI: Yale University Press, 2005.

Agamben, Georgio. *Homo Sacer: Sovereign Power and Bare Life*. Trans. Daniel Heller-Roazen. Stanford, California: Stanford UP, 1998.

Anker, Elizabeth S. "Allegories of Falling and the 9/11 Novel." *American Literary History* 23.3 (2011). 463-482. *Project Muse*. Accessed October 20, 2014.

Anwer, Megha. "Resisting the Event: Aesthetics of the Non-Event in the Contemporary South Asian Novel." *Ariel* 45:4 (2014). 1–30. *Project Muse*. Accessed July 10, 2015. http://muse.jhu.edu.libproxy.albany.edu/article/576070/pdf.

Butler, Judith. *Frames of War: When is Life Grievable?* London: Verso, 2009.

Chow, Rey. *The Protestant Ethnic and the Spirit of Capitalism*. New York: Columbia University Press, 2002.

Darda, Joseph. "Precarious World: Rethinking Global Fiction in Mohsin Hamid's *The Reluctant Fundamentalist*." *Mosaic* 47.3 (2014). 107–22. *Project Muse*. Accessed September 15, 2014. http://muse.jhu.edu.libproxy.albany.edu/article/555665/pdf.

Gui, Weihsin. "Creative Destruction and Narrative Renovation: Neoliberalism and the Aesthetic Dimension in the Fiction of Arvind Adiga and Mohsin Hamid." *The Global South* 7:2 (2014). 173–90. *Project Muse*. Accessed July 19, 2015.

Hamid, Mohsin. *The Reluctant Fundamentalist.* Orlando, FL: Harcourt, 2007.

———. *How to Get Filthy Rich in Rising Asia: A Novel.* New York: Penguin, 2013.

Harvey, David. *Social Justice and the City.* 1973. Columbus: The University of Georgia Press, 2009a.

———. *A Brief History of Neoliberalism.* Oxford: Oxford University Press, 2005.

———. "Right to the City." *New Left Review* 53 (Sep. 2008): 23–40.

———. *Cosmopolitanism and the Geographies of Freedom.* New York: Columbia University Press, 2009b.

Hart, Matthew and Jim Hansen. "Introduction: Contemporary Literature and the State." *Contemporary Literature* 49.4 (2008). 491–513. *Project Muse.* Accessed October 24, 2014.

Jameson, Fredric. *Representing Capital: A Reading of Volume One.* London: Verso, 2011.

Marx, Karl. *Capital Volume 1: A Critique of Political Economy.* Trans. Ben Fowkes. London: Penguin, 1990.

Naqvi, H. M. *Home Boy.* New York: Shaye Areheart Books, 2009.

Srikanth, Rajini. *Constructing the Enemy: Empathy/Antipathy in U.S. Literature and Law.* Philadelphia, PA: Temple University Press, 2012.

Williams, Raymond. *The Country and the City.* New York: Oxford UP, 1975.

## NOTES

1. Georgio Agamben's *Homo Sacer: Sovereign Power and Bare Life* explores the contours of modern biopolitics by looking into the relationship between sovereign power and the *homo sacer*, the bare life "who may be killed but not sacrificed" (8). In his essay "Precarious World: Rethinking Global Fiction in Mohsin Hamid's *The Reluctant Fundamentalist*," Joseph Darda contends that Hamid's novel "offers a counter statement to" understanding the post-9/11 era through the frame of Agamben's account of "bare life" (116). Although I find Darda's observation productive, I also understand that both novels expose the peculiar social/political conditions of the post-9/11 era in which many Muslims found themselves both inside and outside the American society.

2. The relationship between literature and the city has been explored with much depth in many fine works of literary criticism. One of the finest and much cited examples of such efforts is Raymond Williams's *The Country and the City* where he writes:

> "Country" and "city" are very powerful words, and this not surprising when we remember how much they seem to stand for in the experience of human communities. In English, "country" is both a nation and a part of a "land"; "the country" can be the whole society or its rural area. In the long history of human settlements, this connection between the land from which directly or indirectly we all get our living and the achievements of human society has been deeply known. And one of these achievements has been the city: the capital, the large town, a distinctive form of civilisation. (1)

Although city space remains a powerful form as well as object of representation in literature, the relationship between the novel and the city is a more consequential one. Novels' special relationship to bourgeois form of life attests to its affinity to the city and the privilege that novels accord to the city space. As Robert Alter writes in his book *Imagined Cities: Urban Experience and the Language of the Novel* (2005): "it makes perfect sense that novels should repeatedly focus on the city, the principal theater of bourgeois life and also the form of collective existence that undergoes the most spectacular, dynamic growth throughout the modern period" (ix).

3. Judith Butler, who uses the idea of precariousness to explain how injury, loss, and vulnerability are biologically mediated and can be apprehended by the frame of grieveability, also makes a careful distinction between *precariousness* and *precarity.*

According to Butler, *precariousness* is the general biological frame of vulnerability common to beings whereas *precarity* is socially and politically conditioned state of injurability, often mediated by state and political power. In this chapter, I try to maintain Butler's distinction between precariousness and precarity while simultaneously suggesting that under capitalism the distribution of precarity often runs along class lines and precarity—politically distributed condition of vulnerability—is the very norm that conditions the being of the underclass. See Judith Butler's *Frames of War* and Joseph Darda's essay "Precarious World: Rethinking Global Fiction in Mohsin Hamid's *The Reluctant Fundamentalist*" for further discussion on this distinction.

4. In order to further fortify the connection between labor and ethnicity we can perhaps invoke Rey Chow who, in *The Protestant Ethnic and the Spirit of Capitalism*, contends that there is a relationship between ethnicity and certain types of labor. The ethnic's participation in low paying jobs frees up labor at the top, making it possible for the educated classes to monopolize the highly-paid positions. Chow writes:[I]n actual practice in the contemporary world, whereby ethnicity often designates foreignness (which is, in turn, understood as social inferiority), the linkage between certain types of labor and ethnicity are ineluctable. In the context of the United States and other wealthy nations, one does not have to undertake scientific surveys to see that fundamental necessity of society—the lowly, basic services that help to free up well-educated people for more high paid jobs—are most frequently provided by "ethnics" (33).

Chow's insightful reflection on the relationship between ethnic labor and the upper-class urban elites prove particularly useful when we use her idea to understand the relationship between the Wall Street investment bankers who think they make capitalism tick and the labor of the New York City cab drivers whose labor remains invisible, even unacknowledged. Urbanity's internal unevenness is supported by a structure that exploits the ethnic labor through the grids of innumerable informal sectors. Chuck's two jobs put on display two different but connected poles of ethnic labor, offering a glimpse into the internal world of globalized capital functioning through local spatial formations, specifically through metropolitan urban locations.

5. In Megha Anwer's words: "If New York, the ultimate metropolis of the globalised world, is the site of the uber-event, the ideal location for the performance of a theatrical event overloaded with surcharged symbolism, then the relaxed and non-definitional mode of Third World urban spatiality evoked in *The Reluctant Fundamentalist* is one in which an alternative cognitive and emotive relationship to sensory stimuli may be developed. . ." (23–24).

6. Matthew Hart and Jim Hansen foreground the idea that Changez's is a secular nationalism. They write: "If it is neither religious nor ethnopoetic, how then to describe Changez's nationalism? The short answer is that it is political—political because it is predicated on an agonistic relation between two states, the U.S. and Pakistan, and on the judgement that the American response to 9/11 has only worsened Pakistani underdevelopment and insecurity" (510).

However, the novel leaves us with no certainty about Changez's political pedigree and the symbolic import of Hamid's novel's beard points towards a quasi-religious form of nationalism.

# FIVE

# Between Performativity and Representation

*Post-9/11 Muslim Masculinity*
*in Ayad Akhtar's* Disgraced.

Lopamudra Basu

Ayad Akhtar's play *Disgraced*, which won the Pulitzer Prize for drama in 2013, brings to a critical dialogue many contemporary trends in the discourse of racialization of South Asian Muslims in post-9/11 U.S. society. The play is a thoughtful meditation about the fraught political climate that South Asian Muslims encounter in post-9/11 America, where the traditional mythology of immigrant success is harshly undermined by counternarratives of surveillance and deportation of South Asian Muslims. The play posits two different theories of racial formation; the first one treats race as a representational frame for codifying cultural difference in heterogeneous societies, and the second presents race as a performative act by the racialized subject, often in response to the representational frame and an attempt to subvert it. I examine the representation of race in the play, specifically through a close reading of the principal visual artifact of the play, the painting of Amir, the South Asian Muslim protagonist in the play, by his Caucasian wife Emily, in the style of Velasquez's painting of his slave and apprentice, Juan de Pareja. This representation of Amir by Emily parallels mainstream American society's gaze, which is fixed on the South Asian male subject in a post-9/11 America. However, juxtaposed against this representation is Amir's defiant performance of his religious and racial identity as that which is secular, modern, and devoid of any ethnic cultural inflections. The trajectory of the play traces the dialectical tension between Amir's performative agency and the visual representational frame in which he is cast. The second master narrative that frames Akhtar's play is Shakespeare's *The Tragedy of Othello: The Moor of Venice* and its tale of Othello, a Moor and general of the Venetian army, facing alienation in Renaissance Venice, as his marriage to the Venetian noblewoman Desdemona unravels into jealousy, domestic abuse, wife-murder and suicide, following the psychological manipulations of the villainous Iago. Othello demonstrates a precedent of racial performance in which the protagonist underplays his racial and religious background in order to gain acceptance into mainstream society; this performance however does not ensure successful assimilation into Venice. His black skin and his origins as a Moor, and therefore a Muslim, cast him as unassimilable other, in spite of his conversion and ascendancy in the military echelons of Venice. Othello remains the racial and religious "other of Venice," in spite of his concerted efforts to diminish the cultural markers of his difference. As the play *Disgraced* progresses, Amir's own agency seems to be diminished and the overarching framing of himself as a racialized other, in the tradition of Othello the Moor, hastens a trajectory of jealousy, rage, and the tragic breakdown of an interracial romantic relationship, almost predictably playing out a tragic script written by Shakespeare. In post-9/11 America, the play seems to offer a diminished horizon for agency, presenting instead, a deterministic trope for South Asian Muslims as unable to reconcile their cultural and religious identities with American civic and political life. I examine the tragic experience of the play in the light of theorizations of the tragic form and its contribution to social change and revolution. Thus, instead of reading the loss of performative agency and the tragic ending of the play as a re-invocation of the destiny of Shakespeare's *Othello*, I read *Disgraced* as a play that dramatizes social contradictions particular to post-9/11 America and through emotional responses introduced in the audience's sensibility, advocates powerfully for changes to the existing status quo in racial and religious relations.

## FROM VELASQUEZ TO HOLLYWOOD: EXOTICIZATION OF ARABS AND MUSLIMS IN THE U.S.

In post-9/11 America, the media has been saturated by negative images of Arab and Muslim Americans. The vilification of Arabs in Hollywood predates 9/11 by at least a hundred years. Jack Shaheen in *Reel Bad Arabs: How Hollywood Vilifies a People* has meticulously documented a variety of stereotypes about Arabs and Muslims. If we go back further, Edward Said's *Orientalism* in 1979 documents the systematic discourse on the orient that developed concurrently with colonization, in an attempt to subjugate and control it by gaining access to its languages and traditions. The discourse of orientalism led to the progressive dehumanization of Arab and other non-Western cultures and a proliferation of negative images and stereotypes about Arabs and Muslims.

Jack Shaheen in *Reel Bad Arabs* offers a study of over nine hundred films in which Arabs are stereotypically presented as villains. The book, published in 2001, already documents the saturation of negative images about Arabs and Muslims even before the full and damaging effects of 9/11 were felt by Arabs. Along with the inability to distinguish between varied religious affiliations of Arabs in Hollywood representations, Islam and Arabs are automatically equated and Shaheen points out "Islam particularly, comes in for unjust treatment. Today's image-makers regularly link Islamic faith with male supremacy, holy war, and acts of terror, depicting Arab Muslims as hostile alien intruders, and as lecherous, oily sheikhs intent on using nuclear weapons" (Shaheen 2001, 9). Shaheen argues that the overabundance of these negative images and the paucity of any positive images of Arabs is a "grave injustice" (11) as a steady and unrelenting stream of such images "tarnish(es) our image of a people and their culture" (15).

In exposing the common stereotypes of Arabs in Hollywood representations, Shaheen also points to the recurring motif of "Arabs trying to rape, kill or abduct fair complexioned Western heroines" (16). In the trajectory of Hollywood films, Arab men are depicted as lustful and conniving to seduce Western women. There are no scenes of intimacy between Arab men and Western women, as that would be offensive to the American audiences, fueling deep seated anxieties about miscegenation. If an Arab woman is shown to harbor romantic feelings for a white man, the logic of the films is for her to face a tragic death. Arab women are not depicted as objects of lust for Western men in the general trajectory of Hollywood films, but rather depicted as veiled and covered or oppressed by Islamic patriarchy. In Shaheen's analysis of Hollywood films, what emerges is a very narrow and predetermined script for interracial romance between Arabs and Westerners. The sanctioned script seems to be of a male Arab character lusting for a Western, white female. Celia R. Daileader in her study *Racism Misogyny and the Othello Myth: Inter-Racial Couples from Shakespeare to Spike Lee* has coined the term *Othellophilia* to refer to the way Anglo-American culture "is fixated on the coupling of a black male and a white female with the attendant cultural anxieties played out in the story's tragic result"(Daileader 2005, 7). Daileader argues that "masculinist racial hegemony used myths about black male sexual rapacity and the danger of racial pollution at least partly to exorcize its own collective psychological demons: the slave master's sexual guilt . . . (8). She argues that the overemphasis and obsession with Othello's tragic flaw of jealousy minimizes his crime of wife-murder and the preoccupation with the sexuality of a black man deflects attention from the large-scale sexual exploitation of black women within the institution of slavery. Daileader's work interprets a variety of cultural texts through the lens of Othellophilia, ranging from the O. J. Simpson murder trial to films like Spike Lee's *Jungle Fever*. Daileader's study establishes the significance of the Othello story as a master narrative for the reading of interracial romance between a white woman and black man and the ways in which the supremacy of such a master narrative perpetuates stereotypes about the hypersexualized African male and obscures the facts of sexual exploitation of black women by white men.

*Disgraced* consciously plays with the Othello story but the cultural context for applying the Othello myth is somewhat different in this play. This is because the principal character is a Pakistani Muslim man, Amir and his wife Emily is a Caucasian female. The historical context of prejudice against Muslims and Arabs is very different from the history of slavery structuring African American and Caucasian relationships, the lens Daileader uses to interpret the Othello myth in American society. However, as Ania Loomba has pointed out "there is a real difficulty in deciding whether Othello's tragedy has to do with his being a 'circumcised dog' or having a 'sooty bosom'"(Loomba 2002, 92). Loomba argues that it is impossible to decide whether Othello is more African/black or Turkish/Muslim and suggests instead that the play "demonstrates how medieval and newer ideas about blacks and Muslims intersected in early modern England" (92). Loomba maps how Othello becomes a victim of various circulating ideologies in the play and internalizes widespread beliefs about his racial inferiority. Loomba is also highly attentive to the gender politics of the play and points out that "Othello is a victim of racial beliefs precisely because he becomes an agent of misogynist ones" (91). Loomba opines that in early modern England, there was "admiration as well as revulsion" (97) over the tight political and social control exercised by Turks over their women, as presented in reports circulating in England. According to Loomba "English stories of patriarchal violence in Muslim cultures served to both define the incivility of these cultures and to offer models for domestic control of unruly women."(100). Venetian women, also being located in a southern region, were thought to be more prone to lasciviousness than English women. The three female characters in *Othello*—Desdemona, Emilia, and Bianca—are constantly associated with sexual promiscuity and two of them are killed by their husbands. Thus the widespread misogyny in the play and beliefs such as those about women's heightened lustfulness and promiscuity are very much inflected by race and geography. All women are inconstant but those of Venice more likely to cheat than those of northern climes. Finally, Moors and Turks are more subject to jealousy and more likely to seek violent revenge and punish female infidelity. Loomba argues that Iago is able to manipulate Othello successfully and transform him into a wife murderer, because of Othello's deep-seated sense of alienation in Venetian society, due to his race and religion. This alienation exists simultaneously with a sense of racial inferiority with respect to the fair and beautiful Desdemona. He believes that his age, dark coloring, and lack of ease with courtly culture are impediments to his marriage. Desdemona cannot love him for long, especially since women, and particularly women of Venice—are prone to licentiousness and infidelity. The lethal combination of racial and gender stereotypes that Othello cannot resist propels the action of this tragedy.

There is a continuing similarity in the hypersexualization of the Arab/Muslim male, from the Shakespeare's *Othello* to the post-9/11 representation of Muslim identity in Akhtar's play, expressed in the anxiety over interracial relationships and the quest to preserve or protect the white woman from the lusts of the Muslim/Arab man. For the present-day Muslim man, another layer of complexity is added by the association of Islam with misogyny and oppressive treatment of women. There is a re-invocation of this mythology in the context of post-9/11 vilification of Islamic society as violent and misogynist. The stereotypical representation of the Arab/Muslim man as lustful and misogynist deflects attention from the obsession of the Western male with the covered Muslim woman in the harem. There is a long history of Western male gaze penetrating the harem from Delacroix's famous painting of "Women of Algiers in their Apartment" to Malek Aloulla's *Colonial Harem*, which is a an analysis of a visual archive of French colonists' photographs of Algerian women to titillate French male viewers in the late nineteenth and early twentieth centuries. Aloulla argues in this book that the photographs are an inaccurate representation of Algerian women and a projection of colonial fantasy.

The painting of Amir by Emily is a motif that structures the organization of the play, *Disgraced*. Ayad Akhtar devotes a lot of linguistic space in the play to the description of this work of art. It is useful to discuss Emily's painting of Amir in *Disgraced* using John Berger's theoretical framework, which notes how men and women have been represented differently in the canon of European oil painting and the social and historical differences, which undergird these artistic choices. In analyzing the rich archive of European Renaissance paintings, Berger in *Ways of Seeing*, highlights the fundamental relationship of men as viewers of women's bodies. But more significantly, he argues, that women undergo a psychic splitting in being both the object gazed at as well as the surveyor of the object: "Men look at women. Women watch themselves being looked at. . . . The surveyor of woman in herself is male: the surveyed female. Thus she turns herself into an object—and most particularly into an object of vision: a sight" (Berger 1977, 47).

Berger goes on to do close readings of many European oil paintings, particularly nude paintings. He argues that the principal protagonist of these nude paintings is the "spectator in front of the picture, who is presumed to be a man (54). The bodies of women painted are on display in the painting for him. Even when the nude paintings depict a male lover in the painting, the female figure's attention is not directed to her lover in the painting but "towards the one who considers himself to be her true lover—the spectator owner"(56). Berger opines that in the artistic tradition of Renaissance paintings, "The spectator owners were usually the men and persons treated as objects usually women" (63). This "unequal structure," according to Berger, is still pervasive in our culture leading to women constantly surveying themselves as objects of male desire.

In contrast to representations of women in European oil paintings, Berger's study of male paintings sheds light on interesting differences. In discussing the two male figures in Holbein's 1533 painting of *The Ambassadors,* Berger notes how "There is in their gaze and their stance a curious lack of expectation of any recognition" (94). This is in stark contrast to the paintings of many women who seem to be directing their gaze towards the spectator/owner outside of the body of the painting. In contrast to the women, the gaze of Holbein's ambassadors "is both aloof and wary. They expect no reciprocity" (97).

If we examine the historical painting of Velasquez's *Juan de Pareja,* which serves as the model for Emily's painting of Amir, we notice some interesting departures from Berger's theory of the visual tradition of representing different genders. There is no doubt even from internet reproductions that the historical painting of Juan de Pareja is a remarkable achievement of Renaissance oil painting, which before the arrival of photographs produces the closest illusion of lifelikeness. Juan de Pareja, in this painting, is very obviously a man of Moorish descent, fashionably attired in a wool coat with a collar of finely embroidered lace. Most interestingly, his gaze unlike Holbein's ambassadors is not aloof and self-contained. Like many female models and nudes, Juan de Pareja also seems to be directing his gaze at a spectator/owner outside the frame of the painting. This fact becomes even more charged when we take into account that Juan de Pareja was in fact the slave apprentice of Velasquez. Juan's gaze parallels the gaze of many female models who were psychically split between the roles of objects of desire and surveyors of their own beauty. Juan's gaze seems to be seeking the approval of an owner who could be his master Velasquez or the owner of Velasquez's painting. The style of the painting and its expression presents Juan de Pareja as an object of beauty and achievement, desired by his master and other spectators. In a sense, the style of the painting feminizes Juan as a desired object and reestablishes the power of the artist over him.

It is somewhat of a contradiction that Emily's own artistic career, although ostensibly influenced by the traditions of Islam, changes course from initial landscape paintings to the very Western and non-Islamic tradition of portraiture. She is particularly drawn to Renaissance masters like Velasquez and early in the play, she asks her husband Amir if she could paint him in the style of Velasquez's painting of his slave/apprentice Juan de Pareja, who happened to be a Moor. Emily is drawn to this particular painting because she believes it "has more nuance and complexity than his renditions of kings and queens (Akhtar 2013, 7)." For Amir, the most salient point about the painting is that it is the painting of Velasquez's slave and that of a nonwhite man. His first reaction is to suggest that Emily call her "black Spanish boyfriend" to serve as a model for the portrait. This is in response to Emily's request that he serve as a model for the painting. Amir's first reaction, ironically is to remember a former suitor of Emily and thus create a palpable association of the painting to sexual jealousy. Later, he agrees to Emily's request and admires her progress in the sketching but insists that there is something disquieting about this painting and Emily's emulation of it.

This scene signals the problematic position of the Amir/Emily relationship even as it depicts a scene of domestic and sexual intimacy. The problem lies not in the fact that they are members of different racial and religious groups but in the unequal power associated with these groups in post-9/11 America and its impact on their personal lives. In the act of painting Amir, Emily is casting him as the traditional female portrait subject, an object of desire, someone who is gazed at and serves as an object of pleasure and visual gratification for an audience. As the artist, Emily is occupying the active role usually held by male portrait artists and exercising her power over her subject.

The play painstakingly points out that Emily paints Amir in the very style of Velasquez. We can therefore infer that Amir is presented as a handsome South Asian Muslim man. The play specifically alludes to similarities between Emily's painting and Velasquez's. Isaac who is a curator at the Whitney and who is later revealed to be Emily's lover points out that Amir's "six hundred dollar Charvet shirt" parallels Juan de Pareja's ornate lace collar. Later, Isaac also tells Emily that Amir's gaze in the painting is directed at the viewer "that viewer is you. You painted it. He is looking at you." (Akhtar 2013, 70). In the stage directions to the first scene, when Amir is modeling for the painting, it is mentioned that he is wearing a jacket and a crisp collared shirt but only boxer shorts underneath. From these descriptions, it can be inferred that there is objectification and exoticization of Amir's physical beauty taking place. The play even alludes to this self-reflexively, when Isaac, the art critic warns Emily that she could potentially be accused of Orientalism, especially since she even has "a brown husband" (31). Emily's painting does not alter the status quo of power relations vis à vis the minority ethnic group of South Asian Muslims and mainstream white America. Emily may be a female artist reversing the long tradition of the male gaze by directing her gaze at her husband, but in spite of her gender identity Emily belongs to the racial group that has a concentration of power with regard to representa-

Velasquez, Juan de Pareja 1650
*Source:*Metropolitan Museum, New York

**Figure 5.1.**

tion. Amir, following his predecessor Juan de Pareja, is seeking approval of white American society and his gaze is directed at Emily and other representatives of that group who hold power and whom he is always trying to appease. In general, this reversal of traditional gender roles of male artist and female model to a female artist and male model, would have carried with it the possibility of reversing previous gender inequality and injustice. However, within the overall context of post-9/11 American society, this is not a liberating move. This is because in the public sphere, the South Asian and particularly, the Muslim man's body has already been turned into an object of society's gaze. The male body at the overt level is an object of fear and surveillance as a suspected terrorist by mainstream media. In the days following 9/11, the brown body and the turban became synonymous with terrorism and led to many acts of racial profiling and violence.

This sexualization of a Muslim man's body in Emily's painting of Amir stands in conjunction with images of tortured prisoners from Abu Ghraib, which have circulated extensively and which show the bodies of Muslim men in states of sexual shame and debasement as a result of torture. Just like the Abu Ghraib images are the result of unequal power relations between the photographed and the photographer, as theorized by Judith Butler in her essay "Torture and the Ethics of Photography," the representation of Amir as a sexual object also speaks of an unequal power arrangement as it reduces him to an image of a beautiful brown body and not a flesh-and-blood human being. Like the perpetrators of torture in Abu Ghraib were often women prison guards, Emily's gender does not put her in a subservient role with respect to Amir. I do not intend to conflate the two acts, the historical one of physical degradation of the Muslim male body in the Abu Ghraib torture photographs and the fictional artistic celebration of a similar brown body in *Disgraced*. I am arguing, however, that in both instances, the Muslim male body is being acted upon by white society and being denied its own autonomy.

REWRITING OTHELLO IN POST-9/11 U.S.

The common themes linking *Othello* and *Disgraced* are not only the inter-racial relationships in which both protagonists find themselves involved, but the power of racial stereotypes that both protagonists face and which result in their fundamental alienation from the societies they seek to belong to. Edward Berry in an article titled "Othello's Alienation," pointed out the significance of Othello's African identity in Venice "not because of what he is innately or culturally but because of how he is perceived by others and by himself. In this sense, *Othello* like Faulkner's *Light in August* is a tragedy of perception" (Berry 1990, 318). Berry points to the significance of Iago in shaping Othello's own self-perception when he opines "Although Iago's notorious artistry is usually linked to his capacity to shape a plot it extends as well to characterization, for the Othello he in many ways creates, comes to see himself as his own stereotype" (319). The barrage of insults heaped on Othello from the early scenes in the play, when his blackness is linked to monstrosity, evil, black magic, witchcraft, and a host of other evils, ultimately acts as a catalyst in his own transformation and submission to jealousy, rage, and murder.

Gautam Malkani, the author of the novel *Londonstani*, commented in an essay "About Londonstani," on the notion of identity as a performance. He was discussing the role of South Asian ethnic identity in the creation of his characters, who are a group of hypermasculinized South Asian second-generation British youth, coming of age in early years of the twenty-first century. Malkani thinks that the hypermasculinity of his characters expressed through their ethnic identities could be expressed by other forms of behavior, for example, football hooliganism. Malkani is deconstructing the idea of identity as fixed and stable but suggesting instead that identity is a performative act and at any given time, we make choices to perform or emphasize certain aspects of our identity over others.

> That means your ethnic identity can often be something you *choose* to express or not—like other aspects of your identity, you can switch it on or off depending on the context. After all, we all select our identities. Nobody tells us who we are anymore—we just have to "be" us by selecting our "self" from different sources. Nowadays, that means people often have to work really hard and/or imagine really hard instead of just having their identity and life simply handed to them because of their surname or gender or class or caste or whatever. (Malkani 2006)

Malkani's views on identity as performance echo Judith Butler's theorization of gender as performance in her magnum opus *Gender Trouble: Feminism and the Subversion of Identity*. In it, Butler deconstructs the idea of a universal category of patriarchy and opposing it a "seamless category of women." Her work aims to expose the limits of identity politics, arguing instead that the stable binaries of male and female genders are an effect produced by the institutional practices of compulsory heterosexuality. Butler insists that the presence and proliferation of nonnormative gender identities expose the limits of regulatory heterosexuality. Butler uses the term *disordering practices* (Butler 1990, 17), to refer to these acts which destabilize the fixed binaries of gender. In some ways, Malkani's insistence of ethnic identity as performance follows from the same philosophical premise as Butler which rejects essentialized ideas of universal patriarchy and gender. Ethnicity too is multilayered and constructed through performative acts.

If identity, following thinkers like Judith Butler, is a choice of demonstrating some cultural practices as opposed to others, Amir's cultural choice is that of effacement of his ethnic and religious identity. This is not unique to Amir. In literary representations of interracial romance, particularly those following the master narrative of *Othello*, there are many examples of the black or brown man striving very hard to assimilate into the dominant white culture and consciously effacing ethnic and religious markers of his identity. Othello in Shakespeare's play is a convert to Christianity, possibly from Islam given his Moorish ancestry, and explicitly rejects signs of his African identity. However, repressed elements of Othello's African identity resurface as the play progresses. A significant example is the handkerchief which constituted Othello's first gift to Desdemona, inherited by Othello from his mother and carrying with it the superstition that its presence would guarantee the love of the couple who exchanged it as a gift and its loss would lead to the breakdown of the relationship and the loss of love. When Desdemona loses the handkerchief because Emilia has been instructed to retrieve it for Iago, it is planted in Cassio's quarters and becomes the "ocular proof" of her infidelity. Even though, Othello has severed ties with his cultural heritage, the only tenuous material objects that connect him to his family become the source of his private agony and propel him into a trajectory of rage, physical violence, and finally ruthless murder, ironically confirming the very stereotypes of brutality, barbarism, and evil that he has been linked with by native Venetians like Iago and Brabantio, Desdemona's father, who cannot accept Othello's full humanity.

A more contemporary example of interracial romance and more pertinently a marriage between a South Asian Muslim man and a white British woman is offered in Salman Rushdie's *The Satanic Verses*. The protagonist Saladin Chamcha is an immigrant from India in Thatcherite Britain, who has chosen the path of assimilation and effacement of cultural markers of religious and ethnic alterity. He is married to an English woman, Pamela Lovelace, and this marriage is an attempt at acceptance and seamless assimilation into British society. However after the magic realist crash of a flight, Saladin finds himself to be a survivor but one who has been transformed into a goat. This is followed by the discovery that his wife has been unfaithful to him. Rushdie's novel proceeds with the technique of a literalization of the Renaissance motif of cuckoldry; Saladin literally grows a pair of horns and becomes transformed to a beast. In spite of Saladin Chamcha's life long attempts to refashion himself as a brown sahib or mimic Englishman, his wife's unfaithfulness is a source of psychological alienation, and the surveillance that he is subjected to by the institutions of a racist immigration system, strips him of his humanity and transforms him into a beast. Like Othello, Saladin comes to see himself as the stereotype created by the discourse on racialized others, shaping ethnic identity in Britain.

In both the tragedy of *Othello* and *The Satanic Verses*, female sexuality and chastity are invested with a sense of tribal or masculine honor. Women are symbolic carriers of male honor and their infidelity represents a loss of stature and honor for their husbands. Both the Renaissance play and the postmodern late twentieth-century novel represent persistent tropes of female sexuality being integrally connected to patriarchal notions of male honor. Ayad Akhtar's *Disgraced* is an even more direct retelling of the Othello narrative as the consequences of female transgression are once again visited directly on the woman in the form of direct violence inflicted upon her.

How does the Othello theme of a man of color in love with a white woman play itself out in the 2013 play *Disgraced* by Ayad Akhtar? What are the particular kinds of prejudice that the Muslim male protagonist, Amir, is subjected to? To what extent is Amir's fate a repetition of Othello's and what does this repetition say about race relations with regard to South Asian Americans in the first decades of the twenty-first century?

The most striking resemblance that Amir bears to his literary predecessor Othello is in his deep sense of alienation in post-9/11 American
society. Like Othello, Amir stands out in post-9/11 New York due to his
racial and religious difference from American society which is largely
white and Christian. In *Disgraced*, Amir is subjected to a plethora of insults and stereotypes. From the very beginning of the play, the audience
is introduced to the social universe of post-9/11 America, where South
Asians have already been profiled as potential terrorists. In the opening
scene, Amir's cousin comes to persuade him to represent an Imam who
has been charged and held under the provisions of the PATRIOT Act for
purportedly collecting money for terrorist organizations. Abe insists that
the Imam did not do anything that churches in the country are not already doing and appeals to Amir to join the defense team. Amir is very
reluctant to get involved. The Imam's arrest and trial is a direct reminder
of the climate of surveillance and criminalization that has been the reality
for South Asian Muslims ever since the September 11 attacks of 2001.

Not only is the Imam being held on suspicion, Abe, Amir's cousin
who wants Amir to represent the Imam, has already been deeply affected
by the situation of surveillance and presumed guilt. Abe is not the birth
name of Amir's cousin. He has changed his name to Abe Jensen and goes
by that name even with his family to avoid confusion. He insists that
everyday life and interaction have become easier since the name change.
Amir is rather critical of this name change which relinquishes his religious and ethnic origins. In the final scene of the play, we are informed
that Abe and his friend have been reported to the FBI by a barista at a
coffee shop for claiming that Al Qaeda was a creation of the CIA. The two
young men are subjected to interrogation by the FBI. Amir, too, admits to
the excessive surveillance that South Asian Muslims are subjected to at
the airports; Jory, Amir's colleague jokes that the choice at the airport
seems to be between "being ogled or being felt up" (Akhtar 2013, 49).

From early on in the play, Amir, rather than the non-Muslim characters like Emily or Isaac, is the principal voice articulating prevalent
stereotypes about Muslims. For example, in an early conversation with
Abe and Emily, Amir narrates the story of his first crush on a Jewish girl
named Rivkah and his mother's inhuman reaction of spitting at him for
harboring such feelings. Amir was only a young child, in fifth grade at
the time. However the hatred fomented by his mother already affects him
and the next day when Rivkah admits that she is indeed Jewish, Amir
mimics his mother's action and spits on the girl he had harbored tender
feelings for. In narrating this past incident, Amir is perpetuating a stereotype of Muslim bigotry and intolerance, which is already the pervasive
feeling about Muslims, following 9/11. This stereotype of religious fanati-
cism is also emphasized in Amir's comments about his meeting with the
Imam at the prison, after the insistent demands by Emily and Abe that he
help the innocent Imam, who has been held under the PATRIOT Act. The

Imam spends most of the time haranguing Amir to begin to pray again. Amir interprets this as a sign of excessive religious zeal.

Amir declares himself to be an apostate, a person who has renounced his faith. His reasons for rejecting his faith as declared in his own speeches are that he considers Islam to be "a backward way of thinking. And being" (Akhtar 2013, 52). He ridicules Islam's strictures against painting human figures, its aversion to dogs, and other outmoded rules. On a more serious note, he points to passages in the Koran that sanction wife-beating and other forms of misogyny. He also decries Islam's collapsing of institutions of religion and state. These assertions are ironically challenged by Amir's wife Emily, who argues that many of these widely believed Koranic injunctions are highly contested and not universally agreed upon by Muslims. Emily points out that scholars have debated whether the root verb can be translated as "leave" or "beat" in the passage on wife-beating, which would result in very different interpretations. Thus, Amir, the Muslim protagonist in the play, is the most vocal critic of Islam and in many ways articulates dominant media images of zealotry, bigotry, intolerance, and misogyny that are already steeped in mainstream media depictions of Islam.

In the play Amir functions in the play as someone who vocalizes prevalent stereotypes about Islam and also someone who is simultaneously a victim of those very prejudices. Amir, though a successful lawyer in a Jewish firm, is not immune to the climate of prejudice and paranoia about Muslims. Emily, Amir's wife, points out that Amir, too, has changed his name. Amir's change of his last name from Abdulla to Kapoor is the first step in his performance of his religious identity as that of a lapsed, apostate, nonreligious Muslim. This name change is not a simple attempt at assimilation, something that immigrants from varied countries have attempted in the process of simplification of their names for easy usage in America. Amir does not relinquish his first name which is South Asian but not necessarily Muslim. Instead he changes his Muslim last name Abdulla to Kapoor. This name change seems to be part of his general attempt to efface his Muslim identity and reinvent himself. However, Amir does not just stop at changing his name. He also reports his parents' country of birth as India and changes his social security card. His rationale is that the area in the Punjab that his father originated from belonged to undivided India before Partition created the new nations of India and Pakistan. The fact that Amir feels compelled to do this to fit into a Jewish firm proclaims very clearly the inhospitable and intolerant climate of surveillance and paranoia that is rampant in post-9/11 U.S. However, his very act of effacement is seen by the partners of the law firm that he works for to be an example of misrepresenting himself. Steven and Mort, the partners in the firm, use this misrepresentation as evidence to justify their decision not to promote Amir to partner, in spite of the years of seniority he has over Jory, Isaac's African American wife, who is another junior lawyer in the same firm.

Amir's involvement with the case of the Imam who is being held as a terror suspect is also used to fix him as an unreliable Muslim and a terrorist sympathizer. This is very ironic because Amir had no sympathy towards the Imam and was determined not to get involved. It was mainly due to Emily's insistence that the Imam needed a Muslim lawyer that he attends the hearing. At the hearing, Amir makes some comments to the press, stating that the Justice Department did not have a valid case against the Imam and that the Imam had not been given due process under the law. In the media reports of this event, it is subtly implied that Amir Kapoor was the defending attorney. His firm is also named. Amir is outraged that in spite of his protestations that he was not the defending attorney the press report would imply that he was. This publicly reported event along with the discovery that Amir is indeed Muslim becomes the basis for the senior Jewish partners' decision not to promote Amir to the rank of partner. Amir views this as a grave injustice since he has seniority and contributions to the firm beyond those of Jory. This denial of promotion signifies for Amir his failure to get total acceptance in mainstream America, in spite of the deliberate efforts to attenuate all markers of ethnic and religious difference and trying so hard to fit in. He has broken all dietary taboos of Islam and is seen in the play to be drinking wine and eating pork. He has married a white American woman who is an artist, which goes completely against the tradition of endogamous marriage within his community into which he has been acculturated. Yet like Othello, Amir remains fundamentally alienated, when his senior partners interpret his very attempts to efface his identity as duplicity and use those facts to exclude and punish him.

Although Amir's performance of his race is basically one of the lapsed apostate, there are moments in the climatic scenes, when under the influence of alcohol, he reveals that Islam remains a part of his repressed cultural identity that surfaces in odd and sporadic moments. In a conversation with Isaac, he makes this revealing remark; "And so, even if you are one of those lapsed Muslims, sipping your after dinner scotch alongside your beautiful white American wife—and watching the news and seeing folks in the Middle East, dying for values you were taught were purer—and stricter—and truer . . . you can't help but feel just a little bit of pride." (Akhtar 2013, 62). Amir admits that this sense of pride he feels in hearing the jingoism of the Iranian leader Ahmadinejad is wrong but this residual feeling comes from years of being indoctrinated into Islam. This admission provokes horror and disgust in Isaac who immediately brands Amir as a "closet Jihadist" (65). Amir insists that it is Islam's fault that it provokes such reactions among even its lapsed members. Isaac insists that no religion has a monopoly of fundamentalism and blames Amir, the individual, for his feelings of ethnic pride and sympathy for Islamic radicalism.

The climax of the play and Amir's full realization of his alienation happens when in the course of the dinner party, Emily's affair with Isaac comes to light. Jory, Isaac's wife finds Isaac and Emily in an intimate situation and demands to know what is going on. In the high emotional drama that ensues, Amir spits on Isaac's face and Jory gives Amir the crushing news that Mort, Amir's mentor, is retiring and she will be inheriting his case load. Amir is already extremely disappointed with the news that he has not been made partner. This is yet another blow to his personal pride. When Jory and Isaac leave and he asks Emily for the truth, she confesses that she and Isaac have had a tryst on one of their trips to London. She does not tell him that Isaac was propositioning her moments before he left and predicting that she would cheat on her husband again because of Amir's own character flaws of being an alcoholic and a repressed sympathizer of Islamic fundamentalism. The confession from Emily unleashes a wave of fury and Amir beats her violently expressing the "discharge of a lifetime of discreetly building resentment" (75). At the end of the scene Abe enters the room and sees the bloodied face of Emily. This is a moment of shocking violence, something that the audience has not been prepared for in the interactions of Emily and Amir. However, this scene is prefigured in the literary lineage of *Disgraced* as a modern retelling of *Othello*. In *Othello*, Othello strikes Desdemona on stage, building the momentum for the greater violence of the murder and suicide scenes. In *Disgraced*, the scene of Amir's battery of Emily serves as the climax of the tragedy. The scene of Amir's physical violence toward Emily has also been prefigured ironically in the references to wife-beating and misogyny pertaining to Islam in many parts of the play. In spite of his conscious rejection and criticism of Islam, Amir's self-perception of himself as a Muslim male ultimately does get influenced by the stereotype of jealous rage. In spite of vehemently criticizing misogynist passages in the *Koran*, he becomes the wife-beater that he had opposed in the scriptures.

Emily and Amir appear one last time in *Scene Four*, which serves as an opportunity for apology but reinforces the finality of their parting. In the final moments of the play Amir gazes at Emily's painting of him "Study After Velasquez's Moor," that she has left for him as a farewell gift. As the lights dim on stage, Amir stares once again at the painting and reflects on what it has meant to be seen, represented, and framed as a Muslim man. In a 2013 interview with Madani Younnis, Ayad Akhtar reflected on the play *Disgraced*:

> The play begins with a western consciousness representing a Muslim subject. The play ends with the Muslim subject observing the fruits of that representation. . . . Muslims are still beholden on an ontological

level to the ways in which the West is seeing us. And what the play
might be suggesting is that is that we are still stuck there. The play
ends with Amir finally confronting that image. I do believe that the
Muslim world has got to fully account for the image the West has of it
and move on. To the extent that we continue to define ourselves by
saying "We are not what you say about us," we are still allowing someone else to have the dominant voice in the discourse (Akhtar 2013, 96).

These comments by Akhtar point to what is at the heart of Amir's tragedy. His entire attempt at defining his ethnic and religious identity has
been from the perspective of negating or opposing dominant discursive
trends that provide a pretty narrow and limited range of possibility for
Islamic identity. Although, it is not always best practice to accept the
author's interpretation of his work, in this case I tend to agree with Akhtar's view. It also seems to echo Ania Loomba's postcolonial interpretation of *Othello* that I discussed above. At the end of her essay, Loomba
contrasts Shakespeare's *The Winter's Tale* and *Othello* and writes that unlike Othello, for Leontes, the protagonist of *The Winter's Tale*, jealousy is
not attributed to his racial or religious affiliation. On the other hand for
Othello "whether we regard him as noble or debased, challenging or
confirming stereotypes, Othello can only be read against a collective category called 'Moors'" (Loomba 2002, 111). Loomba and Akhtar are both
lamenting the way in which Muslim/Moorish identity remains overdetermined by dominant stereotypes over centuries.

It is true that the Othello story has been rewritten by other postcolonial authors. For example, the Sudanese author Tayeb Salih's novel *Season
of Migration to the North* can be interpreted as a retelling of the Othello
myth. Saree S. Makdisi in "The Empire Renarrated" has argued that the
novel is an attempt in writing back empire. While the main protagonist
Mustafa can be read as an Othello-like figure in his seduction and subsequent murder of a white woman, this novel is also a retelling of Joseph
Conrad's *Heart of Darkness* and therefore has different rhetorical aims.
Written in mid-twentieth century, *Season* is concerned with questions of
Arab modernity; progress versus the contrary force of tradition. In its
plot of Mustafa's wife killing her new husband, the gender roles are
reversed from the Othello paradigm and the strict separation of tradition/
modernity, orient/occident, and north/south are dissolved. *Disgraced* does
not offer us the alternate spaces of the metropolitan center and the colony, with their different temporalities. The action takes place in the heart
of multicultural America, where in the aftermath of 9/11, Muslim identity
has become controversial and volatile again. In the wake of 9/11, circulating discourse on Islam has drawn on centuries of stereotypes about Islamic violence and misogyny. *Disgraced* is thus much more connected to
*Othello* than to a novel like *Season of Migration to the North*, which was
written at a very different historical moment. Written in the immediate
context of decolonization, Salih's novel is more concerned with debunk-

ing myths of the modern West and the feudal/primitive Arab world. Although both works are intimately concerned with race and sexuality, the historical context framing *Disgraced* is very different. Unlike a burgeoning sense of secular Arab modernity, in *Disgraced* we encounter a far more polarized sense of the Arab/Muslim world reverting to Islamic orthodoxy and the United States, increasingly identifying itself as a Christian nation in its opposition. This polarization is much more reminiscent of Renaissance Venice which seemed to be divided along the lines of white Venetian/Christian society and the enemy Moor/Turk. Although written four centuries later, discourses of gender and race/religion in *Disgraced* seem to echo those circulating in *Othello*. Thus even though, Emily is an independent woman and a professional artist who does have an extramarital romance and unlike Desdemona can avoid murder in the play, she cannot avoid the violence of her jealous husband's physical abuse.

In another section of his interview, Ayad Akhtar discusses *Disgraced* as a contemporary tragedy:

> I want the audience to be so humanly identified with the protagonist who acts out in an understandable but tragically horrifying way, that no matter what text you put on top of it, you cannot dissociate yourself from him. . . . What Amir does is an act of political violence, that is to say, a colored male subject who is acting out on a white female love object through violence, in a way rife with political valences. In that respect, the play is drawing on a tradition of representation: Shakespeare and V. S. Naipaul and William Faulkner (Akhtar 2013, 92).

In his own commentary on the play, Akhtar is reading Amir's tragedy as emblematic of a larger political predicament. This is not just a play about one couple's relationship failing and ending in domestic violence and tragedy. It is a microcosmic representation of the social and political ethos of post-9/11 America. Amir's act of violence can be interpreted as his lashing out at the injustices that he has been subjected to for which the political structures do not provide any favorable and just resolution. The only recourse is impotent rage and violence. Even though this violence is destructive of the fabric of intimate domestic relations in the play, it does have a purpose within the tragic aesthetic world view of the play.

Raymond Williams, in his work *Modern Tragedy*, argued for the necessity of revolution in a world which was still rife, in the period of the Cold War when Williams was writing, with profound economic inequalities as well as growing militarization and armament. Williams argued that peace or order could not be achieved "while the full humanity of any class of men is in practice denied" (Williams 2001, 77). Reflecting on the artistic credo of his times, Williams had argued "the only consciousness that seems adequate in our world is then an exposure to the actual disorder"(83). If this theory of tragic violence is extended to a play like *Dis-*

*graced*, it can be argued that although Muslims like Amir Kapoor have been denied their full humanity in post-9/11 America. This is a condition that is still persisting, with recurring negative feelings and prejudice against Muslim Americans. Within the context of this ongoing injustice, the artistic choice available to a playwright like Ayad Akhtar is to expose the schisms and deep-rooted disorder in American society. The ultimate hope of the playwright, as expressed in interviews is for Muslims to be able to refashion their identities without the constant scrutiny and surveillance of rest of America, but that is an utopian dream at this stage. So at present the shocking violence on stage reiterates the deep-rooted injustice structuring ethnic relations in the U.S. and the world, with Muslims facing daily insults and prejudice within the United States, and the violence of imperialist wars, detention, and torture in countries like Iraq and Afghanistan. The play does not provide a vision or path out of the cycle of retributive violence but in exposing the underlying disorder of American society, it is promoting a critical consciousness in its audience.

## REFERENCES

Akhtar, Ayad. *Disgraced*. New York: Back Bay Books, 2013.

Alloula, Malek. *The Colonial Harem*. Minneapolis: University of Minnesota Press, 1986.

Berger, John. *Ways of Seeing*. New York: Penguin, 1977.

Berry, Edward. "Othello's Alienation." *Studies in English Literature* 90. 3 (1990); 315–334. Accessed December 1, 2014.

Butler, Judith. *Gender Trouble: Feminism and the Subversion of Identity*. New York: Routledge, 1990.

———. "Torture and the Ethics of Photography." *Environment and Planning D: Society and Space* 25.6 (2007) 951–66. Accessed January 5, 2016. http://isites.harvard.edu/fs/docs/icb.topic1498626.files/16.%20Butler%20Torture%20and%20the%20Ethics%20of%20Photography.pdf.

Daileader, Celia R. *Racism, Misogyny and the Othello Myth: Inter-Racial Couples from Shakespeare to Spike Lee*. Cambridge: Cambridge University Press, 2005. Print.

Holbein, Hans the Younger. *The Ambassadors*. 1533. National Gallery, London.

Loomba, Ania. "Othello and the Racial Question." *Shakespeare Race and Colonialism*. Oxford: Oxford University Press, 2002. 91–111.

Makdisi, Saree S. "The Empire Renarrated: *Season of Migration to the North* and the Reinvention of the Present." *Colonial Discourse and Postcolonial Theory: A Reader*. Eds. Patrick Williams and Laura Chrisman. New York: Columbia University Press, 1994. 535–50.

Malkani, Gautam. *Londonstani*. New York: Penguin, 2006.

———. "About Londonstani." http://gautam-malkani.squarespace.com/new-gallery/v7e9vv47lyhk3ljfnb1qfdwfg8f2s7. Accessed December, 13, 2014.

Rushdie, Salman. *The Satanic Verses*. London: Viking, 1988.

Said, Edward. *Orientalism*. New York: Vintage, 1979.

Salih, Tayeb. *Season of Migration to the North*. Trans. Denys Johnson-Davies. London: Heinemann, 1970.

Shakespeare, William. *Othello*. New York; Norton, 2003.

Shaheen, Jack, G. *Reel Bad Arabs: How Hollywood Vilifies a People*. New York: Olive Branch Press, 2001.

Velasquez, Diego Rodriguez de Silva. *Juan De Pareja*. 1650. Oil on canvas. Metropolitan Museum of Art, New York.

Williams, Raymond. *Modern Tragedy*. 1966. Peterborough, ON: Broadview, 2001.
Younis, Madani. "An Interview with Ayad Akhtar." n.d. In *Disgraced*, 89-96.

# SIX

# "Sikhs aren't terrorists, those Arabs are"

*Collective Forgetting and Resistive Remembering in Sharat Raju's* American Made

Sarah Wahab

Anant Singh, the protagonist of Sharat Raju's film titled *American Made* (2003), is depicted as a civilized man and American citizen: he is well dressed, well spoken, he drives an American-made vehicle, and he is taking a vacation with his family to a popular American tourist site (the Grand Canyon)—but, he is wearing a turban. The American citizens who drive past Anant and his family—as they are stranded on the side of the highway—are informed by a post-9/11 construct that mistakes Sikh men for Muslims and therefore as "terrorists." Anant's son, Ranjit, vocalizes the accusatory gaze of the American motorists when he tells his father that "no one's gonna' stop for [him] . . . [because he looks] like a terrorist." Ranjit suggests that Anant take his turban off, mentioning quietly that *they* (American citizens) are scared of it, or more aptly, of its misperceived associations with Islam and by extension, terrorism. With Anant's response that "Sikhs aren't terrorists, those Arabs are," he not only separates himself from Arab or Muslim terrorist bodies, but separates the turban from the Muslim hat, implying that Sikhs are not monstrous but that "those Arabs are." Anant's disavowal of "those Arabs" is an attempt to belong as an American citizen but it is also an enactment of a ritual of post-9/11 American citizenship that both establishes and maintains the disconnection of some racialized bodies from other racialized bodies.

103

This separation works to preserve the institution of citizenship while providing an embodiment of evil, figured here as "those Arabs," against which "civilized" bodies may compare themselves in order to preserve their nonterrorist statuses. Anant's comparison of a religious affiliation (Sikh) with an ethnicity (Arab) homogenizes "those Arabs" as "terrorists" *and* as "Muslims," implying that to be an Arab is to be a Muslim and to be a Muslim is to be a "terrorist." Anant's disavowal of "those Arabs" is therefore a disavowal of Muslims and their perceived affiliations with terrorism.

Anant's perception of his Sikh identity as well as his perception of "those Arabs" or Muslims is informed by shared histories of violence. In thinking of the 1947 partition of the Indian subcontinent, in which Muslims and Sikhs (as well as Hindus) were pitted against one another in their respective pursuits of a homeland, Anant's disavowal of "those Arabs" read alongside the act of de-turbaning are both invocations of histories of violence that come to be written into the skin of Sikh and Muslim men. "Sikhs aren't terrorists, those Arabs are" can therefore be read as a testimony that inadvertently expresses multigenerational histories of violence experienced by Sikhs and Muslims under British colonial rule. This chapter examines the ways in which racialized bodies come to be pitted against one another in their quest to belong as American citizens. Using Anant's denouncement of "those Arabs" or Muslims as terrorists, as well as his removal of the turban as points of analysis, I argue that the denouncement of other racialized bodies as well as the removal of all signifiers of previous religious, ethnic, and/or national affiliations are rituals of post-9/11 American citizenship. I suggest that the performance of these rituals allows for the cultivation of a culture of forgetting in which the state and its citizens can forget the violent histories in which they were directly or indirectly implicated. This, in turn, ensures that racialized subjects—in their performance of this ritual of forgetting— maintain divisions between each other and that they do not reach out to bear witness to each other's trauma. In this way, racialized subjects come to be separated from their historical contexts. The act of reciprocal re-membering is therefore a politically defiant act that subverts romanti-cized national histories. Racialized subjects, in their formations of bonds of solidarity, come to reflect the violence of the institution of citizenship *back* to the nation.

Although Anant denounces "those Arabs" in his attempt to belong as an American post-9/11, he reaches out to touch Peter (the black man who offers him help at the film's conclusion). Doing so is a reciprocal act of witnessing whereby both parties come into contact with differing narratives of migration that have come to be written onto the skin of both Anant and Peter (one involving Partition and one involving slavery and the continued violence enacted onto black bodies in America). This bond of solidarity resists the evacuation of historical context when Peter acknowledges that if his car were to break down on the side of the same road, he would also have difficulty getting help, implying that his skin—like Anant's turban—mark him as potentially violent and not worthy of aid.

## MODEL MINORITY STATUS REVOKED:
## TO BELONG, YOU MUST FORGET

Although the Singh family has "made it" as Americans, this identity is challenged post 9/11. The vehicle that the Singh family owns, the clothing that they wear, as well as their blasé discussions of financial matters are signifiers of upward class mobility and as such, come to mark Anant and his family as subjects deemed by the state to be "model minorities."[1] The turban works in opposition to the "model minority" identity, however, and marks Anant—and by extension, his family—as harbouring the *potential* for terrorist activity. The turban's presence produces the affect of fear in the passing motorists but it is not only the fear of the potential for terrorism that keeps them from stopping; it is the fear of "that which cannot be civilized." The fear of the turban is grounded in the fear of *racialized* violence thought to be inherent in the minds and bodies of "Arab" and/or "Muslim" subjects as well as the ways this violence is thought to be capable of infiltrating "civilized" spaces. Immigrant bodies must always work for their citizen status and as such, they must always be *exceptional* (they must excel at everything they do and perform "citizen" better than those born to the nation). Immigrants are also expected to prove that they have the right to feel safe in their new homeland. This means that they must continually demonstrate that they are *not* violent. They must also serve as examples of the potential for humanity among their own religious, ethnic, and/or national affiliations. The struggle for citizenship is thus a struggle for recognition from the state. In her critical analysis of citizenship titled *Exalted Subjects*, Sunera Thobani explains that to be recognized as a citizen by the state is to be marked as worthy of equal treatment under the law (Thobani 2007, 93) and to be recognized as being capable of *human* behavior. The immigrant subject must therefore *earn* citizenship by way of assimilation.

The act of assimilating into the nation-state involves the removal of signifiers that may point to histories perceived as violent by the nation homeland. That is to say that in the acquisition of citizen status, the immigrant must prove that he or she is capable of controlling the violence thought to be inherent in his or her body. The immigrant body is hereby effectively stripped of historical indicators of violence. The "model minority" is therefore not only the immigrant who performs upward class mobility and educational excellence, he or she is also the immigrant who allows the state to forget or ignore histories of violence in which it was or is implicated. Anant aligns himself with the Americans that pass him and his family by and not with "those Arabs" or "Muslims" in an attempt to forget or ignore the historical tie that Sikhs have with Muslims. His turban, however, exists in opposition to this position as it carries with it the very history of violence that he is attempting to forget.

Anant attempts to ground his identity as an assimilated Sikh man and not as an uncivilized Arab man. Doing so allows Anant to align himself and his family with a "terrified" post-9/11 American citizenry, afraid of an impending attack on the very rights and freedoms that are thought to make citizenship worth struggling for. Ranjit points out, however, that white people cannot discern the difference between a Sikh man and an Arab/Muslim man, or, the difference between a Sikh man and a "terrorist." So, although Anant attempts to align himself with Americans by asserting that Arab or Muslim men are inherently capable of terrorism, under post-9/11 constructions of "brown" bodies, he and his family are also feared as potentially volatile and capable of terrorist violence *because* of their model minority status. They are thought to be imbued with a greater capability of infiltrating spaces and infecting civility with their "inherent" potential for violence specifically because they are "model minorities." Ranjit perceives the turban to be the reason for his father's "mistaken identity" but the turban is meant to mark the Sikh *as* a Sikh. The problem is not the turban, the problem is the misconception of the turban but it is also the misconception that to be an Arab is to be a Muslim, and that being a Muslim is akin to being a terrorist.

After Anant's son suggests that he remove his turban, Anant explains that "some things are important to keep" regardless of what others think. Ranjit notes that sometimes, however, what others think *does* matter because modern systems of power—such as the functionality of citizenship in post-9/11 America—control *how* subjects live and under which circumstances they die (Foucault 1984, 138). As the unseen and presumably white motorists pass the Singh family by, they probe their bodies, searching for signs of civility.[2] This probing establishes a boundary between legitimate and illegitimate "Americans" (Zylinska 2006, 526) and Anant, mistaken for a Muslim or a "terrorist," is deemed illegitimate and unworthy of aid. In response to this denial of aid and humanity, Anant attempts to reassert his American citizenship status by peeling the "God Bless America" sticker from the back of his broken-down jeep and holding it like a sign for passing motorists to see. Anant tries to associate himself and his family with a Christian God in order to further distance himself from "those Arabs" or Muslims. Anant attempts to convey to the motorists that pass him and his family by that he, like all American citizens, wishes nothing but the best for America. Anant is misread again, however, and the fear of the turban and its significations of terrorism overrides Anant's performance of post-9/11 American citizenship. The decision of passing motorists to deny Anant and his family aid comes to serve as what Daniel Coleman refers to in *White Civility* as a "necessary" sacrifice (Coleman 2008, 29). That is to say that in searching for signs of civility on the Singh's bodies, the motorists' decision *not* to help is justified by the anxiety of what could happen *if* they were to help.

In this way, the risk of terrorism is "neutralized before actualization" (Puar 2008, 92). Counterterrorism rhetoric, as stated by Jasbir Puar in her article titled "The Remaking of a Model Minority: Perverse Projectiles under the Spectre of (Counter) Terrorism," is hereby stationed in the future. Racialized subjects, like Anant, can be punished for their terrorist *potential* rather than actual terrorist activity. In a poignant moment in the film, Anant drops his "God Bless America" sticker and only his wife is visible to passing motorists. One car begins pulling over, but as Anant straightens and becomes visible to the driver, the car pulls away. Anant's wife and his children are not deemed to be threats unless Anant is visible, asserting that it is Anant that is deemed to be a threat. More specifically, it is the turban which marks Anant as potentially dangerous. The particularly jarring instance of having hope given, then removed triggers a trauma-response in Anant. It brings him to the realization that his turban, and the masculinity connected to it, opens him and his family up to the kind of violent acts reserved for "those Arabs" or terrorists in post-9/11 America. Instead of recognizing, however, that there is potential here to bear witness to the trauma of "those Arabs" or Muslims, Anant works harder to distance himself from them.

The turban, then, is made to be both a means for and an impediment to belonging. While it serves as a symbol of religion and an important indication of a Sikh identity for Anant, it is also made to be a mistaken signifier of terrorism in the collective American psyche. Anant cannot be both turbaned *and* American. In her article titled "The Turban is not a Hat," Jasbir Puar explains that the turbaned man is marked as not only monstrous, but also as inherently difficult to civilize (Puar 2008, 54). Although Anant fits into the category of "model minority," his turban signifies that he maintains a connection to an "uncivilized" past. Anant comes to disrupt or "disturb" American notions of security (54) because, as his son's response signifies, Americans cannot tell the difference between a Sikh man and an Arab man. This "equalizes" the playing field between Anant and "those Arabs," implying that in terms of race, *both* are potentially "terrorists" and *both* are dehumanized. It also implies that neither are *truly* American, meaning that for both, America is not necessarily home. Anant therefore denounces "those Arabs" as "terrorists" while acknowledging that the American citizens that pass him and his family by view *him* as a terrorist. The result is a disavowal of the self, an internalization that controls Anant's body and behavior, leading to the removal of his turban instead of a recognition that both the hat *and* the turban—that both Sikhs *and* "those Arabs"—are bonded in their vulnerability to state-sanctioned violence and probing.

## ASSIMILATING AND FORGETTING,
## RESISTING, AND REMEMBERING

Anant's disavowal of "those Arabs" is a ritual of American citizenship which denies that both Sikh *and* Muslim men have been marked as "dangerous" and as "terrorist" and that these markings are historical by nature. That is to say that they are not objective markings. Both "those Arabs" and Anant have *come to be* marked as potentially dangerous. This ritual of disavowal turns racialized bodies against one another as they fight for the right to belong as American citizens instead of forming bonds of solidarity which may then be mobilized in order to critique and challenge citizenship as an institution. Anant's performance of this post-9/11 ritual of disavowal also works to deny or erase long-standing bonds between Sikh bodies and Muslim bodies that find their roots in the shared history of the Partition of the Indian subcontinent in 1947,[3] in which Sikhs and Muslims came to view one another with suspicion (Raj 2000, 41). Anant's assertion that "Sikhs aren't terrorists, those Arabs are" is not only a ritual of post-9/11 American citizenship but one of post-Partition Indian nationalism. The turban, as well as this assertion, hold an important place in the remembering of Partition and the resulting violence between religious factions and the ways in which Muslims and Sikhs both suffered as a result of colonially drawn borders—at the hands of the state, but also at each others' hands. Anant's accusation of terrorism is both an act of forgetting and an act of remembering; it both refutes and concedes that Muslims and Sikhs have a history of relational violence. It can be argued, then, that the violence enacted onto Sikhs[4] post 9/11 triggers a retraumatization or a reluctant remembering of the violence enacted onto Sikhs before, during, and after Partition. Anant's disavowal of "those Arabs" is therefore an attempt to narrate the trauma of Partition.

Anant may not have direct access to the legacy of trauma for which he bears witness[5] but the testimony is one that he most definitely *feels*. The cumulative traumatic experiences of Partition are inscribed into Anant's skin and expressed via its color and texture (Prosser 2001, 52). Anant is not explicitly stated to have experienced Partition, but as a Sikh man attempting to belong in post-9/11 America—a space in which his body is under similar threats of violence—he experiences the "vibrations" (Puar 2008, 51) of both. These vibrations of history come to be inscribed into Anant's skin because, as asserted by Prosser, the body remembers what the mind cannot or will not remember because "skin is the body's memory of our lives" (Prosser 2001, 52). As such, it is important to read Anant's disavowal of "those Arabs" as an attempt to express, vocally, histories of violence that have come to be written onto the bodies of Sikh men. "Sikhs aren't terrorists, those Arabs are" comes to be a testimony that attempts to express multigenerational histories of violence experienced by Sikhs and Muslims under British colonial rule. In this way, Ranjit is made to bear witness, not only to his father's distress, but to centuries of historical violence. Anant's testimony comes to include the ways in which racialized subjects suffer under the institution of citizenship in post-9/11 America. Anant hereby rearticulates the historical trauma of Partition to include the violence enacted onto brown bodies in the United States post 9/11. Ranjit *ignores* the histories attached to the turban, however, and in so doing, fails to bear witness to the historical traumas his father's testimony invokes. This failure is not by any means intentional. Romanticized versions of traumatic events that serve to maintain the institution of citizenship are upheld while personal tales of suffering are often squelched. If Ranjit were to bear witness to his father's multigenerational testimony of violence, he would be forced to recognize his own traumatic experiences. For this reason, trauma narratives, like the ones attached to Partition, are not transferred intergenerationally.

In order to maintain the institution of citizenship, racialized subjects (like Anant) are prompted to search other racialized subjects for signs of civility. The result is a collective forgetting by which histories of solidarity are forgotten in order to better serve the institution of citizenship. The severing of bonds along racial lines comes to be, in itself, a ritual of post-9/11 American citizenship and it is this ritual that triggers Anant's reluctant remembering of the 1947 Partition of British India. Anant forgets pre-Partition bonds of solidarity between Muslims and Sikhs; he cannot access the potential for solidarity between himself and the Arabs or Muslims that he has been mistaken for. In her article titled "Ignorance, Forgetting, and Family Nostalgia," Dhooleka Sarhadi Raj explains how the first generation affected by Partition *forgets* their personal affiliations with the traumatic event, opting for the nation's record which allows for a "survival" narrative rather than one that recounts both the bodily and psychological suffering of the event (Raj 2000, 43). The desire not to tell the next generation—exemplified by Anant thrusting *Guru Granth Sahib* into Ranjit's chest and shouting "learn about it yourself!"—allows for the "survival" narrative to thrive and for tales of solidarity to disappear. The earlier generations' forgetting manifests as later generations' ignorance: "Ignorance is not forgetting, an erasure of knowledge, rather ignorance is an absence, which occurs when knowledge is not shared. One generation's need not to know produces what appears as systemic ignorance; the absence of some cultural knowledge in the next generation" (Raj 2000, 43).

This does not mean that traumatic histories are totally inaccessible to second and third generations. I suggest instead that trauma comes to be inscribed onto the bodies of individuals and that the narration of such traumatic knowledges is not always verbal but that it can be articulated via the body unbeknownst to its survivor. Trauma, although it may not always be shared by way of "storytelling," is indeed *felt* intergenerationally. It comes to be housed in the bodies of those who experience it both in the moment and residually because traumatic experiences of loss and extreme violence are not stationed in the past, they are projected into the future (Butler 2003, 467) and are therefore capable of manifesting on the bodies of future generations. Anant *feels* the trauma of Partition and expresses[6] this feeling when he discovers that his older son, Jagdesh, has changed his name to "Paul," in honor of his favorite Beatle. In changing his name from one that ties him to India to one that ties him to Britain, Jagdesh demonstrates his ignorance about his ties to India in favor of new Western affiliations. When Ranjit jokes that he should change his name to "Ringo Singh" because it "sounds like Ranjit," Anant attempts to explain to his youngest son that he does not need to change his name, that for Jagdesh, things were different: "there weren't as many Sikhs in America." In so doing, Anant clings to the hope that knowledge can somehow be transferred to Ranjit and that he can somehow articulate to him the importance of holding onto his name. It becomes clear that Anant's turban is his last surviving tie to India and that the importance of such ties has not been transferred to his sons.

Ranjit's dismissal of the turban is therefore an example of collective ignorance and Anant's focus on distinguishing the turban (Sikhs) from the hat ("those Arabs" or Muslims) "forgets" the ways in which the turban historically marked Sikh men for racialized violence during the Partition of the Indian subcontinent. The turban is a memory object imbued with a history of violence that intimately links "those Arabs" (or Muslims) and Sikhs as both the victims and perpetrators of violence during the Partition of India in 1947. To wear the turban in light of its historical affiliations is an act of "survival" for both Anant and the turban as "that which endures" violence. It is also a refusal on Anant's part to divorce his identity as an American citizen from his identity as a Sikh man. The turban marks Anant as a Sikh man and as such, it bears the inscriptions of a violent history in which Sikh men were subjected to violence *because* of their Sikh identity throughout Partition. To be an American is to gain access to all of the rights and privileges that come with citizenship, one of which is the expression of religious affiliation. To face persecution for expressing his Sikh identity as an American, that is, to be "mistaken" for a terrorist, is retraumatizing for Anant because it transforms the turban from a symbol of survival back to a symbol which opens both his body and the bodies of his family to state-sanctioned violence — violence perpetrated by those who *do* belong onto the bodies of those who *do not*. The wearer of the turban throughout Partition *and* post 9/11 is made vulnerable to acts of violence that cite the turban is an indication of monstrosity. To inflict harm onto the turbaned body, then, is to protect the nation — either post-Partition India or post-9/11 America — from that monstrosity.

The fear of the potential for violence — thought to be inherently present in the bodies of racialized subjects — results in "self-surveillance" in which subjects like Anant are made to "probe" the self. This allows state-sanctioned counterterrorist measures to function insidiously in post-9/11 America. Bodies deemed to be monstrous and potentially dangerous come to police themselves in the same way that the state would. Thus, at a climactic moment in the film, Anant removes his turban and as such, enacts a "humiliating" and "emasculating" violence (Puar 2008, 56) onto himself in order to not only assimilate as an American citizen, but also to remove that which marks him as potentially "terrorist" and as a threat to the nation. Removing the turban is akin to "removing" the inscriptions of trauma that have come to be written onto Anant's body. In his attempt to belong as an American citizen, Anant is expected to *ignore, forget,* and *remove* signifiers of violent histories. To do so is to "forget" shared experiences of violence and to "ignore" the potential for solidarity in favor of belonging as a citizen. In removing his turban, Anant loses more than the turban, he loses all that it signifies. In a sense, he is losing history.

Denying the historical bonds that intersect at the site of the turban—bonds such as those that exist between Sikhs and Muslims—allows the state to appropriate the desire to belong in order to maintain the institution of citizenship and to squelch the potential for bonds of solidarity along religious, cultural, racial, and generational lines. Anant's lost homeland does not remain stationed in the past and neither does the turban which comes to signify this lost homeland, they "must be understood as . . . affective and temporal [processes] rather than [places]" (Axel 2001, 426). A place is somewhere to arrive while an affective or temporal process is something to experience or feel. If the turban is a signifier of a lost homeland that Anant wishes to remain connected to, then the removal of such a signifier is his attempt to belong in a *new* homeland. This attempt at belonging requires the removal of an important signifier of history. That is to say that Anant must de-historicize himself in order to belong as an American post 9/11. He must deny the relational history of violence which he shares with Muslims in favor of denouncing them and their misperceived affiliations with terrorism. Anant removes his turban to eliminate the affect of fear that the faceless white Americans experience when they see him on the side of the road. He also removes it as a reaction to his son telling him that he "looks like a terrorist." Anant is therefore removing his turban in order to *belong* as an American citizen. Anant holds the unravelled turban in his hand, signalling that the turban is an extension of the self, that the line between object and subject has been blurred. Unlike the "God Bless America" sticker which he rips up and throws into the wind, Anant holds onto the turban. Doing so sets up an interesting binary in which the destruction of a popular slogan recited after September 11 is set against the turban and all that it signifies. I would like to suggest, then, that in ripping up the "God Bless America" sticker and gripping the turban, Anant quite literally *destroys* this ritual of post-9/11 citizenship—that is, the invocation of a Christian God in the face of a terrifying racialized other—and *holds onto* that which ties him to a legacy in which Muslims *and* Sikhs suffered under British rule.

While Anant holds onto the turban, Ranjit must reach out and touch the very object he suggested his father remove. In order to remember Partition and Anant's experience of "mistaken identity," Ranjit must interact with the turban in an embodied way. In reaching out to touch the turban, Ranjit opens up a "third space," a space that, as theorists like Erin Manning in *Politics of Touch* explain, is said to challenge the limits of self and self as other (Manning 2006, 53). As Ranjit reties his father's turban, fixing it to his father's head, he interacts with not only the garment as object, but he also comes into contact with the histories the turban has come to house. By doing so, Ranjit's skin comes to be inscribed with the very histories of violence that he previously ignored and as such, he bears witness not only to his father's specific trauma narrative of mistaken identity, but to the histories of racialized violence suffered by *both* Sikhs and "those Arabs" or Muslims.

## CONCLUSION: COLLECTIVE REMEMBERING

"I know it's hard when you're young," says Anant to his son, "but you'll learn. Some things are important to keep." The turban carries in it the inscriptions of the cumulative and relational histories of violence shared by Sikhs and Muslims under British colonial rule. To hold onto the turban then, is to hold onto the inscriptions of trauma that it carries. Although Anant removes his turban, he does not let it go, he holds it in his hands and it is this "holding" that ties him to a history of violence which links him to "those Arabs" or Muslims. Anant's disavowal of "those Arabs" is an act meant to protect the signification of the turban. He is attempting to protect it from being associated with terrorist activity in relation to America while simultaneously invoking the ways in which Sikh men were targeted by Muslims during Partition. Anant's disavowal of "those Arabs" is an articulation of a historical wound which is opened with the turban's removal and subsequently healed by its retying. Much like the "American made" vehicle which is said to have been reliable until it broke down, the rites and rituals of post-9/11 citizenship give the illusion of "belonging" without actually affording the racialized subject the rights and privileges of citizenship. Anant is a "model minority" until 9/11. That is to say that the ways in which racialized subjects are made to turn against one another is indeed American or *state*made. It is a way to keep racialized subjects from forming bonds of solidarity. The desire to belong is manipulated or appropriated by the state in order to maintain divisions between racialized bodies so that criticism of citizenship as an institution is squelched before it can begin.

It is significant then, that the man who *does* stop to help the Singh family is a black American and that this moment of solidarity occurs while Anant is wearing the turban. In reaching out to touch this man's hand, Anant opens up another "third space" in which the experience of Partition and the violent legacy of slavery collide. By doing so, Anant *remembers* the ways in which colonialism works to separate racialized bodies from other racialized bodies in order to establish and maintain the institution of citizenship. The black man's skin—like Anant's turban—mark him as potentially violent by the state. Both have histories of violence written onto their skins. Both parties engage in an embodied critique of the institution of citizenship which reflects the shared damages of colonialism and Imperialism *back* to the nation-state.

## REFERENCES

Axel, Brian Keith. *The Nation's Tortured Body: Violence, Representation, and the Formation of a Sikh "Diaspora."* Durham, NC: Duke University Press, 2001.

Butler, Judith. "Afterward: After Loss, Then What?" *Loss: The Politics of Mourning.* David Eng and David Kanzanjian, eds. Berkeley: University of California Press, 2003. (343–71).

Coleman, Daniel. *White Civility: The Literary Project of English Canada.* Toronto: University of Toronto Press, 2008.

Eng, David, and Shinhee Han. "A Dialogue on Racial Melancholia." *Loss: The Politics of Mourning.* David Eng and David Kanzanjian, eds. Berkeley: University of California Press, 2003. (343–71).

Foucault, Michel. *The History of Sexuality: An Introduction.* Trans. Robert Hurley. Harmondsworth, UK: Penguin Books. 1984.

Grewal, J. *The Sikhs of the Punjab.* Cambridge: Cambridge University Press, 1990.

Hirsch, Marianne. "The Generation of Postmemory." *Poetics Today* 29.1 (2008): 103–28. Accessed November 23, 2015. https://webshares.northseattle.edu/cscheuer/Winter%202012/Engl%20102%20Culture/Readings/Hirsch%20Postmemory.pdf.

Manning, Erin. *Politics of Touch.* Minneapolis: University of Minnesota Press, 2006.

Prosser, Jay. "Skin Memories." *Thinking Through the Skin.* Sarah Ahmed and Jackey Stacey, eds. New York: Routledge, 2001. 52–68.

Puar, Jasbir. "The Turban is not a Hat: Queer Diaspora and Practises of Profiling" *Sikh Formations* 4.1 (2008): 47–49. Accessed November 23, 2015. http://www.jasbirpuar.com/assets/The-Turban-is-not-a-Hat-Sikh-Formations.pdf.

———. "The Remaking of a Model Minority: Perverse Projectiles under the Spectre of (Counter) Terrorism." *Social Text* 22.3 (2004): 75–104. Accessed March 10, 2015. https://muse.jhu.edu/article/174060/pdf.

Raj, Sarhadi Dhooleka. "Ignorance, Forgetting, and Family Nostalgia: Partition, the Nation State, and Refugees in Delhi." *Social Analysis: The International Journal of Social and Cultural Practice* 44. 2 (2000): 30–55. Accessed March 19, 2015. http://www.jstor.org/stable/pdf/23166533.pdf?_=1460987972543.

Raju, Sharat. *American Made.* Los Angeles: American Film Insititute, Atomic 6 Productions, 2003. DVD.

Thobani, Sunera. *Exalted Subjects: Studies in the Making of Race and Nation in Canada.* Toronto, ON: University of Toronto Press. 2007.

Zylinksa, Joanna. "The Universal Acts: Judith Butler and the Bio-Politics of Immigration." *Cultural Studies* 18.4 (2006): 523–37. Accessed January 28, 2015. http://dferagi.webs.ull.es/d/social2/docs/THE_UNIVERSAL_ACTS.pdf.

# NOTES

1. A term that Jasbir Puar, in her article titled "The Remaking of a Model Minority," explains as being "often applied to Asian American populations, with particular reference to South Asian Americans. This model minority construct is predominantly a reference to economic exceptionalism, upward class mobility, and educational excellence" (Puar 2004, 77). Furthermore, in "A Dialogue on Racial Melancholia," (Eng and Kanzanjian 2003) David Eng and Shinhee Han write that "The pervasiveness of the model minority stereotype in our contemporary vocabulary works . . . as a melancholic mechanism [that facilitates] the erasure and loss of repressed Asian American histories and identities" (348).

2. "the performance of civility is a way for [citizens of colonized lands] to manage [their] traumatic history . . . and this process means that behind, or within, the optimistic assertions of civility, [they] often find a different cherishing of evil memories, an elegiac discourse by which [citizens] demonstrate their civil sensibilities through mourning the traumatic, but supposedly necessary, losses that were inevitable along the path of progress" (Coleman 2008, 29)

3. The decision to partition British India into India and Pakistan "resulted eventually in the largest transfer of population known to history. Nearly a million people perished, and over thirteen million crossed the borders" (Grewal 1990, 181).

4. Balbir Singh Sodhi was shot five times in the back at a gas station in Mesa, Arizona only days after September 11, 2001, and is cited by Jasbir Puar in "The Turban is not a Hat" as a catalyst for "a wronged Sikh citizenry . . ." as well as "the symbolic and material evidence that Sikhs were, indeed, most certainly not Muslims" (Puar 2008, 47).

5. Unlike events such as the Holocaust, personal narratives of loss were not part of a collective memory of Partition. It is generally understood that the survivors of displacement often repress much of their experience in favour of "starting anew". There is a point of rupture, however, in which traumatized subjects are "jolted" into remembrance, usually by a larger event, not always, but possibly, connected to the original event (Raj 2000, 33).

6. Marianne Hirsch explains that in certain circumstances, memory can be transmitted to those who did not necessarily live an event. She cites a 'temporal delay' in which an uneasy oscillation between continuity and rupture resides. Post-memory is a structure of inter- and trans-generational transmittance of traumatic knowledges and experiences. It is a consequence of traumatic recall but it exists in the realm of a generational remove (106)

# SEVEN

# Terror Narratives

*Art, Music, and the post-9/11 Surveillance Culture*

## Reshmi Dutt-Ballerstadt

Political performative art and music post 9/11 have provoked forms of public responses about the various repercussions of 9/11 on marginalized communities consisting of subjects from the Global South, Middle East, and Africa, that literary texts have failed to do. In fact, the fictions of 9/11, rather than articulating literature's potential engagement with questions of difference, otherness, and strangeness, have underscored such ethical concerns. Critic Clemens Spahr reads novels *Falling Man* by American novelist Don DeLillo and *Saturday* by English novelist Ian McEwan as "symptomatic of the ambivalent literary reaction to the political situation after the collapse of the Twin Towers."[1] This ambivalence is also marked in fiction by a hesitant and late entry into mapping the repercussions of 9/11. Perhaps, like Theodor Adorno once said, "Writing poetry after Auschwitz is barbaric," many fiction writers simply pondered the future of fiction after such a horrific rupture. Kristián Versluys, a Belgian scholar of 9/11 fictions, compares the collapse of the Twin Towers to the category of the "unsayable," and notes that novelists writing in English have shown some serious reluctance to dramatize the events of that day and directly after.[2]

While the fictions of 9/11 demonstrate a "failure of the imagination,"[3] political performative art and music push the boundaries of both the imagination and the reality of the "war on terror" on the civilians. These works, taken together, begin to articulate the gaps that the state spon-

sored surveillance system has overlooked in the narratives of the racialized Other in America, leaving them and their communities displaced
and terrorized. Many of the global artistic responses post 9/11 by non-
U.S. born artists have attempted to *reimagine* by documenting the various
dehumanizing efforts the "war on terror" has produced on the "racialized other"—both citizens and particularly noncitizens of the United
States of America. The double-sided function (of protecting versus terrorizing the foreign-born citizens) is a direct result of the state sponsored
surveillance system post 9/11. These post-9/11 agitations, or what Wafaa
Bilal, a dissident Iraqi American artist calls "domestic tensions" mimic
global tensions represented through provocative art and music, captur-
ing more directly the effects of the "global war on terror" on its racialized
subjects. To put it bluntly, the surveillance system, a system institutional-
ized as a national systematic spying operation, itself has not been a part
of the inclusive war, but rather an exclusive imperial strategy launched to
make subjects from South Asia, the Middle East, and Africa (all emerging
from formerly colonized countries) become both the subject and the object of terrorism and terrorization by keeping them under the watchful
gaze of the empire.

In the light of such a reality, it becomes even more imperative to
include works of these internationally renowned and foreign-born, or
second-generation racialized U.S.-born artists, photographers, and musicians that have a direct impact on our public space and the global consciousness to depict the shadows cast by the events following September
11, 2001. While the past few years have documented an avalanche of
news about the extent to which our communications are being monitored
(WikiLeaks, the phone-hacking scandal, the Snowden files) and what
many think marks an end to various privacy acts and one's right to civil
liberties, what has also been on the rise is an act of "self-tracking,"—that
is, tracking one's self and one's surroundings as an act of both self-awareness, recording of events, and gathering evidence data for one's whereabouts. While an invasion of privacy by any form of surveillance is conducted by outside forces (mainly the government), self-tracking can be
seen as a rather self-absorbed mundane act. Yet only in self-tracking can
one find an alibi, a sense of restorative justice, an explanation of gaps in
one's own narrative, gaps that a surveillance system either is incapable of
documenting, or may have deliberately ignored. Moreover, the glossing
over of such details had resulted in thousands of civilians of South Asian
and Middle Eastern descent being taken into detention facilities, disal-
lowing them any right to due process.

In this chapter I intend to stage an intertwined conversation among
the works of Iraqi-born dissident artist Wafaa Bilal, Bangladeshi interdisciplinary media artist Hasan M. Elahi (who is best known for his work on
"Surveillance art,"), and East Indian–American jazz pianist and compos-
er, Vijay Iyer's, (in collaboration with poet and performer Mike Ladd)

series of musical works about the lives of people of color since September 11, 2001. By probing into Bilal's projects, "The 3rdi" and "Domestic Tensions" and Elahi's exhibition called "Tracking Transience," along with Iyer's award winning albums *In What Language* (2013) and *Holding It Down: The Veterans' Dreams Project* (2013) (documenting the experiences of people of color at the airports and Iraq and Afghanistan war experiences by the veterans of color), this chapter will track the ways in which the culture of surveillance, rather than taking terror out of terrorism, have put terror back into terrorism by terrorizing the "suspects." In other words, the culture of surveillance can also be read as a failure of surveillance both nationally and globally. As several chapters in the collection already articulate various forms of state sponsored "terror" and mechanisms for dehumanizing the racialized Other, namely Muslim citizens as revealed through various literary texts, a simultaneous staging of provocative art forms (music and installation projects) expands the discourse of forms of conscious protest effectively representing traumas, anxieties, and perhaps a sense of hopelessness and despair that the racialized Other continue to feel in a post-9/11 world of surveillance.

Racialization is an act of exclusion, targeting racialized subjects as "suspected terrorists" or collaborators, making such exclusionary practices systemic. Here we are told that the suspected terrorist (mostly foreign born) inflicts calculated use of violence or threat of violence against a civilian population with the intent of causing widespread fear for political purposes. "Terror," imposed by surveillance on the other hand, masked under the shield of "protection from harm" is an overpowering emotion of intense fear, a fear of being watched without knowing who is watching. Can such a logic of state-sponsored terror produced by a system of surveillance (in the name of protection) ever be justified? How can such terror be understood by civilians and citizens both nationally and globally in order to move the terrorized subject from his/her disempowered state to a state of justice? Bilal, Elahi, and Iyer all attempt to explore the above inquiries as they boldly deconstruct the logic of state-sponsored surveillance as a deliberate and sustained terror-producing mechanism to keep the racialized bodies and voices suppressed.

## WAFAA BILAL

Both Elahi and Bilal provoke the issue of surveillance in their various installation projects. For instance, in Iraqi dissident artist Bilal's 2010–2011 installation project "The 3rdi" Bilal had a camera surgically implanted in the back of his head to spontaneously transmit images to the web twenty-four hours a day. Such an installation was not just a provocative act "of seeing and of being seen . . . [in which] Bilal uses his body as the primary vehicle of communication,"[4] but also serves as an act

of social commentary to expose to the public the terror of being constantly watched in a public space. Ironically enough, such a system of surveillance is not attached or implanted in the head of either a CIA or FBI
undercover agent, but a common civilian, an Iraqi dissident. The camera
in Bilal's head immediately prompted a reaction from the *Wall Street
Journal* in an article titled, "Sir, There's a Camera in Your Head."[5]

> Because Mr. Bilal is an active professor, teaching three courses this
> semester and scheduled to teach this spring, his special camera could
> capture not just his personal activity, but also his interactions with
> students. The possibility of exposing private encounters without partic-
> ipants' consent has raised concerns among NYU administrators and
> faculty: "Obviously you don't want students to be under the burden of
> constant surveillance; it's not a good teaching environment," said Fred
> Ritchin, associate chairman of the Department. (Orden 2010)

It is worth noting here the anxiety expressed by the NYU administrators
against "exposing private encounters without participants' consent" as
perhaps also a national concern that many citizens of the United States
and around the world have felt and expressed against the secrecy embed-
ded within the logic of a government-sponsored surveillance system. Just
as the NYU administrators' critique of Bilal's camera open to the public
surveillance system seems to be in conflict with student privacy and
hence "not a good teaching environment," a U.S. government-mandated
and -sponsored surveillance system must also then be violating a good
cultural and secular environment, especially in the light of a surveillance
system that watches not all citizens but only citizens who are "suspects"
based on their race, religion, and countries of origin. An act of monitoring
only a selected group of "non-citizens"/"foreigners" of the United States
is an act of exclusion in and of itself, yet for Bilal such an installation
serves not so much a political statement but as a benign observation on
everyday surveillance that every citizen globally (some more than others)
was subjected to post 9/11. Such an ordinary and a mundane act of being
watched post 9/11 has become a normalizing act, an act of which Bilal
says, "I see myself as a mirror reflecting some of the social conditions that
we ignore." For Bilal, however, in his controversial project called The
3rdi,[6] his intention was not to provoke any commentary on surveillance
but to use it as a platform for recording stories. Bilal had been arrested as
a dissident artist, critiquing the Saddam Hussein regime and fleeing Iraq
in 1991. He recalls his own story, a story that longs to preserve his lost
memories of people, places, and things left behind.

> During my journey from Iraq to Saudi Arabia, on to Kuwait and then
> the U.S., I left many people and places behind. The images I have of
> this journey are inevitable ephemeral, held as they are in my own
> memory. Many times while I was in transit and chaos the images failed
> to fully register, I did not have the time to absorb them. Now, in hind-

sight, I wish I could have recorded these images so that I could look back on them, to have them serve as a reminder and record of all the places I was forced to leave behind and may never see again. [7]

Bilal's benign intentions here of processing his memory and his environment (memory past as a way to move forward) is glossed over by the media. Instead the initial news of such a surgical implant spread in every major news outlet, from CNN to FOX and other international news outlets. The *Daily Mail Reporter*'s headline read: "Artist has camera surgically inserted so he can have 'eyes at the back of his head' for a year." [8] Furthermore the paper reported, "This project was commissioned by a museum in Qatar. The camera will broadcast everything he 'sees' to the public and will be transmitted to *Mathaf: Arab Museum of Modern Art* in time for their December 30 [2010] opening." So here, the issue immediately shifted from a personal reflective agenda to an ulterior political motive, where both what is recorded and more importantly, who will see such recordings (namely Middle Eastern subjects and citizens) came under scrutiny. While Bilal makes it clear that "the installation is intended to provide a broad viewing experience, similar to that of the Internet, for the 3rdi apparatus," the reports provide a suspicious motive, especially since Bilal's surgically implanted camera will transmit these images to the Arab Museum of Modern Art. These transmitted images, according to Bilal's artistic lens, are nothing more than "the extension of the 3rdi into physical space explor[ing] issues of perception, image recognition, surveillance, internet viewing, and information saturation." (Bilal's 3rdi website). Yet the fact that Bilal himself and his viewers are Arabs, provoked the same irrational fears that Edward Said in his seminal work *Orientalism* [9] had reminded us, that is, the Western representations of the Orient as being irrational, menacing, untrustworthy, anti-Western, and dishonest. Here, the media begins to mimic Bilal's intentions as a spy, documenting the daily lives of U.S. civilians in New York City post 9/11 and reflecting them back for viewership in Qatar. Bilal is no longer just a photographer, but an agent for the surveillance system in Qatar.

What is, however, overlooked is Bilal's own interest in raising a state of consciousness among common citizens about both the real and the residual effects of the U.S.-led war on terror in Iraq, arguments that are perhaps more personal than political. In an age of virtual reality where one doesn't have to confront dead civilians living in other countries and continents (both in the virtual games of war and the real combats from the sky called drones) there seems to be a real loss of humanity and a disconnect from humanity in terms of the actual war zone. So Bilal and Lydersen's book *Shoot an Iraqi: Art, Life and Resistance Under the Sun* emerges out of a concern, or what Bilal calls "Domestic Tension," where people mindlessly shoot without knowing the lives of their victims, victims living in other parts of the world with drastically different cultural realities. "Domestic Tension" is a game, a game that Bilal uses to both interrogate and raise an awareness of the state of disconnect that virtual realities produce on the psyche of the subjects. Such an act of interrogation and awareness raising becomes the stage for a live art installation, where Bilal becomes the Iraqi subject, the citizen, the civilian, that hundreds of virtual shooters begin to shoot. Here, Bilal creates a makeshift room in the FlatFile Galleries in Chicago in 2007. In the makeshift room, Bilal lives for a month, "going about my daily routine with a robotically controlled paintball aimed at me, which people could shoot live and over the internet, 24 hours a day" (Bilal and Lydersen 2008, 1). According to Bilal, "Domestic Tension" was intended to be a provocative commentary on the nature of modern technological warfare, and a lack of surveillance for such warfares, in which a soldier sitting in comfortable safety at a computer somewhere in the United States can drop a bomb somewhere else in the world causing death and devastation in remote locales, with absolutely no physical or psychological connection to their targets. Yet there is no global surveillance system in place that documents such misfirings, or fatalities from the U.S.-operated drones.

Bilal had conceived the project earlier that year in 2007, and he calls it "a product of my grief at the deaths of my brother and father in my hometown of Kufa, Iraq (a holy city near Najaf) in 2004, and my intense need to connect my life as an artist in the comfort zone of the United States to the terrors and sorrows of the conflict zone in which my family and so many others were living out their daily lives" (Bilal and Lydersen 2008, 1). After Bilal's own brother was killed in Iraq by a U.S. drone, it became even more crucial for Bilal that his viewers make an attempt to understand this disconnect between one's action and how this action causes great devastation elsewhere.

Bilal provides some background that explains further his impetus behind his art installation project "Domestic Tension."

> In early 2007 I saw a TV interview with a young female American soldier whose job was to drop bombs remotely on Iraqi targets. . . . The reporter asked if she had any doubts or remorse about what she was doing. She perkily answered that she trusted the orders and information she got from her superiors. My brother had been killed by explosives dropped from an American helicopter that flew in after an unnamed U.S. drone had scoped out the area. It struck me that Haji's death had been orchestrated by someone just like this young woman, pressing buttons from thousands of miles away, sitting in a comfortable chair in front of a computer, completely oblivious to the terror and destruction they were causing to a family—a whole society—halfway across the world. . . . Born and raised in the United States, an encapsulated sphere of privilege and safety, it's not surprising they would be unable to fathom the reality of a distant, foreign society and the ramifications of their actions. [10]

Bilal is convinced that if common citizens/civilians around the world begin to understand this "disconnect" in our own domestic space, there may be hope globally to intervene into such mindless aggressions. For Bilal then, the surgically implanted camera, or his project "Shoot an Iraqi" are artistic renditions of not as much "being seen by" but "being shown to" the citizens who actively support the invasion of Iraq and the repercussions of the U.S.-led Global War on Terror. It is an act of raising the level of awareness to a point where such inhumane and horrific acts are condoned and treated with sensitivity, rather than celebrated as acts of winning a misdirected U.S.-led war on Iraq. Bilal's own camera begins to provide an alternative narrative, a more empathetic surveillance, and an inclusive narrative of the fear, unease, and trauma experienced by the Iraqi civilians. Here the surgically implanted camera at the back of Bilal's head begins to act as the "third eye" — the eye of the State made visible to the public by the public. Post 9/11 Bilal thinks there has been a resurgence of political art — art that challenges the depiction of the terrorist to reduce xenophobia, or art that makes provocative commentary on the extremity of the surveillance system, like Elahi's exhibition called "Tracking Transience." These installation projects, according to Bilal are an attempt to move citizens from the "comfort zone to the conflict zone."[11]

Bilal's installation project, titled "I Don't Know Their Names," at Linfield College in 2014 at the James Miller Fine Arts Center was a durational performance in which Bilal painted on the walls in Arabic in white semitranslucent paint the names of one hundred thousand Iraqi civilians who have died in the Iraq War. The space became one of remembering and haunting, a "subtle memorial" that became an

> [I]nvisible testament to the humanity of those who lost their lives in the Iraq War conflict. . . . "I Don't Know Their Names" answers a common refrain in conflicts that as casualties escalate, the personal stories of each tragedy are lost in the dehumanizing scale of modern warfare. Faces and stories denigrate to names; names denigrate to numbers. War memorials often name the soldiers whose lives are lost in combat, but rarely is equal attention given to the civilians of conflict. The exhibit responds to questions such as what are the names behind the numbers? And who were they?[12]

For Bilal such installations are necessary acts of empathetic readings and empathetic actions, readings and actions that are imperative to unmask the masks of threat and terror. While Bilal's empathy stems from his brother's violent death by a drone attack, Elahi's Bangladeshi-Muslim identity connected him to the complex grid of terror based on the culture of surveillance post 9/11. Elahi in his artistic renditions begins to expose the overbearing approach to documenting terror by not the terrorist, but by those like Elahi who have been terrorized by mindless U.S. surveillance. Unlike Bilal (who wanted to document the movement of ordinary

civilians, Elahi wanted to log every movement in his life (self-surveillance) and make his life transparent to the FBI by thoroughly documenting his every move.

## HASAN M. ELAHI

In 2002, US government mistakenly listed Bangladeshi born artist Hasan
M. Elahi on its terrorist watch list. As Elahi stepped off a flight from the
Netherlands, he was detained at the Detroit airport. In the *New York
Times Sunday Review* "You Want to Track Me? Here You Go, F.B.I." Elahi
reported:

> On June 19, 2002, I ran into a bit of a problem that turned my life
> upside down. It happened at the Detroit airport as I was entering the
> country. I realized something wasn't right when the immigration agent
> at United States Customs slid my passport through the reader, then
> froze. "Is there something wrong?" I asked. He was still frozen. After a
> few moments, he said, "Follow me please," and I ended up at the
> Immigration and Naturalization Service's airport office. [13]

While Elahi waited at the INS's airport office in Detroit, a man in a dark
suit approached Elahi and said, "I expected you to be older." Elahi asked
if the man could explain why he was being held and the man said, "You
have some explaining to do yourself." (*New York Times Sunday Review*,
October 29, 2011). This was followed by an interrogation where Elahi was
asked to "retrace the path [he had] taken since [he] had left the United
States" and finally out of nowhere said, "Where were you on September
12?" [14]

> While this interrogation at the Detroit airport marked the beginning of
> what Elahi refers to as "turn[ing] my life upside down," (where he had
> to produce a minute-by-minute record of his whereabouts) the interro-
> gation focused on a storage unit that Elahi had rented in Tampa near
> the university.
> "You had a storage unit near Tampa, right?
> "Yes, near the University."
> "What did you have in it?"
> "Boxes of winter clothes, furniture I can't fit in my apartment, some
> assorted junk and garage sale materials."
> "No explosives?"
> "I'm certain I didn't have any explosives."
> "Well, we received a report that you had explosives and had fled on
> September 12."

This type of interrogation continued for six months, finally ending with a
series of polygraph tests. In Elahi's case, lie detector tests convinced the
FBI that Elahi was not their "wanted" but only their "suspected" terrorist. While Elahi's ordeal with a six-month interrogation ended, his own

plans to continue to travel did not. Yet, such a withholding without a cause gave Elahi serious pause, and perhaps even a determination to document his every movement in case he was withheld again as a suspected terrorist. After all, images don't lie! Elahi began to log thousands of images of his movements every day, and invited the FBI to follow him and his movements on his site. Elahi thought,

> You want to watch me? Fine. But I can watch myself better than you can, and I can get a level of detail that you will never have. . . . By putting everything about me out there, I am simultaneously telling everything and nothing about my life. Despite the barrage of information about me that is publicly available, I live a surprisingly private and anonymous life.[15]

Such a conscious and categorical self-documentation, or what is called *self-surveillance* became the subject of Elahi's installation "Tracking Transience."[16] His server documents hits from the Pentagon, the Secretary of Defense, and the Executive Office of the President, among others, tracking Elahi's movements through the photographs that he loads in an act of what I call *self-surveillance*, or as Elahi himself says, "In an era in which everything is archived and tracked, the best way to maintain privacy may be to give it up" (*New York Times Sunday Review*, October 29, 2011). Also, given that FBI agents had provided Elahi with their phone numbers, he called the FBI before each trip he undertook to notify them of his whereabouts. Elahi's project represents indeed a shift in not *where* one travels (locally and globally), but a moment by moment capture of *how* one travels. Here Elahi begins to document details of his own whereabouts since the "truth" is not in his passport, but in the details of his own documentation.

As presented in a panel discussion on "Sousveillance-culture" led and curated by Marisha Olson citing Thompson Clive says,

> Poke around his site and you'll find more than 20,000 images stretching back three years. Elahi has documented nearly every waking hour of his life during that time. He posts copies of every debit card transaction, so you can see what he has bought, where, and when. A GPS device in his pocket reports his real-time physical location on a map. . . . Elahi's site is the perfect alibi. Or an audacious project. Or both.

What Elahi undertakes is a subset of the global *Sousveillance-culture* called "Inverse Surveillance." An *inverse surveillance*, in other words, studies and critiques the surveillance system itself and is generally undertaken by the subjects that are under surveillance. While Foucault's Panopticon operates through implied surveillance by someone else (namely the police or the guard) Elahi's *sousveillance* is an act of self-surveillance to provide documented evidence in anticipation of any future interrogation. According to Mann, Nolan, and Wellman, "One way to challenge and problematize both surveillance and acquiescence to it is to resituate these technologies of control on individuals, offering panoptic technologies to help them observe those in authority. We call this inverse panopticon 'sousveillance' from the French words for 'sous' (below) and 'veiller' to watch."[17] In other words, it is a system that both exposes and protects one's self from any countersurveillance or interrogations as a result of mistaken identities. It is an act of empowering the suspected subject to produce his/her alibi. On Elahi's website, various databases document each airport he has been in; the food he has eaten at home, on the road, at hotels and other random places; hotel beds he has slept in; various parking lots off Interstate 80 where he has parked his car; empty train stations he has seen; as well as "specific information like photos of tacos [he] ate in New Mexico between July 5 and 7, and the toilets [he] used."[18]

Such a meticulous attempt at self-surveillance is a brief attempt by Elahi to unmask the terror that a National Security State continues to impose on its predominantly "foreign-born" citizens, particularly those that originate from the countries as identified by the "National Security Entry-Exit Registration System (NSEERS)[19][20] His project turns the logic of "being watched" into "an invitation to watch" one's movements, providing citizens with a kind of self-agency that has been denied post 9/11. Elahi also explores another kind of domestic tension, namely a tension produced by the state and managed by the public. Here the public response to the tension caused by constant surveillance becomes self-regulated, self-determined, self-exposed. In a *New York Times* article called "Sousveillance," Jascha Hoffman clarifies that, "Surveillance, from the French for 'watching over,' refers to the monitoring of people by some higher authority—the police, for instance. Now there's sousveillance, or 'watching from below.'" [21] If both Bilal and Elahi explore the world of terror inflicted by the War on Terror and surveillance through their installation projects, Vijay Iyer, an East Indian American jazz pianist, brings together such acts of terror(isms) in a blended and hybrid form through his musical collaborations with various poets, war veterans of color, and civilians.

## VIJAY IYER

In 2013, Iyer won the prestigious MacArthur Genius Fellowship, and 2013 also marked his three years of effort to capture the poetry of war. Trained as a jazz pianist, Iyer's intervention into the politics of 9/11 is through a collaboration of the written word and music to represent the various effects of the war on terror on the communities of color in the United States and beyond. Iyer has worked with poet and performer Mike Ladd on a series of musical works about the lives of people of color since September 11. His award winning album, *Holding It Down: The*

*Veterans' Dreams Project*, features lyrics composed from interviews that he and Ladd conducted with Iraq and Afghanistan veterans, veterans who shared with them their still-fresh memories of combat. In an interview given to NPR's Arun Rath in 2013, Iyer spoke quite candidly about the impetus behind his albums, *Holding It Down: The Veterans' Dreams Project*, *In What Language?* and *Still Life With Commentator*, and about his collaborative projects considering American life since 9/11:

> We came to realize we were sort of looking at life in the shadows of war—you know, these two wars that the U.S. has been conducting on our dimes for the last decade or so. But we also realized that we hadn't really come face to face with the lived experience of war. So it seemed like if we were going to continue in that vein, the thing to do was to speak with veterans. As two civilians, we couldn't just make a piece about wartime experience; we really had to feature the voices of those who had lived through it. [22]

Iyer collaborated with Maurice Decaul and Lynn Hill, both African American war veterans. Decaul served in the Marines in Iraq and Hill served in the Air Force. The narratives emerging from the war on terror cannot be complete if we ignore the impact on the communities of color within the United States and how such a global war on terror has had serious repercussions on those at home, namely the minority citizens of the U.S. and their complex subject positions of being deployed to fight a war with Other racialized subjects abroad. Hill, in particular, was tasked with piloting drones over Afghanistan from a base in Las Vegas, a task that Hill narrates in her performance poetry titled as "Name" in Iyer's *Holding it Down*. Iyer was quite deliberate about such collaborations with racialized Other subjects in order to represent their state, stakes, and voices, and perhaps their lost visions of what it meant to be an American citizen in the aftermath of September 11, 2001. Hill's chilling poem "Name" is a sharp reminder of the loss of one's identity and the pain of not knowing who or where the drones were falling—all in the name of protecting one's nation against the terrorists.

After Bilal's own brother was killed in Iraq by a U.S. drone, Bilal made an artistic commitment to make his viewers attempt to understand the disconnect between one's action and how such action causes great devastation elsewhere. In her poem "Name", Lynn precisely takes readers inside the world of a drone operator (like herself) as she articulates her own transformation from her birth to destruction:

**Name**
**Lynn, Bronx, NY**
Born Tamika Lynn Hill
My dad's arms as he named me
he gave a name that made your mouth
work

hard . . .

The poem begins with the act of a father naming her daughter at birth, a naming that becomes the first symbolic gesture in one's identity formation specifying one's gender, one's imagined personality as one evolves. While the name Tamika means "people" it is derived from the word *tamu* which means "sweet." Yet, every symbolism associated with the uniqueness of a name is reduced to a state of homogeneity as Tamika emphasizes her transformation from being a "civilian to servicemen" where one surrenders their personality, individuality, and as the poet says, "everyone looks like me":

> In one day, I went from civilian
> to serviceman
> became Airman and Sergeant
> referred to only as
> female
> a gender
> no personality
> no individuality
> everybody look like me
> the straight backs and creased pants
> and hair pulled back so tight in a bun
> skirts
> everybody look like me.

Here the very meaning of her name that indicates sweet or sweetness transforms into a state of being a tough soldier ready for combat. Also, the politics of such an erasure of identity, as names are replaced to erase one's gender and racialized identity is a deliberate psychological manipulation to make the subject disidentify with his/her consciousness, a consciousness that may rebel against the operation of drones. Such invisible operations, or what Susan Sontag calls "cowardly," where the predators can neither be seen nor identified killing civilians, and committing acts of murder (in the name of national security)

> Unmanned
> aircraft
> called drones
> predator
> came with no formalities
> courtesies
> no ranks
> no last names
> it was a club
> the good ole boy system and
> what you did there was attached to your
> name
> but your first name.

> And they said Lynn
> pull the trigger
> and they said Lynn
> hit that target
> and they would say Lynn
> are you hot?
> bombs away

Who are the "they" that Lynn refers to? "They" appears to refer to masked commanders asking racialized subjects to pull the trigger on other racialized subjects abroad, invisible and unseen. While the rise of the "National Security State" post 9/11 focuses on identifying act of criminality and terrorism, there appears to be no such surveillance for the unknown and invisible commanders who order subjects like Lynn to pull the triggers.

> And I said
> is this happening
> on base?
> When the mask was taken off
> and I could no longer
> hide behind
> the rank that was on my sleeve
> it was the name my dad had given me
>
> That name that I had carried
> gets switched off
> when a man comes and gives me his
> and that name was Torres
> and it's a new culture
> and it doesn't fit me like the number 8
> it just swirls
> and when I sign it, it doesn't even look like
> mine
> God, what's in a name?
> What's
> In a name?

And the horrors of such killings unfold as Lynn is no longer Lynn but "Torres"

As Lynn questions her own name and ponders about the crimes against humanity that she has now committed, perhaps unknowingly she is falling apart, perhaps disoriented by the reality that she, too, has blood in her hands. She, too, has been made into a 9/11 war criminal. Will she ever be restored?

And then comes her powerful self-reflection in her poem, "Capacity" as Lynn's own voice conveys self-awareness and anger at the destruction she has caused by her involvement in the U.S.-led war on terror. Here her first-person awareness should not be read as justification for the killings, but rather as her remorse at her transformation into a dehumanized subject, devoid of feelings.

> I have a capacity for war
> I have a capacity for hate
> I have a capacity for insanity
> for anger
> for lies . . .
>
> A capacity for destruction
> A capacity for loss
> A capacity for death
> Violence
> Nothingness

Lynn in her poems "Name" and "Capacity" exposes one's destroyed sense of self and justice and the terror that the war on terror imposes on those that are trained to fight the war. While the U.S. government shielded its civilians from witnessing the horrors of the war by prohibiting photographs of coffins and video footages of war, soldiers like Lynn did live among the terrors of what they were commanded to do. Her words and her testimony call for our understanding and empathy and perhaps even restorative justice (as a form of protection) from her U.S. commanders. Her sentiments and her incapacity to feel the consequences of her drone operations, killing civilians abroad are a sharp reminder of how the U.S.-led war on terror has been launched on people of color (globally) by the veterans of color—a systemic racial violence perpetuated by those who have been least affected by the war on terror.

While *Holding it Down* brings together voices of war veterans of color and their experiences of serving in Iraq and Afghanistan post 9/11 (as they examine their past, their traumas, their frequent nightmares, their guilt, their pleas for restorative justice), Iyer's album *In What Language?* represents people of color in airports, namely foreign nationals both before and after 9/11 and their shared experiences of surveillance and paranoia. In Iyer's interview with NPR he makes a poignant commentary both about the cost of the war in Iraq and Afghanistan.

> . . . because these two wars in Iraq and Afghanistan are so racialized, because the way that the enemy was construed and talked about was in very racialized terms, and because we just saw brown and dark-skinned people being targeted as suspects across America over the last decade, both through airport surveillance and through homeland security roundups and all of these things. . . . So, there was this double-sidedness to the whole effect of these wars. On the one hand, the enemy is racialized, or thought of in very racialized terms—you know, all the terms that they use to dehumanize the enemy. But on the other

hand, people on our side are possibly finding some point of connection with people on the other side of the rifle."[23]

The project *In What Language?* takes its title from a pre-9/11 experience of the Iranian filmmaker Jafar Panahi. In spring 2001 Panahi had been scheduled to travel from Buenos Aires to San Francisco and later to Los Angeles for the opening of his acclaimed new film *The Circle*, but was detained for twelve hours by immigration officials at JFK Airport in New York, (where he was changing planes en route from the Hong Kong to the Buenos Aires film festivals). While he was detained, Panahi was "shackled to a bench in a crowded cell for several hours, and ultimately sent back to Hong Kong in handcuffs." (Inside the album cover of *In What Language?*). Angered by his treatment, he canceled the trip. Panahi's description of his detention was widely circulated online, as he wanted to explain to his fellow passengers the anxiety, humiliation, and the absurdity of his ordeal. According to the *Los Angeles Times*, "Panahi's troubles started when he refused to be fingerprinted, which he has said he finds humiliating. (The State Department requires that citizens of some countries be fingerprinted in an attempt to prevent members of terrorist organizations from entering the country.)"[24]

Later, in an open letter written "To The National Board of Review of Motion Pictures," Panahi writes:

> But as soon as I arrived at JFK airport, the American immigration police took me to an office and asked that I be fingerprinted and photographed because of my nationality. I refused to do it, and I showed them my invitations from the Festivals. They threatened to put me in jail if I would not be fingerprinted. I asked for an interpreter and to make a phone call. They refused. Then, they chained me like the medieval prisoners and put me in a police patrol [car], and took me to another part of the airport. . . . I could not move. I was suffering from an old illness. However, nobody noticed. Again, I requested that they let me call someone in New York, but they refused. They not only ignored my request, but also that of a boy from Sri Lanka who wanted to call his mom. Everybody was moved by the crying of the boy, people from Mexico, Peru, Eastern Europe, India, Pakistan, Bangladesh and . . . I was thinking that every country has its own law, but I just could not understand those inhuman acts . . . I could not stand the other travelers gazing at me and I just wanted to stand up and cry that I'm not a thief! I'm not a murderer! I'm not a drug dealer! I . . . I am just an Iranian, a filmmaker. But how could I say this? In what language? In Chinese, Japanese or in the mother tongues of those people from Mexico, Peru, Russia, India, Pakistan, Bangladesh, . . . or in the language of that young boy from Sri Lanka? Really, in what language?[25]

It is these last couple lines of Panahi's letter that serves as an inspiration for Iyer's album *In What Language?* For Iyer, such treatment is a narrative that holds fellow brown skinned travellers together bringing them to an understanding of global solidarity in their fight for racial justice. "We could not ignore this tale," said Iyer. "It served as a point of departure for what this project became: a song cycle about people in airports, narratives of lives in transit."

While a system of surveillance post 9/11 has reached a point of banality for the common civilian, and the act of "being watched" has become normalizing, each news story that outlines the continuous and continuing system of surveillance imposed upon the noncitizens of the United States and around the world in the name of protecting our "national security" raises serious concerns about the right to one's civil liberties. Each of these three artists have outlined for us both the dangers and the everyday experience of not just surveillance, but also the act of self-regulating one's movements. Bilal's and Elahi's projects directly stem from their own encounters with the various facets of the War on Terror and their ironic and political renditions only extend their analysis. Nicholas Mirzoeff, in his book *Watching Balylon: The War in Iraq and the Global Visual Culture*, notes that "the image has undergone a further stage of capitalist development and accumulation. If in the 1960s capital has become an image, by 2003 the image has become a smart weapon" (Mirzeoff 2005, 73). In what ways then does Bilal's "3rdi" project, or Elahi's project "Tracking Transcience" become political statements of acts of "watching from below"—watching that begins to expose the various inconsistencies and malpractices of the state of "National Security?" In what ways can art and music be used as "smart weapon[s]"to destroy some of the misconceptions that have circulated against the racialized Other post 9/11?

While the surveillance system is sold to the citizens as a mechanism for keeping the terrorists or what is referred to as the "enemy of the state" off U.S. soil and other Western nations, the findings in *The 9/11 Commission Report* are certainly not consoling in terms of the protection that subjects within the U.S. either assume or expect. The chapter "The System was Blinking Red" concludes its findings by saying:

> In sum the domestic agencies never mobilized in response to the threat. They did not have directions, and they did not have a plan to institute. The borders were not hardened. Transportation systems were not fortified. Electronic surveillance was not targeted against a domestic threat. State and local Law enforcements were not marshaled to augment the FBI's efforts. The public was not warned. The terrorists exploited deep institutional failings within our government. (265).[26]

Yet, the new hauntings are the masking of threats managed, mismanaged, and micromanaged at various airports, produced and reproduced by our foreign policies in the name of national security. These hauntings are joined by further hauntings, or what Susan Sontag once called "kill[ing] from behind." of documented human rights violations (as exposed through various photographs and detainee logs) of detainees in the Abu Ghraib prisons and Guantanamo Bay, and the detention of thousands of "mistaken identities." Where is the surveillance system that has documented all these horrific tortures of the detainees and killings sanctioned by the CIA and the U.S. Government? Why such a lopsided representation of justice, where those that terrorize the public (and we are reminded over and over again that terrorists are cowards and their mindless killings are cowardly acts) are tortured, torture that is in fact sanctioned by the State, while the torturer suffers no consequence? While the surveillance system and the post-9/11 system of "Special Registration" detained thousands of these so-called cowards of Middle Eastern and South Asian origins, in the September 24, 2001, issue of *The New Yorker* in the segment called *The Talk of the Town* Sontag reminded us of the following: "And if the word 'cowardly' is to be used, it might be more aptly applied to those who kill from beyond the range of retaliation, high in the sky . . ."[27]

In an opinion piece titled "Malala and Nabila: Worlds Apart," Murtaza Hussain reported the following:

> On October 24, 2012 a Predator drone flying over North Waziristan came upon eight-year-old Nabila Rehman, her siblings, and their grandmother as they worked in a field beside their village home. Her grandmother, Momina Bibi, was teaching the children how to pick okra as the family prepared for the coming Eid holiday. However on this day the terrible event would occur that would forever alter the course of this family's life. In the sky the children suddenly heard the distinctive buzzing sound emitted by the CIA-operated drones—a familiar sound to those in the rural Pakistani villages which are stalked by them 24 hours a day—followed by two loud clicks. The unmanned aircraft released its deadly payload onto the Rehman family, and in an instant the lives of these children were transformed into a nightmare of pain, confusion and terror. Seven children were wounded, and Nabila's grandmother was killed before her eyes, an act for which no apology, explanation or justification has ever been given. . . .While testifying in the congressional hearing, Nabila's father said, "My daughter does not have the face of a terrorist and neither did my mother. It just doesn't make sense to me, why this happened. . . . As a teacher, I wanted to educate Americans and let them know my children have been injured."[28]

As the War on Terror continues and more lives of civilians are lost, hopes and dreams of families shatter, parents grieve holding their dead children in their arms, and then, heartbroken like Bilal's father, they die too. Perhaps our only hope is a new kind of surveillance, a surveillance system that begins to document the real stories of terror and terrorists lurking within the walls of protected offices, asking drone operators like Lynn Hill to "pull the trigger," "shoot the target." A surveillance system that can bring to justice those who perpetrated the inhumane treatment of the prisoners in Guantanamo Bay, Abu Ghraib, and the thousands of foreign nationals, whose stories are unheard, that were taken to various detention camps within the United States within days of September 11, 2001. Only then can a transnational restorative justice be served because "restorative justice requires us to focus on the victims, but also widens the scope to include the offender and the communities in which both live" (McCarthy, 135). In *Collateral Language: A User's Guide to America's New War* Erin McCarthy in her chapter, "Justice" posits the following:

> After 9/11, citizens of the United States have something in common with *all* victims of terrorism around the world, and *this* bond, whether one lives in the United States or Rwanda or Bosnia, *this* is the power that can be harnessed to foster peace in the world. Restorative justice recognizes the complexities of a situation—it requires that, rather than backing into a corner, we step into a space of dialogue and recognize that framing the conflict in terms of "good versus evil," "light versus darkness," "freedom versus fear," "justice versus cruelty," does not serve to restore peace, but to justify war. (124)[29]

Similarly, a system of surveillance that only focuses on the "suspects" based on their race, religious affiliation, and national identity without including within its scope not the so-called suspected terrorists, but those that terrorize innocent civilians (in the name of justice—restorative or otherwise) ought to be exposed, widely and clearly. And only through such exposure can one's faith in any state-sponsored surveillance be restored.

The genres of installation art and music provide a space to trace new patterns of South Asian and Middle Eastern cultural representations post 9/11, as well as expand the representations of histories of "terror." The diverse forms of threat imposed on both the body and the mind of these racialized subjects are not isolated but everyday experiences and spectacles of state surveillance, spectacles that are masked in the mainstream media. As a result these state-sponsored interventions on the South Asian and the Middle Eastern subjectivity and geopolitics post 9/11, these "brown" bodies continue to experience patterns of systemic exclusion and racialization. These various exclusions are the masks of threat that continue to haunt the space of racialization and threaten their sense of belonging and citizenship in contemporary America and beyond.

*I would like to thank my students in my "9/11 Literatures" course during Spring 2014 for their stimulating discussions. Both Wafaa Bilal and Vijay Iyer's works and their respective presences were invaluable for this study. I also want to thank my very able student Dawn Wyruchowski for her editing and Aparajita De for her astute feedback. I am grateful for receiving the "Marvin and Laurie Henberg International Scholarship Award" that allowed me the much-needed*

*time to complete this chapter. I remain thankful to Lynn Hill-Torres for granting
me permission to use her poems in my work.*

## REFERENCES

Adorno, Theodor. W. "Cultural Criticism and Society." *Prisms*. Cambridge: MIT Press, 1981.

"Artist has camera surgically inserted so he can have 'eyes at the back of his head' for a year." *DailyMail.com*. December 5, 2010. Accessed August 5, 2015.

Bilal, Waffa and Kari Lydersen. *Shoot An Iraqi: Art, Life and Resistance Under the Gun*. San Francisco: City Lights, 2008.

Collins, John, and Ross Glover. *Collateral Language: A User's Guide to America's New War*. New York: New York University Press, 2002.

Davis, Laura. "Interactive exhibit features 100,000 civilian names." *Linfield News* April 2, 2014. Accessed August 5, 2015. http://www.linfield.edu/linfield-news/wafaa-bilal/.

Elahi, M.Hasan. "You Want to Track Me? Here You Go, F.B.I. *The New York Times* October 29, 2011. Accessed August 5, 2015. http://www.nytimes.com/2011/10/30/opinion/sunday/giving-the-fbi-what-it-wants.html?_r=0.

Hoffman, Jascha."Sousveillance." *New York Times Magazine* December 10, 2006.

Hussain, Murtaza. "Malala and Nabila: World's Apart." *Aljazeera*. Nov 1, 2013. Accessed December 14, 2015.

"Iranian director protests harassment by US immigration officials" World Socialist Web Site May 4, 2001. Accessed December 14, 2015.

"I See You: Wafaa Bilal's 3rdi" in "Vocabulary of the Body" *wordpress* January 4, 2011. Accessed August 5, 2015. trackingtransience.net. Web. August 5, 2015.

Iyer, Vijay and Mike Ladd. *Holding It Down: The Veterans' Dreams Project*, PI Recording, 2013. CD.

———. *In What Language?*, PI Recording, 2003. CD.

Mann, Steve, Jason Nolan, and Barry Wellman. 2003. "Sousveillance: Inventing and Using Wearable Computing Devices for Data Collection in Surveillance Environments." *Surveillance & Society* 1(3):331–55.

McCarthy, Erin. "Justice." *Collateral Language: A User's Guide to America's New War*. Eds: Collins, John and Ross Glover. New York: New York University Press, 2002. Print.

Mirzoeff, Nicholas. *Watching Balylon: The War in Iraq and the Global Visual Culture*, New York: Routledge, 2005.

Orden, Erica. "Sir, There's a Camera in your Head." *The Wall Street Journal*. November 16, 2010. Accessed August 5, 2015. http://www.wsj.com/articles/SB10001424052748703670004575617083483970398.

Rath, Arun. "Vijay Iyer On Learning from War." On *NPR's* "All Things Considered" Interview. September 29, 2013. Accessed August 5, 2015. http://www.npr.org/2013/09/29/226844535/vijay-iyer-on-learning-from-war

Rothberg, Michael. "A Failure of the Imagination: Diagnosing the Post 9/11 Novel: A Response to Richard Gray." *American Literary History* (2009) 21 (1): 152–58.

Said, Edward. *Orientalism*. Vintage: New York, 1978.

Sontag, Susan. "Tuesday and After." *The New Yorker*, September 24, 2001. Accessed August 5, 2015. http://www.newyorker.com/magazine/2001/09/24/tuesday-and-after-talk-of-the-town.

Spahr, Clemens. "Prolonged Suspension: Don DeLillo, Ian McEwan, and the Literary Imagination after 9/11," *Novel* (2012) 45(2): 221–37.

The 9/11 Commission Report: Final Report of the National Commission on Terrorist Attacks Upon the United States. *The 9/11 Commission Report: Final Report of the*

*National Commission on Terrorist Attacks Upon the United States.* New York: W. W. Norton & Company, 2004.

Thomas, Kevin. "Iranian Director Detained, Sent Home. *Los Angeles Times* April 2, 2001. Accessed December 14, 2015. http://articles.latimes.com/2001/apr/20/entertainment/ca-53195.

Thompson, Clive. "The Visible Man: An FBI Target Puts His Whole Life Online." *Wired News.* May 22, 2007. Web. April 22, 2016.

Versluys, Kristián. *Out of the Blue: September 11 and the Novel,* New York: Columbia University Press, 2009.

*Wafaa Bilal.* Wafaabilal.com/thirdi/ Accessed August 5, 2015. http://wafaabilal.com/thirdi/.

# NOTES

1. Spahr, Clemens. "Prolonged Suspension: Don DeLillo, Ian McEwan, and the Literary Imagination after 9/11," *Novel* (2012) 45(2): 221–37.

2. Versluys, Kristián. *Out of the Blue: September 11 and the Novel,* New York: Columbia University Press, 2009.

3. Rothberg, Michael. "A Failure of the Imagination: Diagnosing the Post 9/11 Novel: A Response to Richard Gray. *American Literary History* (2009) 21 (1): 152–58.

4. http://vocabularyofthebody.wordpress.com/2011/01/04/i-see-you-wafaa-bilals-3rdi/

5. http://www.wsj.com/news/articles/ SB20001424052748703670004575617083483970398?mg=reno64wsj& url=http%3A%2F%2Fonline.wsj.com%2Farticle%2FSB20001424052748703670004575617083483970398.html

6. The "3rdi" is a small digital camera permanently surgically mounted to the back of Bilal's head with a USB connection. The function of the apparatus, according to Bilal is as follows: "The camera though no intervention of the artist, captures an image automatically once a minute and send this image through the USB connection to the receiver (the computer) on my body. The receiver then sends this image through the 3G network to the website, where the images are archived and made available to the public." http://wafaabilal.com/thirdi/.

7. http://wafaabilal.com/thirdi/.

8. http://www.dailymail.co.uk/news/article-1335469/Wafaa-Bilal-camera-surgically-inserted-eyes-head.html.

9. Said, Edward. *Orientalism.* Vintage: New York, 1978.

10. Bilal and Lydersen 2008, 10

11. An artist talk held on Wednesday, April 2, 2014, in the Linfield Gallery in the James Miller Fine Arts Center at Linfield College, McMinnville, Oregon.

12. http://www.linfield.edu/linfield-news/wafaa-bilal/

13. *New York Times Sunday Review,* October 29, 2011.

14. *New York Times Sunday Review,* October 29, 2011.

15. *New York Times Sunday Review,* October 29, 2011.

16. http://trackingtransience.net/

17. Mann, Steve, and Jason Nolan, Barry Wellman. 2003. "Sousveillance: Inventing and Using Wearable Computing Devices for Data Collection in Surveillance Environments." Surveillance & Society1(3):331–55.

18. *New York Times Sunday Review,* October 29, 2011.

19. Special Registration under NSEERS

20. For citizens or nationals of Afghanistan, Algeria, Bahrain, Eritrea, Iran, Iraq, Lebanon, Libya, Morocco, North Korea, Oman, Pakistan, Qatar, Saudi Arabia, Somalia, Tunisia, United Arab Emirates, Sudan, Syria, or Yemen

21. Hoffman, Jascha."Sousveillance." *New York Times Magazine.* Dec,10, 2006. (p.74)

22. NPR Interview, http://www.npr.org/2013/09/29/226844535/vijay-iyer-on-learning-from-war

23. NPR Interview, http://www.npr.org/2013/09/29/226844535/vijay-iyer-on-learning-from-war.

24. http://articles.latimes.com/2001/apr/20/entertainment/ca-53195.

25. http://www.wsws.org/en/articles/2001/05/iran-m04.html.

26. *The 9/11 Commission Report: Final Report of the National Commission on Terrorist Attacks Upon the United States.* New York: W. W. Norton & Company, 2004.

27. Sontag, Susan. *The New Yorker, The Talk of the Town,* "Tuesday and After" September 24, 2001.

28. http://www.aljazeera.com/indepth/opinion/2013/11/malala-nabila-woIn an rlds-apart-201311193857549913.html.

29. Collins, John, and Ross Glover. *Collateral Language: A User's Guide to America's New War.* New York: New York University Press, 2002.

# Epilogue

## Racialization and Resistance:
## The Double Bind of
## Post-9/11 Brown

### Nitasha Sharma

*After 9/11, the Bush administration decided to ignore its own history. It was almost a crime to suggest that the wars to come would merely exacerbate the problem—throw fuel on the fires of hatred. A few days after that violence, I wrote, "nothing good comes from terror. It never did and it never will." What I meant was not only the terror of those who attacked the US, but also the terror that was to follow.* —Vijay Prashad, "We are in pitiless times," Open Democracy, November 15, 2015

*[S]ince 9/11, the scene has already been set for a backlash in coming weeks and months, in large part due to federal infrastructure and resources allocated towards the targeting of Muslim, South Asian, and Arab communities, and to the rise in anti-Muslim and anti-immigrant groups in the nation.* —Deepa Iyer, "Here We Go Again," *The Nation*, November 16, 2015

In his article, "We are in pitiless times" cited in the epigraph, Vijay Prashad (2015) troubles French President Francois Hollande's call for a "pitiless war" in response to ISIS attacks on Paris in November 2015. Prashad ends his piece with the statement: "Western policy-makers are like little boys playing with their little toys. They don't see the human suffering and the terrible outcomes of their terrible polices" (Prashad 2015). This volume expresses such "human suffering and the terrible outcomes of their terrible policies." *Masks of Threat* traces the lives of South Asians, Muslims, and Arabs impacted by Islamophobia (racio-religious hatred) through state and vigilante surveillance, detention, and deportation amplified in the past decade and a half. It joins Deepa Iyer's *We Too Sing America: South Asian, Arab, Muslim, and Sikh Immigrants Shape our Multiracial Future* (2015) and Moustafa Bayoumi's *This Muslim American Life: Dispatches from the War on Terror* (2015) to illustrate life from the vantage point of Brown and Muslim people in the contemporary United States. However, the contributors uniquely focus on cultural productions that speak (back) to these processes to reveal a variety of expressive reactions

137

to the racialization of "Muslim looking" people since 2001. Literary and cultural studies support the authors' analyses of plays, literature, and music to shed needed light in these dark days. The darkness of being Muslim and Muslim-looking in America as targets of fear and loathing has been the focus of recent ethnographic and descriptive studies (Nguyen 2005; Bayoumi 2008; Maira 2009; Rana 2011). A foreboding sense of more darkness to come builds as we continue to terrorize one another in a perpetual loop of reaction and justification.

President Hollande declared war in response to the ISIS attacks in Paris on November 13, 2015, which followed bombings in Beirut two days earlier and a downed Russian airplane on October 31. Yet a less publicized war—the backlash faced by Muslims across these nations— took place just as quickly. A camp housing Syrian and Sudanese refugees in Calais, France, was set aflame soon after the Paris attacks; U.S. governors illegally declared their states closed to Syrian refugees; mosques in the U.S. South were vandalized and received threatening phone calls; and Western extremists shot at and beat Muslims in the U.S., Canada, and in Europe. September 11 haunts and frames this cycle of attack–declaration of war–Islamophobic backlash. The experiences of a forcefully racialized population after 9/11 taught us to brace for backlashes to similar events that include the *Charlie Hebdo* attacks and the 7/7 London bombings in 2005, which raise echoes of 9/11. Except this time, as Deepa Iyer states in the epigraph, the infrastructure and xenophobia are already in place, quickly mobilized to strike.

While mainstream media focuses obsessively on small sects of anti-Western terrorists, it underreports the devastating effects faced by a population—potential "Muslim terrorists"—that the media helped create. This volume centers the voices and creations of a different "collateral damage" in its study of artistic and aesthetic responses to being Brown in a post-9/11 era.

## POST-9/11 BROWN AS A RACIAL PROJECT

Before 2001 South Asians, Arabs, and Middle Easterners fell under the racial radar, not fitting into U.S. conceptions of Black, White, or (East) Asian. Subcontinentals, for instance, experienced a legacy of miscategorization in the U.S., from "Hindoo" to White, Asian, and Muslim. Race was not the primary paradigm through which scholars understood the experiences of these groups in the U.S. Ethnicity, culture, immigration, and diaspora were our central tropes. Studies centered on people's movements around the globe and the flow of commodities and cultures with them (Hall 1990; Gilroy 1993; van der Veer 1995; Appadurai 1996; Brah 1996; Clifford 1997). However, the relative inattention to South Asians, Muslims, and Arabs prior to 9/11 did not shield these groups from having to negotiate U.S. racial dynamics. They experience racialization in their attempts to claim citizenship and negotiate the black/white binary. Since 9/11, however, this process has become explicit, as "Muslim-looking people" see themselves through other's watchful eyes, mirroring Du Bois's notion of a double consciousness. Explicated in his 1903 classic *The Souls of Black Folk* as a "peculiar sensation" experienced by Blacks in America, Du Bois describes double consciousness as "this sense of always looking at one's self through the eyes of others" ([1903] 1995:45).

September 11, or rather its aftermath, constitutes a *racial project* for South Asian, Arab, Muslim, and other "Muslim-looking people," shaping both the ways others see Brown people and the ways they see themselves. According to Omi and Winant, a racial project

> *is simultaneously an interpretation, representation, or explanation of racial dynamics, and an effort to reorganize and redistribute resources along particular racial lines.* Racial projects connect what race means in a particular discursive practice and the ways in which both social structures and everyday experiences are racially organized, based upon that meaning. (2nd edition, italics in original, 1994, 56).

A racial project links structure and representation (Ibid.). In this case, media and politicians repeat images of Middle Eastern and South Asian Muslim men as foreign, patriarchal, and oppressive religious fanatics to highlight the disloyalty of these people *now in living in our country* as enemies of the state. These representations are linked to structures of white supremacy, nativism, and imperialism through profiling, detainment, expulsion, militarization, and other forms of violence against people thought to occupy this constructed Orientalist category of the Western imagination (Said, 1978). The racial project of post-9/11 Brown (Sharma 2016) also wedded older stereotypes of East Asian Americans (the model minority myth and the perpetual foreigner) to stereotypes of West Asians (terrorist, oppressed veiled woman, religious fanatic) grouping together people who come from a vast landscape including Eastern Europe, West Asia, South Asia, and East Asia (their Americanness is unrecognized). Some of this is new; much of it is not.

The scale, reach, and technological sophistication of today's surveillance and suppression through U.S. imperialism in the Middle East (or West Asia) and detentions at home via the PATRIOT Act are remarkable. Yet, Islamophobia preceded 2001 as did technologies of surveillance. Simone Brown's *Dark Matters: On the Surveillance of Blackness* (2015) details the technological surveillance of Black people in the United States over time. Brown requested from the CIA "documents pertaining to Franz Fanon" and received three unclassified documents. With this opening to her study, Brown illuminates a different "pre-history of 9/11" (Hutnyk, this volume), back in time and through the experiences of Black people upon whom the U.S. has employed the science of seeing, searching, and detaining. These practices have, since 9/11, the War on Terror, the Arab Spring, the ongoing Israel-Palestinian conflict, and the refugee crises in Syria, captured the attention of entire fields of Security Studies, Muslim American Studies, and Middle East and North African Studies to which this volume speaks. But the current heightened "infrastructure" that Deepa Iyer (2015) mentions consolidates much older ideological constructs of Orientalism and Black inferiority: of Muslims and Arabs and South Asians as foreign, different, and threatening (see Said 1978); of Blacks as surplus, expendable, and subhuman (see Fanon 1967).

*Masks of Threat* is attuned to this longer and expansive connection across groups targeted by the state for exclusion, expulsion, and eradication. Illuminating these connections across time and race can lead to an overwhelming sense of the overriding nature of state violence. However, the racialization of Brown people and the consequent development of post-9/11 Brown unearths connections that can foster coalitions and inspire shared resistance among seemingly divided groups. Racialization not only connects people across racial categories; it is also what can hold together the diversity within these overarching categories. This book captures the intensity and specificity—and intentional clumsiness and expansiveness—of "Muslim" or Brown racialization.

The ferocity with which Muslim-looking peoples are racialized and typecast as model minorities who could be terrorists has created bonds across differences like religion whereby Hindus, Sikhs, atheists, and Muslims alike are read as Muslim. Their shared experiences with migration, community formation, racism, and nonrecognition can bond people and create empathy across religious, national, and regional divisions. Sharing is not only rooted in experiences with migration. We also see how experiences with settlement, including racism and non-belonging in the West, create empathy among racialized minorities. The Black driver in "American Made" who stopped to help Anant's family signified the driver's understanding of a Brown person's humanity (where others saw "danger") quite possibly based on his own people's legacy of oppression (Wahab, this volume). Thus, while a gulf develops between hardened and repeated images of Muslims as dangerous outsiders and their everyday lives in the West, what happens on the ground includes heartbreaking divisions alongside potential connections among Black, Brown, Hindu, Sikh, and Muslim.

Recent work on race and religion (specifically Blackness and Islam) showcases the difficulty in disarticulating Black from Muslim: not all Muslims are Brown in the U.S. and thus surveilling Muslims today and the surveillance of Blacks since enslavement are not separate processes enacted upon distinct groups. Reviewing Sohail Daulatzai's *Black Star Crescent Moon* (2012), Chris Tinson writes, "The presence of Muslims and their perception as quintessentially both non- and anti-American at key points in U.S. political history intersects with the racialization and criminalization of African Americans, resulting in mutually reinforcing discourses and practices of marginalization" (Tinson 2013).

A particular cannon of race theorists including Fanon are instructive to comprehending the differential and relational racialization of Black and Brown people and attend to the plurality within these labels. Race scholars often draw from Fanon (whose concept of "the mask" is central to this collection) to understand the racialized experiences of Black people. Simone Brown examines Fanon's statement, "Look, a Negro!" to discuss the "imposition of race on the body" (2015, 14) in her work on surveillance (note the "veil" in surveillance) and Blackness. Aparajita De (Introduction, this volume) draws upon another Fanon passage, "Mama, see the Negro! I'm frightened!" to describe the racialization of "Arab, Muslim, non-Muslim Sikh, and Brown identities." De further illustrates how differentially racialized groups (Black, Asian, and Brown people, for instance) experience racial formation in connective ways, locating the Brown Peril within the historical construction of the Yellow Peril. Japanese American activist Yuri Kochiyama's expansive and historical understanding of contemporary racial profiling and violence inform her placement of Islamophobia within the trajectory of racist and nativist Yellow Peril discourses that were used to justify the internment of Japanese and Japanese Americans during World War II. Thus De's transposition of theories of Blackness and Kochiyama's application of the Yellow Peril upon our understanding of the conditions of Brown life in contemporary America showcase how racism and its practices (including surveillance) impact and unite racialized groups.

## CREATIVE RESPONSES TO RACIALIZATION

Much of the work cited in this volume details the mechanisms of surveillance and racialization. *Masks of Threat* illustrates the *agentive and creative artistic responses* by South Asian, Muslim, and other Brown communities to their oppressive racialization. These creative expressions ground the impacts of processes and representations that at first glance appear disembodied and abstract. Thus they illustrate the double bind of post-9/11 Brown: on the one hand, post-9/11 racialization details the imposition of ideas and practices that create and curtail this racialized "group" through repeated stereotypes and oppressive practices; on the other hand, it engenders empowering resistance and creative collaboration. As a global political identification across national, religious, and racial borders, post-9/11 Brown understands the historical roots of racialization and rearticulates "Brown" in empowering ways that contest the flattened stereotypes in media portrayals and mainstream nativism (Sharma 2016). Some responses evoke troubling divisions between "us" and "them" while others build solidarity through shared experiences.

South Asians in the U.S. employ various tactics to contend with their racialization. Some engage distancing strategies: soon after 9/11, Indian Hindus waved American flags and clarified, "we are not Muslims, we are not the enemy" just as non-Japanese Asians did during WWII. Others distance themselves not only from co-ethnics, but also from their ethnic and cultural backgrounds in an attempt to soften their racial difference. Louisiana Republican governor Bobby Jindal exemplifies desires to belong through citizenship, assimilation (using his nickname), whitening, and anti-Blackness through his draconian policies that hurt the most vulnerable members of his State.[1] Jindal illustrates Wahad's argument in this volume that claims to belonging through citizenship limit both a recognition of shared racialization and a critique of national belonging. Basu's (this volume) reading of *Disgraced*, Akhtar's Pulitzer Prize–winning remake of Shakespeare's *The Tragedy of Othello*, shows how racialization heightens divisions among Muslims. The play features Muslim protagonists who attempt to assimilate by changing their names (like Jindal), eating pork, drinking, and intermarrying. Yet in the end, the stakes are not about cultural or ethnic difference, but about race. Attributes of the foreigner—always dangerous when Brown or, in the case of Latinos, always already "illegal"—are linked to bodies read as having a fixed Muslim "essence" regardless of how they act, how self-disparaging they are, or whether or not they remove their turban.

In addition to distancing, Al Zayed's careful handling of two "novels of return" illustrates another immigrant response to the "precarity" and "persecution" faced by South Asian immigrants in post-9/11 New York City. Mohsin Hamid's *The Reluctant Fundamentalist* (2007) and H. M. Naqvi's *Home Boy* (2009) feature male protagonists who abort their attempts at belonging and return home with dashed dreams. How could their experience of America diverge so drastically from their dreams and expectations? Post-9/11 cultural productions like these seem to "offer a diminished horizon for agency, presenting instead, a deterministic trope for South Asian Muslims as unable to reconcile their cultural and religious identities with American civil and political life" (Basu, this volume). Yet al Zayed offers an alternate interpretation of the protagonists' "desertions": he reads their return to the subcontinent not just as acts of defeat, but rather as "performative gestures geared towards the rejection of post-9/11 imperial muscle flexing" (al Zayed, this volume).

Ronak Kapadia uses the term "insurgent aesthetics" to describe "how "contemporary artists have contested the violent projects of U.S. empire and the recent global war on terror" (Kapadia unpub). Kapadia and this volume's contributors analyze artists like Wafaa Bilal who perform yet another response to being targeted: they "self-surveil." Bilal, an Iraqi-born artist and New York University professor, lodged a camera in the back of his head as part of his project "3rdi" to track his movements and those of the people around him. He explains, "[a] camera temporarily implanted on the back of my head, it spontaneously and objectively captures the images—one per minute—that make up my daily life, and transmits them to a website for public consumption."[2] In this volume, Dutt-Ballerstadt places Bilal in conversation with Bangladeshi media artist Hasan Elahi, who logged his every movement in response to being questioned for six months, and Indian American Vijay Iyer's album *In What Language?* to show how the War on Terror has terrorized the "suspects." Each artistic production grapples with the themes of post-9/11 Brown—hypervisibility/invisibility, mobility/immobility—with a focus on airports as sites of misrecognition and detention. Dutt-Ballerstadt suggests restorative justice through another kind of surveillance: artists exposing state-sponsored violence. This collection reminds us to look past the impending doom to the light shed by cultural workers who illuminate future imaginings through their alternative readings of this world.

This volume is about the reactions and initiatives carved out by those the dominant narrative increasingly circumscribes. It features music, plays, and writings in which protagonists resist and return; they distance and enact empathetic politics of solidarity. Like many South Asians living in the U.S., they allow their bodies to be misread and refuse to clarify who and what they are and are not. South Asian, Latino, and Black men who may or may not be Hindu, Muslim, or atheists wear "Muslim-looking" beards. Muslims rappers across racial and national backgrounds record tracks in support of the Arab Spring and against anti-Black and anti-Brown racisms in the United States.[3] Yet are cultural producers doomed to a life of reaction?

## THE FIX OF STEREOTYPES

Coalitional experiences emerge out of the lumping of broad-scale technologies that do not decipher who is an actual terrorist. The purpose of such science is to *create* the terrorist with little grounding in reality through the rules and regulations of the PATRIOT Act, the TSA (formed in direct response to 9/11),[4] ICE, the War on Terror, and school administrators who decide clocks made by young boys with Muslim names are threats.[5] September 11 is a racial project. It quickly altered the terrain upon which formerly unremarked-upon populations became marked and disciplined whether or not they displayed a propensity for terrorist actions.

Japanese American activist Yuri Kochiyama attended a packed event in the Bay Area soon after the Twin Towers fell on September 11, 2001, and forecasted what she, as a former internee, knew was going to be the swift and sweeping arm of the U.S. government in creating its fiction as fact. Kochiyama's fears were not unfounded. Following ISIS attacks in Beirut and Paris, a Democratic mayor in Virginia stated: "I'm reminded that President Franklin D. Roosevelt felt compelled to sequester Japanese foreign nationals after the bombing of Pearl Harbor, and it appears that the threat of harm from ISIS is now just as real and serious as that from our enemies then." That two-thirds of Japanese internees were American and the fact that U.S. intelligence agencies denied that Japanese Americans had committed any wrongdoing seems irrelevant in this renewed demonization of Asian Others.[6] The stereotype of Asians—South, East, and West Asians—as perpetual foreigners with divided loyalties lives on and is produced through the U.S.'s incessant wars across Asia. Thus we see what Bhabha described as stereotype's "repeatability in changing historical and discursive conjunctures" (1994, 95).

According to Homi Bhabha, who also draws from Fanon, colonial discourse (and its central strategy, the stereotype) is dependent on "the concept of 'fixity' in the ideological construction of otherness" which paradoxically operates through repetition (that is, if something has a fixed essence, why would it need to be repeated?) (Ibid.). In this way Americans read Brown bodies through a lens shaped by the repeated images in the news and popular media—or what Patricia Hill Collins (2008) calls "controlling images"—of the cultural foreigner, terrorist, and religious extremist. Racialization consolidates differences, cementing them into stereotypes analyzed in this volume: model minorities, model immigrants, model mourners (Chakraborty), nerds, and terrorists (Thangaraj, Wahab). It is not the case that individuals occupy one or the other stereotype; that one (the terrorist) can masquerade as the other (the model minority) implicates all terrorist-looking immigrants and "justifies" state and vigilante suspicion.

Aparajita De reminds us that the racialization of the Muslim terrorist not only references the body, but also speaks to the way that cultural and religious markers, such as the headdress, become racialized and gendered. The turban—which is not a hat (Puar 2008)—becomes a mask, according to De's explication. "[M]asks," writes De, "refers to a cover or an imposition that hides the other aspects of a racialized identity to show only the façade of an identity that is over determined and always already exoticized and vilified" (6). Thus, in "American Made," the Sikh father's turban must go. "No one's gonna' stop 'cause you look like a terrorist," says young Ranjit to his turban-wearing father. The older man agrees to remove his turban—an item and practice so meaningful to his sense of self yet deemed so offensive to other Americans (Wahab). The body and its accouterments are the target of looking: if you see something, say something. However, we often misread racial cues, thinking a Sikh is a Muslim or that a Latino is an Arab through the imprecision of perception and misperception, reading and misreading, recognition and misrecognition, identification and misidentification. As Puar writes, "The overdetermined reliance on narratives of visibility . . . both privileges an epistemological knowing over an ontological becoming, and foregrounds a process of panoptic racial profiling" (Puar 2008, 68). The turban is like a veil that, according to Bhabha, "becomes the object of paranoid surveillance and interrogation" (1994, 90). The hegemonic processes of Islamophobia and nationalism combine such that it is able to contain all of these differences.

In this oppressive context, resistance emerges in multiple expressions of political action and expressive forms. South Asians, Muslims, and Arabs create art—film, literature, music—that unearths these processes. Authors, filmmakers, thinkers, and doers analyzed in this volume contest flattened images and in their work, pluralistic and humanized representations flower.

## DIVIDED DISCOURSES

This volume's contributors illustrate the gulf between official discourse (such as Harper's Canadian governmental apology about the Air India flight discussed in Chakraborty's chapter) and the worldviews of non-white people in North America. This gulf—illustrated but irreducible to Homi Bhabha's (1994) iteration of the stereotype—functions to justify the status quo and gives little sense of the fullness of people's everyday lives. Ethnography and cultural texts flesh out the latter. The mainstream press may consolidate the heterogeneity of basketball-playing Muslims and South Asians in Atlanta, but Thangaraj fleshes it out. His work is attuned to the internal dynamics among desis, including debates over intermarriage, intraethnic contestation, and the intergenerational incorporation of sport into American and Muslim belonging. The racial diversity of league members is further complicated by class distinctions that, according to Thangaraj, differentially impact how desis experience the aftermath of post-9/11. While post-9/11 Hindu professionals relate feeling that something terrible has happened to their country, working class Muslims face the devastating effects of surveillance and deportation.

The gulf between mainstream depictions and the everyday lives of people takes on a different dimension here: what does it mean if ethnography reveals the distancing strategies of some South Asian, non-Muslim professionals like Bobby Jindal, whereas the fictional representations like "American Made" reveal oppression despite the Sikh family's professional class status? To what extent does the omnipotence of hegemonic discourses of Muslims in the post-9/11 era shape and constrain expression? *Masks of Threat* reveals the extent to which Muslim, South Asian, Sikh, and Arab artists engage—by conforming or confronting—dominant ideologies. Volume contributor Lopamndra Basu, says of Amir, the protagonist in the Pulitzer Prize–winning play, *Disgraced*: "His entire attempt at defining his ethnic and religious identity has been from the perspective of negating or opposing dominant discursive trends that provide a pretty narrow and limited range of possibility for Islamic identity" (Basu, this volume).

The post-9/11 racial project catches Muslim-looking people in a bind: on the one hand, maltreatment, terror, and violence may motivate South Asians, Arabs, and Muslims to critique the state; yet the state explains dissidents' anger as evidence of their danger. This explanation is used to justify state and vigilante surveillance and violence against Muslim-looking peoples, which then motivates some of the targeted to then critique state violence, and so on in a loop. Has this impossible bind "pushed many young, secular Asians towards Islamism as an alternative worldview" as Malik (in Hutnyk, this volume) suggests? Hutnyk diagnoses another unsettling result: he notes a "quietening of a critical, sexually and intellectually rampant and promiscuous radical tradition" (Ibid.). The diversity and vibrancy expressed in so much literature by South Asians and Muslims is "now reduced to no more than a single image" (Ibid.).

Artists focus their attention not on the pathology of Islam, but on the society that created the spectacle of the terrorist everyman: "Within the context of this ongoing injustice [of the recurring negative feelings and prejudice against Muslim Americans], the artistic choice available to a playwright like Ayad Akhtar is to expose the schisms and deep-rooted disorder in American society." Like the themes in rapper Chee Malabar's "Feral Child" LP (Malabar inverts "the New World" into Kipling's "Jungle") cultural producers indict the United States.

These chapters repeat the expressions of South Asians, Muslims, and Arabs in the United States, Canada, and England following 9/11. But the cultural productions, including plays, literature, and sport articulate a variety of responses to racialization. Some South Asians produce art that reiterates stereotypes through protagonists who discard their cultural and religious practices in favor of assimilation; there are those who write novels of return and unfulfilled expectations (al Zayed); and others respond through self-surveillance art. These chapters humanize the very people who have been dehumanized through U.S. racism, Islamophobia, and the War on Terror. More importantly, research on the agentive responses to racialization highlights intersections with other communities of color.

This volume's amalgam of South Asian American Studies, Muslim Studies and research on race and religion theorizes the impacts of post-9/11 state and vigilante practices upon expansive and vibrant communities. It also explicates a variety of responses to the condition of racialization—a process that, like hegemony, is never complete or totalizing. This book emerges from the dialogic contestation of hegemony and resistance, between the formation and imposition of the mask and the refusal of that mask, the evocation of what lies beneath it: the humanity that racio-religious hatred cannot extinguish.

*Masks of Threat* brings together scholarship that interprets tensions of contemporary Brown life through the lens of cultural and literary analysis. The choices and actions of the protagonists in films, writings, and theatrical performances attest to the power of dominant stereotypes and the ability of the state and vigilantes to reinforce a one-dimensional and racist depiction of "bearded terrorists." We see in these pages the responses of self-tracking, whereby self-surveillance becomes an artistic and actual response to life after 9/11. However, alongside self-regulation, self-surveillance, and self-consciousness emerges a fullness of humanity the authors illustrate through their attention to the interactions among those who live as post-9/11 Brown.

## REFERENCES

Akhtar, Ayad. *Disgraced.* New York: Back Bay Books, 2013.

Appadurai, Arjun. *Modernity at Large: Cultural Dimensions of Globalization.* Minneapolis: University of Minnesota Press, 1996.

Bayoumi, Moustafa. *This Muslim American Life: Dispatches from the War on Terror.* New York: New York University Press, 2015.

———. *How Does it Feel to be a Problem.* New York: Penguin, 2008.

Bhabha, Homi. *The Location of Culture.* New York: Routledge Classics, 1994.

Bilal, Wafaa. "3rdi." http://wafaabilal.com/thirdi/. Accessed September 27, 2015.

Brah, Avtar. *Cartographies of Diaspora: Contesting Identities.* London: Routledge, 1996.

Brown, Simone. *Dark Matters: On the Surveillance of Blackness.* Durham, NC: Duke University Press, 2015.

Clifford, James. *Routes: Travel and Translation in the Late Twentieth Century.* Cambridge, MA: Harvard University Press, 1997.

Daulatzai, Sohail. *Black Star, Crescent Moon: The Muslim International and Black Freedom Beyond America.* Minneapolis: University of Minnesota Press, 2012.

Du Bois, W. E. B. *The Souls of Black Folk.* New York: Penguin, 1995.

Elahi, Hasan. "Tracking Transience." http://elahi.umd.edu/track/. Accessed December 2, 2015.

Fanon, Franz. *Black Skin, White Masks.* New York: Grove Press, 1967.

Gilroy, Paul. *The Black Atlantic: Modernity and Double Consciousness.* Cambridge, MA: Harvard University Press (Reissue edition), 1993.

Hall, Stuart. "Cultural Identity and Diaspora." *Identity: Community, Culture, Difference.* Ed., Jonathan Rutherford. London: Lawrence and Wishart. 393–403. 1990.

Hamid, Mohsin. *The Reluctant Fundamentalist.* Orlando, FL: Harcourt, 2007.

Hill Collins, Patricia. *Black Feminist Thought: Knowledge, Consciousness, and the Politics of Empowerment.* New York: Routledge, 2008.

Iyer, Deepa. "Here We Go Again? Muslim Americans Brace for a Backlash After Paris." *The Nation,* November 16, 2015. Accessed November 17, 2015.

———. *We Too Sing America: South Asian, Arab, Muslim, and Sikh Immigrants Shape our Multiracial Future.* New York: The New Press, 2015.

Iyer, Vijay, and Mike Ladd. "In What Language?" Pi Recordings, 2003. CD.

Khabeer, Su'ad. *Muslim Cool* (forthcoming, New York University Press).

Malabar, Chee. "Feral Child." Red Bench Records. January 2015. CD.

Maira, Sunaina, *Missing: Youth, Citizenship, and Empire after 9/11.* Durham, NC: Duke University Press, 2009.

Naqvi, H. M. *Home Boy.* New York: Saye Areheart Books, 2009.

Nguyen, Tran. *We are All Suspects Now: Untold Stories from Immigrant Communities after 9/11.* Boston, MA: Beacon Press, 2005.

Offendum, Omar, The Narcicyst, Freeway, Ayah, and Amir Sulaiman. "#Jan.25." Produced by Sami Matar. Single. 2011. Accessed December 1, 2015.

Omi, Michael and Howard Winant. *Racial Formation in the United States: From the 1960s to the 1990s.* New York: Routledge. 1994.

Prashad, Vijay. "We are in pitiless times," *Open Democracy,* November 15, 2015. Accessed November 17, 2015.

Puar, Jasbir. "'The Turban is Not a Hat': Queer Diaspora and Practices of Profiling." *Sikh Formations: Religion, Culture, Theory* 4.1 (2008): 47–91.

Raju, Sharat. *American Made.* Los Angeles: American Film Institute, Atomic 6 Productions, 2003.

Rana, Junaid. *Terrifying Muslims: Race and Labor in the South Asian Diaspora.* Durham, NC: Duke University Press, 2011.

Said, Edward. *Orientalism.* New York: Random House, 1978.

Sharma, Nitasha. "Rap, Race, Revolution: Post-9/11 Brown and a Hip Hop Critique of Empire." Eds., Ronald Radano and Tejumola Olaniyan. *Audible Empire: Music, Global Politics, Critique.* Durham, NC: Duke University Press, 2016.

Tinson, Christopher. "Book Review – Black Star, Crescent Moon." *Blog of the American Studies Journal.* https://amsjournal.wordpress.com/2013/01/28/book-review-black-star-crescent-moon/. January 28, 2013. Accessed November 8, 2015.

van der Veer, Peter. *Nation and Migration: The Politics of Space in the South Asian Diaspora,* Philadelphia: University of Pennsylvania Press, 1995.

# NOTES

1. Social media circulated an unofficial portrait of Bobby Jindal (not his official portrait) that depicted him as much fairer—white, actually—than he is in person. Jindal took this opportunity to state that "the left is obsessed with race." http://onpolitics.usatoday.com/2015/02/09/bobby-jindal-portrait-white-race/. Accessed November 2, 2015.

2. Wafaa Bilal, "3rdi." http://wafaabilal.com/thirdi/. Accessed November 15, 2015.

3. For instance, Palestinian American Sami Matar produced a hip hop track, #25Jan (referring to the dates the protests in Egypt began during the Arab Spring). It featured a number of Muslim rappers, including Syrian American Omar Offendum and African American poet Amir Sulaiman.

4. The TSA website describes its formation:

> "On the morning of September 11, 2001, nearly 3,000 people were killed in a series of coordinated terrorist attacks in New York, Pennsylvania and Virginia. The attacks resulted in the creation of the Transportation Security Administration, designed to prevent similar attacks in the future. Driven by a desire to help our nation, tens of thousands of people joined TSA and committed themselves to strengthening our transportation systems while ensuring the freedom of movement for people and commerce."

https://www.tsa.gov/about/tsa-mission. Accessed on December 1, 2015.

5. In September 2015, a high-school boy in Texas, Ahmed Mohamed, was arrested for bringing a homemade clock to school. School officials feared it was a bomb.

6. http://korematsuinstitute.org/institute/aboutfred/. Accessed November 10, 2015.

# Index

# About the Contributors

**Hasan al Zayed** is assistant professor of English at the University of Liberal Arts Bangladesh (ULAB), where he teaches literature and cultural studies. He completed his BA (Hon) and MA from Jahangirnagar University, Savar, Dhaka. Zayed's academic interests lie in Marxism, postcolonial studies, and cultural theory. His scholarly and creative works have appeared in *South Asian Review, Journal of Third World Studies, Harvest, Six Seasons Review,* and other journals and anthologies. He is currently working on a book-length monograph on Akhtaruzzaman Elias, one of the most important literary figures writing in the latter half of the twentieth century.

**Lopamudra Basu** is an associate professor of English and director of the Honors College at University of Wisconsin–Stout (UW-Stout). She grew up in Calcutta, India, and attended the University of Delhi, India, where she received BA and MA degrees. She earned her PhD in English from the City University of New York. She is the coeditor of *Passage to Manhattan: Critical Essays on Meena Alexander,* Cambridge Scholars Publishing, UK, 2009. Her articles, interviews, and reviews have been published in *South Asian Review, Nebula, Social Text, Journal of Commonwealth and Postcolonial Studies, Remarkings,* and in the anthologies *Rites of Passage in Postcolonial Women's Writing* (2010) and *Drawing From Life: Memory and Subjectivity in Comic Art* (2013). She recently developed and taught the course "After 9/11: American Literature of Trauma and Public Crisis" at UW-Stout.

**Chandrima Chakraborty** is associate professor in the Department of English and Cultural Studies at McMaster University, Canada. She has published widely on nationalism, masculinity, and cultural memory, with a focus on South Asia and the South Asian diaspora. Her publications include *Masculinity, Asceticism, Hinduism: Past and Present Imaginings of India* (2011), *Mapping South Asian Masculinities: Men and Political Crises* (2015), and a Feature Section in *Topia: Canadian Journal of Cultural Studies* on the 1985 Air India bombings. She has also published in journals such as *Economic and Political Weekly, ARIEL, Postcolonial Text, Journal of Postcolonial Writing, Studies in Canadian Literature,* and *Journal of Commonwealth and Postcolonial Studies.*

**Aparajita De** is an assistant professor in the Department of English at the University of the District of Columbia, Washington, DC. She was formerly assistant professor at City University of New York's Kingsborough College, where this project was initiated. She has published widely on diaspora literatures and South Asian studies. Her select publications include essays in *South Asian Review* and *South Asian Popular Culture*. She has a coedited collection of essays titled *Subaltern Vision: A Study in Postcolonial Indian English Text*. Her current areas of research include the study and intersections of race and raciality in popular culture and politics. She is currently working on a project examining the intersections of civil and political movements in contemporary America.

**Reshmi Dutt-Ballerstadt** is professor of English at Linfield College in Oregon. She is the author of the scholarly monograph *The Postcolonial Citizen: The Intellectual Migrant* (2010) and her scholarly and creative works have been published in the *Journal of Asian American Renaissance, Jouvert: Journal of Postcolonial Studies, Naming Jhumpa Lahiri: Canons and Controversies, Saranac Review, Rocky Mountain Review*, and others. Her current book projects are on the discourse of 9/11 literatures and she is editing a collection of essays on the relationship between civility and marginality in academia.

**John Hutnyk** is currently guest professor at the Graduate Institute for Social Research and Cultural Studies, National Chiao Tung University, Taiwan. His books include: *The Rumour of Calcutta: Tourism, Charity and the Poverty of Representation* (1996); *Critique of Exotica: Music, Politics and the Culture Industry* (2000); *Bad Marxism: Capitalism and Cultural Studies* (2004); *Pantomime Terror: Music and Politics* (2014); and coauthored with Virinder Kalra and Raminder Kaur: *Diaspora and Hybridity* (2005).

**Nitasha Tamar Sharma** is associate professor of African American studies, Asian American studies, and performance studies at Northwestern University. She is the author of *Hip Hop Desis: South Asian Americans, Blackness, and a Global Race Consciousness* (2010). She is currently writing an ethnography of Blacks and mixed race Blacks in contemporary Hawaii, where she is from.

**Stanley Thangaraj** is an assistant professor of anthropology at the City College of New York. His interests lie at the intersections of race, gender, sexuality, and citizenship. He studies immigrant and refugee communities in the U.S. South to understand how they manage the black-white racial logic through gender. His monograph *Desi Hoop Dreams: Pickup Basketball and the Making of Asian American Masculinity* (2015) looks at the relationship between race and gender in co-ethnic-only South Asian

American sporting cultures. He has coedited the volumes: *Sport and South Asian Diasporas* (2014) and *Asian American Sporting Cultures* (2016).

**Sarah Wahab** is a PhD student at McMaster University. She completed her BA with honors at Laurentian University and obtained her MA at McMaster University. Her doctoral research is focused on embodied responses to historical trauma. She is particularly interested in challenging traditional understandings of the witnessing process and writes primarily about embodiment as a means of decolonization and healing for traumatized subjects. Her areas of research include dance, protest, mourning, and oral histories as they apply to making invisible traumas visible.

www.ingramcontent.com/pod-product-compliance
Lightning Source LLC
Chambersburg PA
CBHW030649110726
47901CB00002B/634